A Windfall Homestead

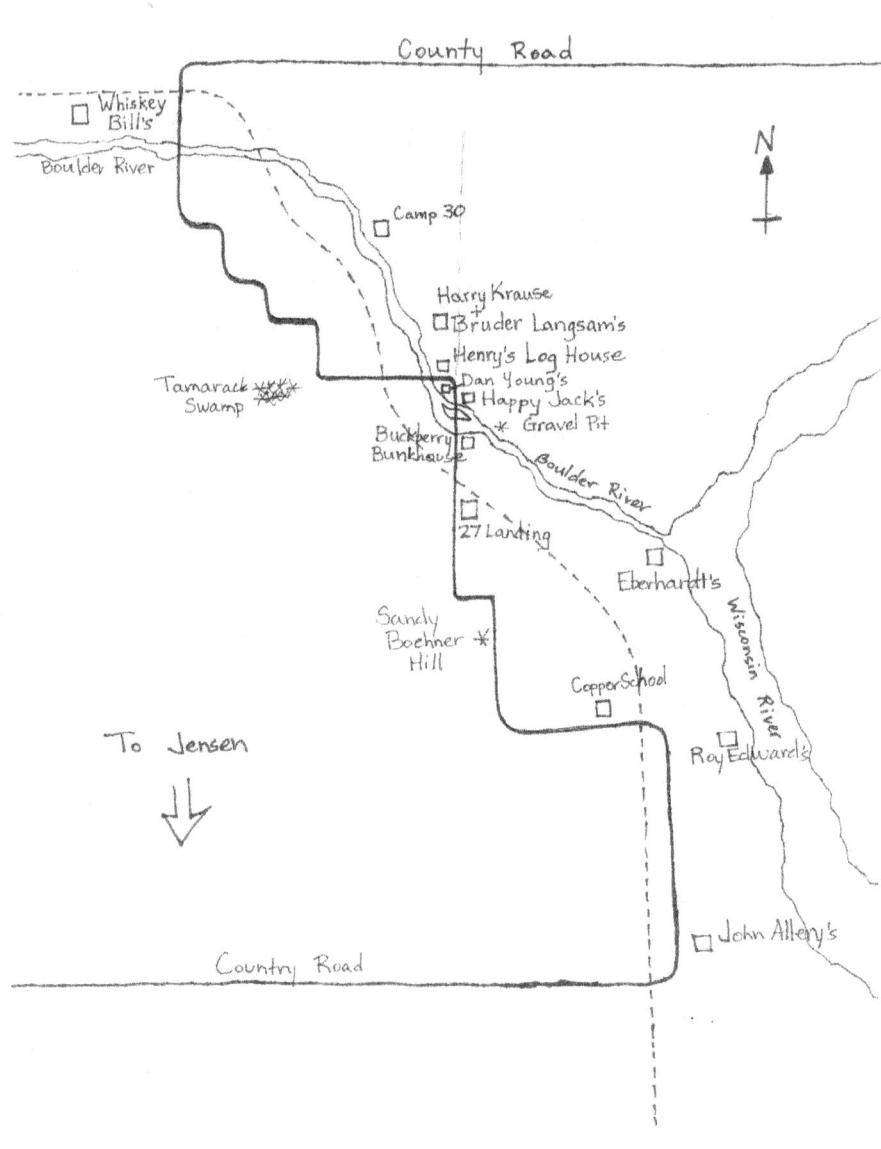

A Windfall Homestead

The Life and Times of Henry Buckberry

SEEDY BUCKBERRY

Two Introductions by
Efrazima Fiddlehead

Afterword and Henry Buckberry's Obituary by
Seedy Buckberry

RESOURCE *Publications* · Eugene, Oregon

A WINDFALL HOMESTEAD
The Life and Times of Henry Buckberry

Copyright © 2013 Seedy Buckberry. All rights reserved. Except for brief quotations in critical publications or reviews, no part of this book may be reproduced in any manner without prior written permission from the publisher. Write: Permissions, Wipf and Stock Publishers, 199 W. 8th Ave., Suite 3, Eugene, OR 97401.

Resource Publications
An Imprint of Wipf and Stock Publishers
199 W. 8th Ave., Suite 3
Eugene, OR 97401

www.wipfandstock.com

ISBN 13: 978-1-62564-236-3

Manufactured in the U.S.A.

For Jack

*I should not talk so much about myself
if there was anybody else
whom I knew as well.*

HENRY DAVID THOREAU
Walden; or, Life in the Woods, p.1

Contents

Editors' Foreword | ix
Acknowledgments | xi
Efrazima Fiddlehead's First Introduction | xiii
Efrazima Fiddlehead's Second Introduction | xv

1. Full a Soot an Dirt | 1
2. A Canthook Man | 13
3. Full a Little Tricks | 20
4. The Biggest Walleye I Ever Caught | 26
5. A Peculiar Kind of Exercise | 32
6. A Cocky Little Wretch | 41
7. Orange Pajamas | 51
8. Married Two Days an Broke | 59
9. When Enuff's Enuff | 68
10. Gettin Over that Flirtin Business | 73
11. Life's Little Accidents | 84
12. Caught His Limit | 95
13. Mark My Words | 98
14. These Bits an Pieces | 106
15. The Most Worthless Piece a Land | 114
16. Way Too Fast | 122
17. Comin Home With Both | 130
18. Changes on the Farm | 138
19. Too Big ta Ketch an Swallow | 144

Seedy Buckberry's Afterword | 149
Henry Buckberry's Obituary | 160

Editors' Foreword

WE'RE GOING TO PRESS with the second volume of Henry Buckberry's stories, *A Windfall Homestead*. Our schedule is tight, and we can't wait any longer for Mr. C. D. Buckberrry in Wisconsin and Ms. Efie Fiddlehead in Oregon to resolve their apparent confusion (if confusion is what it is) over which of Ms. Fiddlehead's Introductions we're to print. So we've decided to print them both. Editors also have their prerogatives.

Truthfully, we seem to detect a certain degree of family tension here, and that makes it hard for us to get on with the job. We do publishing, not family counseling. But we hope all concerned will feel we've done the best we could under the circumstances.

Acknowledgments

Henry's dead, but—needless to say—without him there would be nothing to acknowledge. Without his love of stories, there would be no *Get Poor Now, Avoid the Rush* or *Windfall Homestead*.

But it wasn't just Henry's love of stories that prompted these books. I think there's another layer here. It seems to me that, in some strange, unconscious way, my brothers and I selected me to be, you might say, Henry's designated driver. That is, as we get older we're realizing with greater clarity what it's meant for us to have failed to remain in Henry's world. Most narrowly, that meant we let Henry's farm get away from us. We failed to "take it over."

But that's not all, and maybe that's not even the main point. Well, we all left. Nearly everyone in our generation left. Not everyone left the area, exactly, but only Mark Lemmer's grandson Matthew hung on as a farmer. All the rest of us walked.

What I'm trying to say is that these stories—Henry's stories—constitute both homage and hope. The homage is obvious, and needs no explanation, but where's the *hope*?

The hope is embedded in a deep, deep conviction—call it a feeling if you want to—that the richest and finest aspects of this homesteading life are destined to return. It'll be different, probably (in some ways) a lot different. But the core grounded earthiness is going to return. Mark my words. The Town of Boulder will come back to life. And it'll be a place where Henry Buckberrry will feel right at home.

And, if at first he's a bit befuddled as to where he is, Henry can thank Sarah Blake for providing him not only a clear electronic manuscript of memory-jogging stories, but also with a hand-drawn map by which he'll be able to find his way home, even in the dark.

Efrazima Fiddlehead's First Introduction

WHO WOULD'VE THOUGHT (IF we date this project from late September 1987) that it would take over twenty years to produce two thin volumes of Henry Buckberry's stories? It's the fault of that no-good son of Henry's, Charles Darwin Buckberry, AKA C. D. Buckberry, AKA "Seedy" Buckberry.

Once that no-good seedpod had kicked himself with sufficient omph in the rear templates, volume one (*Get Poor Now, Avoid the Rush*) made it from nibbled start to reasonable finish in just over two months—just in time for Christmas 2006. Volume two got underway in mid-January 2007, but spring had the nerve to show up before a hundred pages were complete. Seedy (less an author than a mere transcribing medium with a cheap tape recorder he was barely smart enough to operate) has a thing about naps in warm weather. Once the Wisconsin snow was gone, he put on his summer Rip Van Winkle hat and didn't wake up until December.

Henry, meanwhile, cut, split, and stacked enough firewood for two more Wisconsin winters, before he, too, chose December—not to wake up, but to make a practice run at dying. It might've been little strokes. Nobody knows for sure. There was worry that he wouldn't even show up for his ninety-sixth birthday cake on January 9, 2008.

Well, by Christmas 2007, Uncle Henry apparently had learned what he needed to know from his practice run at dying, and his appetite for birthday cake proved (nearly) as strong as ever. Seedy, meanwhile, had gotten something of a jolt from his father's playing footsy with the proverbial bucket, and he began to buckle down, or wake up, or whatever it is he had to do to get on with this foozled project. Before, you know, it was altogether too late.

A Windfall Homestead

By all accounts (though he's a sly one), Seedy kept at it modestly well—if anything Seedy has a hand in can be called "modest."

Here, at any rate, is volume two of Henry's stories, as submitted by S. B., complete with the latter's aggravating notes and some pretense of an "Afterword"—intellectualized B. S. is what I'd call it. (If you write Seedy Buckberry's initials backwards, what do you get?)

But I am glad Uncle Henry's stories are getting published. I know it's only my opinion, but I think Henry Buckberry is a beautiful man who's lived a beautiful but pretty rugged life. Reading these stories is like listening to him talk. So absolutely wonderful.

A West Coast Cousin,
Efrazima Fiddlehead
April 1, 2008

Efrazima Fiddlehead's Second Introduction

My cousin Seedy B. has, on occasion, shown a certain impulsive generosity. That's hard for me to say, but it's true. For instance, after *Get Poor Now, Avoid the Rush* was finished, he wrote to me—longhand, of course, in his nearly illegible scribble—asking if I'd be willing to write an Introduction to *A Windfall Homestead*, the second volume of Uncle Henry's stories. With that letter, Seedy included a copy of *Get Poor Now*, in the form of an 8½-by-11, blotchy photocopy of the original manuscript, obviously done on an out-of-date manual typewriter with a worn-out ribbon that should've been thrown away years ago. So typical. Such an impossible, selfish, stingy skinflint.

But (rather to my amazement) Seedy had actually done a pretty good job of putting down Uncle Henry's stories, complete with a reasonably accurate conveyance of Uncle Henry's dialect or vernacular or idiom or whatever you call it. Uncle Henry's voice. Or maybe Seedy just miraculously failed to screw it up. And, in all honesty, I loved my Uncle Henry—I loved him a lot—and so I wrote a sort of puffball Introduction, a happy piece of praise, and I did it because I was *so* happy for Uncle Henry. Hugs and kisses. Kisses and hugs.[1]

However, I wrote that puffy Introduction without seeing a single page of the second manuscript. *That* was a big mistake. And then there was a terribly long silence—except for a wonderfully sweet "I love you" note from Uncle Henry, written in his bold but shaky hand—and then, *after* Uncle Henry had his final set of strokes, *after* my dear Uncle Henry had died, *after* his wake and his funeral, I got this last-minute, urgent note from Seedy

---

1. Ms. Fiddlehead apparently means by "a happy piece of praise," what we're calling the First Introduction. The editors.

A Windfall Homestead

(nearly illegible, as usual), telling me—well, I'd say *demanding* of me—to edit my puffy Introduction immediately because the publisher was getting ready to print *A Windfall Homestead*, a book I'd never yet seen.

By then, of course, I'd learned from west coast family that my dear, sweet Uncle Henry had passed. And here's Seedy B., not exactly the sharpest knife in the drawer or the brightest bulb in the chandelier, who'd never even bothered to tell me Uncle Henry was dying, suddenly *demanding* that I polish up my happy Introduction and get it to the publisher pronto, because—well, because Seedy said I had to.

Not only did I take my good-natured time to read and reread the ready-to-be-printed manuscript—I drove up to Eugene and got a copy of *A Windfall Homestead* from the publishing firm—friendly editors, I have to say—but my huffy-puffy, sweet little Intro has been neatly inserted into my favorite scrapbook as a momento to my love for Henry.

In other words, I'm starting this Introduction over from scratch, and Seedy won't get to see a word of it until *A Windfall Homestead* is published.

Surprise, Seedy! I'd love to be watching your face when *this* puffball explodes in your furry mug.

The stupid Afterword of Seedy's in this book is bad enough, but the unbelievable Obituary makes me want to scream. Or take karate lessons. Or learn what the rules are for concealed carry.

I was willing to choke down Seedy's omissions and misrepresentations in the Afterword he wrote to *Get Poor Now*. You know, when he said he knotted my pigtails so tight it took my mom three hours to get them loose. What he *didn't* say—the damned nasty bully—was that he caught me outside, knocked me down, sat on my back, and methodically rubbed a big glob of pink bubblegum into each pigtail knot. And it took him quite a while to get each glob of bubblegum soft enough to smear in. So I had to lie there, on my belly, in the wet grass, shivering with cold and mad as hell, while he's smacking and slobbering mouthfuls of pink bubblegum, drooling on my back, and pressing that pink crap into my hair. My dear cousin Seedy . . .

Henry was *so* mad. I think he would've spanked Seedy half to death if I hadn't intervened. I told Uncle Henry I thought Seedy had learned his lesson. At which point Seedy got to sit in a corner, snorting and blubbering, snot all sticky down his face, tears dripping off his chin, while Henry held me on his lap and apologized over and over for the vicious behavior of his

Efrazima Fiddlehead's Second Introduction

worthless son. Which was exactly true. Worthless. Except maybe he was worse than worthless.

There's more I could say (a *lot* more), but I'm not going to hang even more dirty laundry on the family line. Except I *do* have to say one more thing. It's none of Seedy's goddamned business what Henry and I did or did not do in my "psychedelic hippy shack" in the Oregon Cascades. You can daydream about it all you want, C. D. Buckberry, but you'll never get another word about it from me. Stick *that* in your tobacco can and chew it. Eat your heart out, you jealous runt.

For Henry's sake, however—and it is for dear, sweet Henry's sake—I have to say I love these stories. Henry, whatever his faults may have been—and we all have some faults (although Seedy seems to have picked up a truly oversized load)—Henry lived an amazingly real life. I miss him *so* very much.

I frankly don't care if I ever see Seedy again. But Henry—in the form of two slim volumes of stories—will be by my bedside for the rest of my days. And for *that*, even though it's awfully hard for me to say it, I'm grateful to that devious, crude snot—Charles Darwin, C. D., "Seedy" Buckberry.

Rot in hell, you crew cut, worthless brat.

A Cousin no longer,
Efrazima Fiddlehead
April 1, 2013

1

Full a Soot an Dirt

It was a Sunday noon, the middle a September, 1933, when I got off the train in Jensen, Wisconsin, next town north a Wausau. I was full a soot an dirt becuz I'd hoboed behind the coal tender on a train from New Lisbon ta Wausau. But becuz another hobo had told me I'd get kicked off the train north ta Jensen, I bought a ticket for thirty-five cents an got ta sit on my ass for the last twenty miles. I thought the conductor'd throw me off becuz I was as black as the Devil an probably jest as ornery.

But he didn't throw me off. Maybe he thought Jensen was the pits a hell an I was jest one a Jensen's little devils goin home for a weekend of fun. Takin a day off ta do whatever it is devils do on their day off. Dress up in their best suit of sooty dirt and then go scare the crap out of a few little kids. Happy Halloween.

In Jensen I walked the mile or so west to Grampa an Gramma Coster's place, a big brick house with a barn an seventeen acres an a crick running through it, right off South Foster Street, in the Sixth Ward.

I was one tired fella, I kin tell ya that.

After shoutin at the Devil an then gettin me a tub a hot water, Gramma went back into the house to make me somethin ta eat. As I was washin, out in the yard, Grampa told me—he was sittin on the steps, watchin me soap up—that I had to fix up my log shack cuz him an Gramma were gonna come live with me.

I jest stood there, bent over that tub a water, an stared at'em.

A Windfall Homestead

They'd lost their home an land, an they were jest waitin for the last axe ta fall. An it was gonna fall soon.

After Gramma'd fed me somethin, an I'd rested up a bit, I decided I had ta go home. It was two o'clock in the afternoon, two-thirty maybe, an I walked north on South Foster Street until I came to the railroad track, an then I followed the track west an north to the Town a Boulder, eight, ten miles a walkin, an when I got home—not to the log shack, but to the old logging camp bunkhouse where the folks lived, right next to the Boulder River—there was hardly ennybody there, only Ethel babysittin a couple a the real little kids. Pat an Paul fer sure (they were the twins), an maybe Jannette as well.

Ethel was one a my younger sisters. Two of us plus eleven more equals thirteen. We were a big family. Not countin Ma an Pa. Lots a kids.

"Ma an the rest of'em are up workin in yer potato patch," Ethel told me. An so—I guess I hadn't walked far enuff yet that day—I walked a couple more miles north an west, up to the log shack, an there they were, Ma an a whole flock a the kids, pickin the potatoes they'd dug earlier in the day, an puttin'em in the buckboard Old Jack was pullin.

I don't know who was more surprised—Ma, to have me show up like that, all soot an dirt except for my hands an face, or me, cuz the forest fire that'd come through while I was gone ta Lyndon Station over summer had burned the country black as the ace a spades. It was like a prairie rubbed with coal dust. Burnt! The land was as black as my clothes. Almost as if the Devil had spread out a welcome mat fer me.

Welcome home, Henry. I hope ya like how I fixed things up for ya.

Ma's big garden, in the sandy flat by the river, had dried out over summer, an so she'd turned her attention to my potato patch. It was new, heavier soil, an those potatoes *grew*. She took a hunnerd bushel an put'em down the bunkhouse cellar.

But as I stood there lookin at that black prairie, I realized that what'd kept my potato patch from burnin, an the log house with it, was that half-moon road Old Jack an me'd made with the stoneboat, haulin load after load a brush an rocks from the little potato field an dumpin that stuff in a pile. Our little road had blocked the fire.

It was kind a funny becuz I'd thrown the brush in a heap on the east side a that half-moon road, an the road had kept the brushpile from burnin. See, the fire had come from the west an north, and that stoneboat road'd kept both the potato garden *and* the log house from burnin.

Full a Soot an Dirt

If I'd been smarter, I wudda put that brushpile on the west side a the stoneboat road an hired the fire ta burn it up for me, though it probably wudda done it fer free. As it turned out, I had ta burn it myself, later.

Ma an the kids had even left the bunkhouse an stayed a couple days with Happy Jack, up at his speakeasy, when the fire was at its worst, but the county road an the river blocked the fire, so the bunkhouse was spared.

If yer house or yer shack burnt down, then you *really* had nothin. We were spared that. But it was close.

Ennyway, when I told Ma what Grampa Coster had said about him an Gramma havin ta move in with me, she was totally surprised. Well, first she was surprised an then she was mad. She knew things were bad, but I guess she didn't know how bad.

Her getting mad had ta do with her sister Minnie, cuz it was Minnie an her husband Jack Dixon who had got Grampa an Gramma Coster ta mortgage their brick house an loan'em the money for a restaurant they started, down in Ohio or Kentucky. Wherever it was. An that restaurant didn't prosper, an then the Depression hit. An so Grampa an Gramma were left holdin the bag. An the bag was empty. Worse than empty.

Ma usually went ta town once a week ta buy groceries. She'd hook Old Jack to the buckboard an drive on in. The next time she went ta town she went ta see Grampa an Gramma, an she took'er anger with'er.

But what good did that do? All the losin was over. Nothin ta do now but make the best of a bad situation.

Pa was still fightin fire, though by the middle a September there wasn't much left ta do but squirt a little water on scattered puffs a smoke. None a the men had got paid a nickel since they started ta fight fire, way back in July. So when Pa got home, I shared with'em some a the sixty dollars I'd come home with, from Lyndon Station.

But it wasn't long an there was a shower a rain, an that put an end even ta huntin up the smoke.

Since the drought had been so severe, there was a ready market for potatoes. I still had more ta dig, an I took a trailerload of'em ta town, behind the Model T, an sold'em on the street. One dollar an twenty-five cents a bushel. Quinten Ament had jest got married, an he came over an bought a bushel.

Wasn't long an I dug a little cellar hole under the log shack an stored some potatoes there, cuz it wasn't gonna be but a little while before

A Windfall Homestead

Grampa an Gramma would come out. There was a long winter comin, an we all had ta eat.

So I got ta work on the log house. Well, Pa an me. He made window frames out a that raft wood I'd salvaged before goin ta Lyndon Station, from the boards I'd floated down the Boulder, an I split pieces a wood ta fill cracks between the logs, nailed'em in, an plastered'er up.

Pa said I needed a better floor—those deadhead raft boards were all cracked an knotholed—so I bought shiplap from Ollhoff's mill an laid down a second floor, a better one.

Now Gramma had got in touch with Mike Stevens to see if Mike would buy her two Jersey cows. He said he would, but he'd only give'er ten dollars apiece, an Gramma wouldn't sell at that price.

So now what were we gonna do? I didn't have a barn; but the forest fire had swept right through a swamp in the middle a my forty, an on the north end a that swamp there'd been a nice stand a black ash trees, most of'em a foot, foot an a half in diameter. Nice ones.

Well, ya can't burn green black ash if ya build a fire right under it. But the roots were shallow an that swamp had been six, eight inches deep in moss, an since it had got bone dry, the moss burned. An the roots stuck out.

So those black ash trees tipped over in the wind. An there they were, layin down.

So Pa an me looked'em over an cut logs out of'em with a crosscut saw an, with Old Jack pullin, we got'em over by the log shack an we built a log barn. When we were done, there was room in there for three, four cows, and a corner for Gramma's ten, twelve chickens.

What hay there was in Grampa's barn, in town, I hauled out on the trailer behind the Model T—it wasn't enuff, an I had ta buy more that winter—an then Pa an me led the cows out, all the way to the log barn, walkin'em out along the railroad track, all the way from South Foster Street. Took us half a day, at least. They were kinda city-slicker cows, not eager ta go livin in the brush. Too far from the beauty parlor and the movie house. They were, ya know, scared a wild animals, like chipmunks an porcupines.

Ennyway, they came from a nice barn in town to a shack of a log barn out in the country; but, as far as I could tell, those cows didn't say nothin bad about their new home once they got used to it. Better'n a butcher shop. An they managed ta give a little milk all winter.

A man named Julius Ranke lived jest up Frostbite Avenue, an he hauled milk to Rindt's cheese factory, which was over along Natzke Road in the Town a Corning. The milk check'd come once a month, but those were Gramma's cows, so she got the money. Milk sold for ninety cents a hunnerd pounds. Gramma wasn't gettin rich, I kin tell ya that.

But I'm gettin a little ahead a myself.

I hauled out Grampa an Gramma's stuff, which wasn't much, before I hauled them out. I got their cookstove an round potbelly stove, an a table with (I think it was) three chairs, a corner cupboard, some dishes, a woodbox, an a few barn tools. An their bed.

Now you gotta remember the log shack was sixteen feet by eighteen feet, an for room dividers I had cloth hangin ta separate bedrooms from the kitchen, an another piece a cloth ta separate bedrooms from each other. Mine, a course, was smaller'n theirs.

An then I brought Grampa an Gramma out in the Model T. It was November, bare an black an cold. Gramma sat in front with me. Grampa sat in back.

They'd never been to the log shack before, never seen it. This was the first time. So you got to imagine how all this looked to'em, Seedy, how it musta felt. I don't know if yer imagination is workin today, but give'er a try, ennyway.

They'd jest left their big brick house fer good, an I'd jest drove'em twelve, thirteen miles out in the brush, on a bad road, in a cold car, on a cold, grey November day. I pulled up in front a the log shack an turned the motor off. They didn't say nothin, an they didn't move. They jest sat there an stared.

I think the whole thing was a shock to'em. Two elderly people. Nearly eighty years old. Welcome to the log house. Yer new home.

I'm amazed they didn't jest break down an bawl.

Athough it was several years before I put a ceiling in the log shack, it was a warm little place, easy ta heat. Most of the time, the cookstove was all we needed.

But I never stayed in the log house much, except ta eat an sleep, if I could help it. It was perty small for three people, an I always had somethin ta do.

The fire had burned almost everything blacker'n the ace a spades. I still believe somebody set that fire, jest so there'd be some work that'd pay. You gotta remember this was Depression, when ya couldn't buy a job. So jest maybe some—what a ya call'em?—*entrepreneur* got himself a box a matches an made some work fer lots a people. I ain't sure about this, and it ain't ennything I kin prove, but I always did wonder.

Ennyway, I'd written a letter to the Universal Engineering Company in early July a 1933 becuz I didn't want ta fight fire. See, I'd fought fire once before, over by the cranberry marsh, with a tank on my back, an a little hose fer squirtin water, an it was one hell of a job jest to keep from chokin ta death on all that smoke. I had no desire ta do that again. None.

In the fall, I also saw that the fire had not burned in the timber, which convinced me even more that the fire had been set—though there had been several hunnerd thousand feet a logs in rollways, down along the 27 landing, close to the folks' bunkhouse, an they had all burned up. Gone ta smoke an ashes. An to the south a those rollways was that alder swamp I used to hunt rabbits in, with our dog Gyp, when I was a kid with a .22, an that alder swamp had burned right down to the ground. George Ament had bought that forty, an the fire did all his brushin for'em. Helped'em start a farm.

Even Happy Jack had got his winter's wood burned up. See, there were lots a old pine logs, stuff that was no good for lumber, but good enuff fer burnin, an every year Old Jack'd cut an split a bunch of 'em for his winter's wood. When that fire came, Old Jack had his winter wood all cut an split an stacked, an so the fire didn't have ta go lookin for somethin ta burn, but found Jack's wood all ready in nice, neat piles. Burnt it all up. More smoke an ashes.

After Pa'n me had put up the black ash barn for Gramma's cows, we both got hired by the WPA to cut brush alongside the county road. My brother-in-law Stub Lohff got a job, too. Stub was my sister Clara's husband.

But after a month, the foreman came to me an said he was sorry but he had to lay me off. When I asked'em why, he said it was becuz I didn't have a family to support. Well, I told'em, What about Grampa an Gramma? But that didn't make enny difference to him. They weren't my kids, he said, an I couldn't argue with that. I thought, maybe, I'd try'n adopt'em, but that monkey business costs money, too, and I couldn't afford a lawyer. (Ya know, Seedy, that wudda made yer great-granparents yer brother an sister. Even then, I wasn't sure how you would feel about that.)

But on that job I'd got acquainted with Ned Fox, who was also out there brushin. Ned an his wife Martha, an however many little kids they had already, were livin in a tiny little house Frank Kurth had built, jest up

Full a Soot an Dirt

Frostbite Avenue, on a little clearing, an that house was so poor it was held together with car wire.

Now I was out a work, pokin around, Grampa an Gramma already livin in the log shack, adopted but not adapted, if ya see what I mean, an I saw where a patch a small timber, pulp-sized hemlock, had survived the fire, jest acrost the Boulder from the mouth a Kelly Crick. So I talked ta Ned about it. He had come from the Doering area, northeast a Jensen, an he knew a guy who ran a little store up there who also was a agent for buyin pulp. An it ain't long an Ned sez the guy is interested.

So I went to the courthouse to see if I kin figger out who owns that land with the patch a hemlock on it, an it's a Mrs. Frank Lambrecht, from down in Marathon County.

Ned an me went ta see her, an her husband's there, but it's her that does all the talkin. She was willing ta let us cut the wood, but she wanted twenty-five dollars fer stumpage. Up front. It took a while, but I kept jawin an jawin, an perty soon I had'er down ta twenty-two fifty. I had the money an I paid'er, right then an there.

Ned was jest along. He was maybe ten years older'n me. He was my partner, but he was broke, an I did all the talkin. All the talkin an all the payin.

By Christmas, Ned an me had pertner all that wood cut. Some of it had been burnt a little, by the forest fire; but enny a that we jest sliced off with our axes. Snow up to yer knees. It was winter.

But then the weather got warm, an it started ta rain. End a December, an all it did was rain an rain an rain. All the snow left, an the river raised jest like in spring breakup, an we didn't know what to do.

Well, winter tends to come back, ya know, specially that time a year, an this one did. It got cold an it froze—froze hard, froze that water in the river, high up over the riffles. An very little new snow.

I was down to the river nearly every day, checkin out the ice, an I sez to Ned, "I believe the ice'll hold my car." So we gave it a try, got it out there perty easy, but a course I had to step on'er too much right away, an I spun that Model T in a couple a circles before I got'er settled down.

We put chains on the rear wheels, an threw a couple heavy sacks a feed fer Gramma's critters in the back a the car, jest ta weigh'er down, an up the river we went.

A Windfall Homestead

With all the curves an bends in the river, it was probably three-quarters of a mile upstream to the place where our hemlock pulp was layin in little, scattered piles among the stumps.

Now Ned had a little bobsled an a old plug of a horse he called Dick. Black Dick. Mostly Dick. An Ned skidded that hemlock up to the riverbank with Dick, an I pulled load after load a that skidded wood down the ice to the bridge there by Batchelders', all of it on that little bobsled.

The only problem I had was gettin started with the bobsled loaded. The car'd jest sit an spin, even with chains on. But Ned had a long skidding chain, an one end a that chain had a ring on it, so he'd loop that ring over the back end a the nearest bobsled runner an, with him an Dick up on the bank, he'd have Dick give that sled a little jerk. That was all I needed ta git a move on, an down the ice I'd come. Load after load. Cord after cord.

Ned'd skid more pulp to the edge a the bank, an I'd be back for another load.

In the end, we took out a full carload a pulp, twenty cords, pulled down the river behind the Model T, an stacked by the side a the county road.

But it was still a couple a miles to the 27 landing, so we hired one a Ned's brothers, who had a Model T truck, ta come an haul for us. We loaded by hand, an Ned's brother made trip after trip until we had'er all down at the landing. In fact, the county road was breaking up, getting wet an muddy an sloppy, an we worked all one day, all night, an kept right at it till we were done, which was about ten, ten-thirty the next morning.

An then I went home, to the log shack, an Gramma fixed me somethin to eat. Grampa was sittin acrost the table from me, an all of a sudden I could hear'em laughin in his deep, growly voice—"Ho, ho, ho!"

I'd fallen asleep with a forkful a food almost up to my mouth. His laughin woke me up. An there he was, sittin acrost the table, lookin at me, laughin.

On that same piece a land where we cut the hemlock, Ned an I also cut some nice big hard maples. We took'em down the river to the bridge, jest like we did the hemlock—on Ned's bobsled, hooked behind my Model T.

Most a that hard maple we had up alongside the road, cut into firewood lengths. By then it was election day in April, an we still had maybe a cord ta cut, still in pole lengths, layin on the ice. I kept at'er all day—never did go ta vote—until I got'er done. But it got too late, or I was jest too tired, so I didn't carry those last blocks a wood off the ice. Thinkin, ya know, ta do it tomorrow.

That seems, ya know, ta be almost everybody's favorite day, Seedy. It's jest plain amazing the amount a work that'll get itself done *tomorrow*. The sheer gumption that's gonna happen *tomorrow* is always bigger than all a last week's gumption stuffed in a sack. It's kinda like the sign August Smite used ta have in his tavern, down by Grampa an Gramma's old brick house—"Free Beer *Tomorrow*."

Ennyway, the ice went out overnight, an that cord a wood went right down the river with it. But we had a lot more wood alongside the road. A fella from east a Jensen bought it from us, hauled it away on a big truck, though we had to help'em load. He paid us seventy-five cents a face cord, which is a stack a wood eight feet long, four feet high, an sixteen inches acrost. For seventy-five cents.

You kin see how close we were ta bein millionaires. Almost put us through the roof.

That was the spring a 1934.

But we still had our pulp ta ship. An, ta do that, I had ta get the railroad ta let us use a car. Now John Oestreich and Clarence Samuelson had wood to ship, too, so instead a gettin one car, I got two.

There were two places where the train went perty slow, coming down from the northwest, loaded with logs. One a those slow places was east a Doc Sievert's cottage, and the other was Rock Cut, down toward Eberhardts'. So I walked up the track, east a Doc's (though Doc wasn't in there yet), an I waited for the train. I knew the spot where it went slow, an when it came by I swung up on the back a the caboose an walked on in.

The conductor was kind a surprised to see me stroll into his cubbyhole (it wasn't every day a fella'd hop the caboose in the woods), but I told'em what we needed, an he wrote it all down. We had enuff time ta do our little business before the train grunted up ta Rock Cut, an I swung down again.

Did the same thing when our cars were loaded an ready ta be shipped.

My Pa helped us load.

But Ned an me weren't done yet with that piece a land acrost the Boulder from Kelly Crick. We cut more firewood for ourselves, an we discovered a big, hollow yellow birch that had honey bees in it—a bee tree.

A Windfall Homestead

We cut that big birch down—had to contend with some unhappy honey bees who weren't too thrilled ta see their house get wrecked—but we each got about a washtub full a honeycomb. Gramma was busy quite a while, heatin an strainin all that honey—lots a sawdust an pieces a punk in it, ya know—it's hard ta be real careful about things like that with a lot a unhappy bees tappin on yer shoulder. But we had honey for a long time afterwards.

So Ned an me got lots a use out a that piece a land owned by Mrs. Frank Lambrecht. For twenty-two dollars an fifty cents.

I ain't even sure she knew where her land was.

In the spring a '34, I bought a couple pounds a seed, clover an timothy, an jest broadcast it by hand on three, four acres a burnt-over land north a the log barn. An then I put up a fence, posts an two wires, an when that clover an timothy came up an got kinda lush, I turned Gramma's cows in there.

Did those cows ever milk! Eat an lay down, eat an lay down. That's all they did.

One month Gramma got a milk check for thirty dollars. One month! An she had a 6.1 butterfat test at Rindt's for those two cows.

Julius Ranke told everybody—Old Gramma Coster got a check for thirty dollars, for one month, an her Jersey cows had a 6.1 butterfat test!

Eat an lay down, that's what those two cows did.

Gramma was perty happy. She didn't smile too much, but she was fit ta burst over that thirty-dollar check, the 6.1 butterfat test, an—maybe most of all—that she was, at least for a day or two, the center of gossip an envy in the Town a Boulder.

Gramma Coster was a little woman, active an quick. She couldn't read or write, but she could *count*. When it came ta money, she knew how ta add an subtract real well.

She was little, but Grampa was big an tall, well over six feet, an he probably weighed more'n two hunnerd pounds. He walked stooped—not bent over, exactly, jest stooped.

At some earlier time, even before they'd been ta North Dakota, they'd lived a while in Colorado. I think Grampa had some sort a mining job out there. But it musta been kinda off-an-on work, cuz he said he'd sometimes hitch a ride with a man who ran a general store, go with'em part way as that man'd take a horse an buckboard out to a ranch ta buy eggs an whatnot,

Full a Soot an Dirt

an Grampa'd get off somewhere with his double-barrelled shotgun an go huntin.

He said he shot a mountain lion once, on one a those trips. He was sittin on a rock, or a stump, or a cactus—I ain't sure *what* it was, Seedy, cuz I wasn't there—an jest lookin, when out a the corner of his eye he caught a movement, kinda to the side an behind'em, an he turned an shot, an it was that mountain lion. But one shot didn't kill'em, so he had to give'em the second barrel.

When the man with the buckboard came back, Grampa had a mountain lion for'em ta haul, an he said folks looked at'em kinda funny when they got back ta town, like it was perty risky business, kinda reckless, ta be shootin a mountain lion with a shotgun. But that's what he did.

He also said he knew Frank James, one a the famous robbers, an he liked'em. Said Frank was a nice man. But not Jesse, though. Jesse, he said, was kinda stuck up an proud. But he liked Frank.

But Gramma could be perty sharp—with'er tongue, I mean. That same winter Ned Fox an me cut hemlock pulp, acrost from the mouth a Kelly Crick, I caught a medium-sized beaver an I skinned it. Well, to sell it, you had ta stretch an dry the hide, so it had ta be hung a while where it was warm. I tacked that hide on the inside a the log house door for two, three days, an Gramma didn't like that very much. But Ray Trantow'd give me three, four dollars for a hide like that, an that meant groceries, so she didn't complain too much. Jest enuff ta let me know that beaver stink wasn't her favorite perfume.

Musta been in the spring a '34, I came into the log house about nine o'clock in the morning, an there's Gramma sittin at the table with a cup a coffee an a little lunch. See, I'd be out workin, pickin stones, cuttin brush, by seven o'clock, an I never knew Gramma'd have a lunch in the middle a the morning. Kinda bothered me. Kinda ate on me. Got to the point where I'd go to the barn an take a egg or two an suck'em.

See, when I was jest a big kid, I'd gone one day with Arnold Schreurs, who was on the town board, to see where some smoke was comin from. We walked an walked—I saw a big pile a cedar posts get burned up that day, an not a thing ta do about it—but there were some people livin perty close to the cranberry marsh, poor as rats, an Arnold asked'em if they had somethin for me ta eat. An they did, though I don't remember what it was. No TV dinner, I kin tell ya that. Nothin ya stick in yer microwave. No frozen pizza.

A Windfall Homestead

But when they asked Arnold if he wanted somethin, too, he sez, "I'll take care a myself," an he went out a the house.

When we left, he told me he'd gone to the barn an sucked a couple eggs, an he told me how ta do it.

So that's what I did, a few times ennyway, ta steer clear a Gramma an her lunches.

Maybe this seems kinda silly ta you, Seedy. I see you got a funny, puzzled look on yer face. I mean me gettin bothered by Gramma sneakin a lunch. An maybe she wasn't sneakin at all. Maybe she always ate a little lunch in the middle a the morning. But nobody wudda dared ta do that at home, in the bunkhouse. There we barely had enuff ta eat, an havin a private lunch in the middle a the morning wudda been jest like stealin. Maybe I misunderstood Gramma's lunchin, but I think you kin see how I might a come ta see it as I did. Maybe this is one a those places you kin sort a sense what discipline it takes ta be really poor an yet treat everybody fair'n square. An then how mad you kin get if you catch somebody violating the rules. Or are we all too fat an well-fed now ta be able to understand such a thing? What do ya think, Seedy?

Suckin eggs is awful, though, jest like suckin a big glob a snot. But if ya kin get the first one down, the second one's not so bad. An I'll tell ya what, there's poost in raw eggs. It'll turn yer guts ta eat one, but if ya get'er down an keep'er down, why you can damn near fly. A few more a those raw eggs an I think I wudda growed feathers an started ta crow.

2

A Canthook Man

WHAT'S NEXT? WHAT'S NEXT? What's next? You gotta, remember, Seedy, I never wrote ennything down. My head jest isn't big enuff ta have all that stuff stored away neat'n nice. An even if it is in there somewhere, how ya gonna find it in that dustbin?

I think you better put that vacuum cleaner away. It ain't exactly the sweetest sound I ever heard. Plus yer likely ta suck stuff out you might not care ta see.

Well, in the summer a '34, I went up west a Joe Smitty's, on Conservation Road, ta see about gettin a job from a gypo who was loggin for Rib Lake. There were two brothers who ran the outfit, an their last name was Lamberti.

The younger brother was Matt. He was the woods boss, the foreman, an the men didn't like'em very much. They called'em The Weasel becuz you'd be workin in the woods, an all of a sudden there's Matt poppin up, from behind a tree or a pile a brush, like he'd been sneakin in ta see if you were workin hard enuff.

The older brother was Lambert—Lambert Lamberti—an he perty much stayed in the office. So if Lambert was the boss, it was Matt ya had ta deal with in the woods.

There ain't a lot ta tell about this job, cuz all I did was roll logs. Well, I worked for Lamberti from the summer a '34 till breakup in the spring a '35, though the last couple a days in the spring I drove a team a horses an drayed logs, dawn to noon. We had ta quit by noon becuz the drays'd cut up an wear out the snow, on account a the sun turning everything ta slush.

But except for those couple a days drayin, I was a canthook man. In the summer an all fall I rolled logs up into big, long stacks, rolled'em up on spiked skids, an in the winter I rolled'em down ta be loaded on rail cars an hauled away to the sawmill.

Lamberti had lots a canthooks, an it took me a while ta find one that fit, but once I found it, that canthook was *mine*, an nobody else got ta use it. An if it's possible ta be a *expert* with a canthook, I was a expert. Or I learned ta be one.

Logs, ya know, are always bigger on one end than on the other, so when ya roll'em, one end goes fast an the other goes slow. So ta keep the logs rollin straight, ya got ta learn ta cut'em, an by *cuttin'em* I mean gettin'em ta move the way you want'em ta move—straight. I ain't talkin about cuttin with a saw. I mean turnin'em—cuttin'em—with yer canthook. Ta do that, the log's got ta be movin. So yer cuttin'em while they're rollin. An so you got ta be strong an quick an always payin attention.

I had lots a partners, but none of 'em lasted. I got really good at rollin logs, an I even got ta like it. Kinda like a athlete with a canthook.

Once Matt came an got me an took me over to a skidway where a couple a men couldn't keep up with the skidders an had a awful mess. Logs were comin in too fast for'em ta deck. Logs layin everywhere.

Well, I saw right away that they needed more skids put down, so I sez to'em—an ya gotta remember I'm only twenty-two years old, an all those men were older'n me—I sez, "Here, grab hold! Let's put more skids down here an here!" An we did, an in a half-hour we had that mess perty well straightened out.

Then Matt comes an takes me back ta where I'd been workin, an there's *two* men doin what I'd been doin by myself, rollin logs down from the stacks, an he sends those two men away.

So I was a canthook man for Lamberti. An I was good at it. Maybe I'm braggin, an maybe I ain't.

Is it braggin, Seedy, ta be proud a somethin ya know yer good at? You, fer instance, cudda been a world champion napster, if you ever had a notion to compete.

What was the pay? Are ya tryin ta change the subject? It was either twenty-six or twenty-seven cents a hour, nine hours a day, six days a week, an they took ninety cents a day out a yer pay fer room an board. So you kin do the arithmetic if you want to, if you got yer slide rule handy, ta see how rich I got workin for Lamberti. I probably cudda been President with all that money—advertising on TV, ya know, billboards—but I wasn't quite old enuff ta run. Plus, the Lumberjack Party wasn't very big those days. An, ya know, ta be a member in good standing ya had ta have a axe ta grind. But I was only a canthook man.

Now while I was up workin for Lamberti, stayin in Lamberti's bunkhouse, some a the kids'd come help Gramma in the log barn, help'er with the cows an chickens an chores.

In the summer an early fall, I'd sometimes walk from camp down to the log shack, after a day a rollin logs, an dig in the cellar hole for a hour or two, go to bed, an walk back to Lamberti's in time for breakfast in the cook shanty. That'd be seven, eight miles, one way, but I never did it more'n a couple times a week.

My shoes were wearin out, an I must a told Ned Fox about it, cuz one day he showed up in camp an he had a new pair a shoes fer me. Had to pay'em, a course, but I was awful glad to get'em, an they fit.

Late in the summer there was a terrific rain—water over the road by the Sixth Ward bridge in Jensen, jest to give you a idea a how much it rained—an the cellar hole under the log shack filled with water, right up to the hewed floor joists.

Gramma got all excited about it, scared to death. I guess she thought the log shack was gonna float away, down the Boulder to the Wisconsin, an down the Wisconsin to the Mississippi, an down the Mississippi to the Gulf a Mexico, an she didn't have no sunglasses or inner tube or nothin. Not even enny fishin tackle. Plus she wasn't big on alligators.

Ennyway, I jest told'er not to worry, the water'd go down again. An it did.

Grampa wasn't well, an he was gettin worse an worse. He could hardly get out a bed ennymore. Now Grampa Buckberry, before he died, always had a trimmed beard an a full head a hair. But Grampa Coster was perty thin on top an he didn't want a beard. It got to be my job to shave'em, once a week, while he was sorta sittin up in bed.

I still got his razor.

It was in the fall a '34 when he died. He wasn't yet eighty years old. I wasn't home when he kicked the bucket. I was rollin logs for Lamberti. But

A Windfall Homestead

the funeral was at the Catholic church in Jensen, an he was buried in the big cemetery on the east side a town. I was one a the pall bearers.

After Grampa was buried, Gramma stayed on at the log house through the winter, though one or another a my sisters usually stayed with'er. I don't think enny of'em liked it very much, cuz Gramma was perty sharp. She was not a happy woman, an it ain't easy to be around somebody who's got a sharp tongue an ain't afraid to use it, especially when yer a kid, an ya don't dare talk back.

Cudda been in the spring a '35 when Gramma went to live with my sister Daisy, cuz by then Daisy was married to Jim Meier, an they were livin on Third Street, in Jensen.

But I'd come home every Saturday night. Except once, in the winter, when the weather was too bad. So I stayed in camp on a Sunday. I think that was the hardest day a my life. Nothin to do. Toss an turn an pace the floor. I thought that day'd never end. An, besides, it cost me ninety cents fer room an board! I decided I'd never do that again.

One a the times I was shavin Grampa Coster, he sez to me, "Everything here is yers." I guess he meant table an chairs an stove an such as that. But it didn't turn out that way.

Well, it did an it didn't. But we ain't up to that yet.

When the big brick house was sold, I went to the auction. See, there was about seventeen hunnerd dollars worth a debt against it. I spoze that was Minnie's restaurant, mostly. With interest an unpaid taxes, the total debt came ta over two thousand dollars.

Those days it had to be a public auction, maybe on account a the unpaid taxes, an the sheriff was the auctioneer. It was held right out the front door a the court house. An I think it took longer fer people to assemble than it did to do the auction. Couple a minutes an it was all over.

Later, somebody came up to me an sez, "I heard you bought yer Grampa's place." I jest laughed, though it wasn't a happy laugh. I didn't have seventeen hunnerd cents, much less seventeen hunnerd dollars.

I offen thought about it—big brick house, an a barn, an seventeen acres a woods an field an pasture, with a crick runnin through it, in town but at the edge a town—all that for jest over two thousand dollars.

Kinda makes ya sick to think about it. Even now.

A Canthook Man

Before he died, one a the times I was shavin'em, Grampa told me to go get the top buggy an the cutter he had stored in the barn by the big brick house. He said they still belonged ta him. But I could have'em. But I had no place to put'em, so I never went ta get'em.

When the place got sold at auction, the cutter an buggy went right along with the sale a the big brick house.

Seems like, when yer poor, things sometimes get away from you even when they shouldn't. Maybe, if I hadn't already been thinkin cars, I wudda found a place for that buggy an cutter.

But, at that time in my life, I didn't even own a horse. What use did I have for a buggy an a cutter?

While I was workin for Lamberti, I heard that Joe Smitty had shot a wolf. But by the time I got ta see it, that wolf was layin on the back seat a Lonzo Ward's car.

The Wards lived less'n half a mile east a Smitty, right alongside a Conservation Road. Him an her had a couple kids—two, three—well, two, cuz the baby had died—an I even hired the older boy to help me make hay one summer. He was fifteen, sixteen, kinda small an mouthy. Paid'em a dollar a day. An fed'em.

Ennyway, it wasn't a timber wolf, only a brush wolf, though now everybody calls'em coyotes. An though Smitty had shot'em, this Ward boy was talkin like *he* got'em, an made it sound like it was a dozen of'em he got. Big long string a bullshit. That boy was a talker.

It was the Wards who took that brush wolf ta town an got the bounty. I guess at the time I figgered Joe Smitty didn't take it down becuz he didn't have a car. An so he jest kept his nose out of it.

But, years later, when Smitty died at the county home, when they printed his obituary in the paper, why his name wasn't Joe Smitty at all! That was jest an assumed name—though now I can't remember what his real name was. He was still Joe Smitty ta me.

But then I got ta thinkin about that brush wolf an why Smitty didn't go along ta town ta collect the bounty. Maybe he was keepin his distance from ennybody who might figger out who he was. Though what he'd done, or what he was hidin from, I never did know or learn.

All I know is Joe Smitty liked to drink a little, an I guess that's all there is ta tell, other than he had his house built right over top of his barn. A little drinkin, a little wolf, an a couple a cows an a team a horses in the cellar. Maybe he saved on firewood. Maybe he jest liked the smell of his critters. Who knows?

How to tell ya this one? I kin look right at it an see it, right in front a my eyes, right now.

Jest imagine yerself layin in bed, sound asleep, and all of a sudden somebody's poundin on yer door. It was a bright moonlit night, an I got up. Two guys were at the door. Hard to make'em out at first, but then I recognized'em. Both of'em kinda wobbly.

One was Cat Zortman an the other was Joe Smitty. They were drinkin pals. An they said their car was tipped over in my field.

So I got dressed an walked with'em ta see the problem. An there was Cat's Ford, not far from my driveway, acrost the ditch, layin on its side.

Well, they wanted it straightened up, so I got my car an rigged a chain up an over Cat's car an I pulled real easy an up she came. Every single window was busted out, even the windshield.

But Cat an Smitty climbed in, Cat hit the starter an she ran, an off they went, headed west, up towards Smitty's. I had to laugh. I think they still had more drinkin ta do.

The only bad thing, besides all the broken glass, was that they had got me outa bed.

I told ya Ned Fox'n me put sacks a Gramma's cow feed in the back a the Model T, when we pulled that hemlock pulp down the river on Ned's bobsled, but I didn't tell ya ennything about paying for the feed.

See, this was Depression, with drought on top a that, an jest about everybody was short a hay, short a feed. So Uncle Sam came up with a program called Feed Loan. You could get so much hay, so much ground-up cow feed, but you had ta work off yer debt.

Town a Boulder got a big dose a that program, an it was roadwork you had ta do to work off yer debt. Pa worked off his feed loan, an I was spozed to work off Gramma's. She had maybe fifteen, twenty dollars worth a Feed Loan debt.

Pa worked his off up on Whiskey Bill Road. They were jest puttin that road in. He was up there a couple weeks, workin off his debt. Brushin.

Throwin off rocks. Whatever he did. But I was workin for Lamberti by that time.

It was on a weekend when I saw Pa, an he sez, "They want you ta come work off yer loan." He was jest done workin off his. An I told'em, "I can't come. I can't quit my job ta do that." But Pa told me I couldn't ignore it, I had ta do somethin about it. So I asked'em if he'd work it off for me, a couple weeks work probably, an I'd give him my wages from Lamberti ta make it worth his while.

Well, he wasn't too happy about it, but he did it. See, twenty-six, twenty-seven cents a hour, an take room an board out a that, an there wasn't much left fer me to give'em. But Pa worked off Gramma's Feed Loan, an I paid'em my wages from Lamberti ta do it.

I think Gramma's cows were tickled pink.

I don't think I told ya, either, that Aunt Minnie didn't come ta Grampa Coster's funeral. Well, ta be honest, I don't think ennybody told'er he had died.

Ma was awful mad at'er.

So I guess Minnie couldn't come to her Pa's funeral if she didn't know he was dead.

3

Full a Little Tricks

Ya know, I said Gramma went to live with Daisy an Jim in the spring a '35, but now I ain't so sure it was that soon. Seems ta me Gramma was still livin in the log shack when I was workin for Kinzel, which was from the summer a '35 right through till breakup, in the spring a '36.

Maybe there wasn't enny '35. Maybe the calendar went from '34 right to '36, jest so we could get through the Depression a little quicker.

Roosevelt, ya know, was full a little tricks ta help poor folks. Every month now I get one a those little tricks, an I take it to the bank an turn it into money. Thirty years worth a tricks, so far. Easiest money I ever made. Don't get me wrong: I ain't complainin.

But, ya know, it's probably a good thing Methuselah was dead before Social Security came along. It says in the fifth chapter a Genesis that Methuselah was nine hunnerd an sixty-nine years old when he kicked the bucket. All by himself he mighta broke the system, not countin the other old geezers way back then. Jest think, if he'd gone on the dole at age sixty-five, he'd a been getting a check every month for the next nine hunnerd an four years. Go ahead, multiply nine hunnerd an four times twelve an see what ya get. That's a lot a money. There wudda been nothin left for the rest of us!

Ennyway, I jest went up to Kinzel's Camp 41 an asked for a job, an I got one. Actually, Pa an me went up together, but Art Bus—he was the foreman—he sez to Pa, "You ain't a lumberjack," an it's only me he hired.

Full a Little Tricks

Well, I wasn't exactly doin lumberjack work at first, either. See, there's a lot a little garbage jobs to do around a big camp, an it was jest those little things they gave me to do, those first few weeks.

First thing Art Bus got me doin was to unload a railroad car full a what they called hog fuel, an the man I worked with was Hank Fau Fau.

Hank Fau Fau was Indian, or part Indian, an he lived on the east side a the Wisconsin River, acrost the 107 bridge, on Fau Fau Road, in the Town a Rock Falls. He was a middle-aged man, never talked much, but he was my boss.

Hank an me had to unload hog fuel into a box that was sittin on a dray. An when we had a load, we had a team a horses to pull that dray down the road leadin into camp. We'd dump the hog fuel on the road an spread it. Load after load. Trip after trip.

I spoze I should tell you what hog fuel is. It ain't nothing but ground-up waste wood, sort a like wood chips, but made a all kinds a garbage wood. Kinzel used it instead a gravel on places where cars'd come in or park. See, Kinzel had a big sawmill operation in Jensen, an he had railroad cars, so this was a way a gettin rid a some a the junk wood by puttin it to use.

Ennyway, that's what I did with Hank Fau Fau. Took us about a week. Next job I had with Hank was making skidding roads an skidways for piling logs, over near the fur farm, next ta Averill Crick. Axe an saw an grubhoe, those were our tools. Sweat and deer flies.

We were over a mile from camp, but we always walked back for dinner in the cook shanty. Hank'd get a little impatient with me, cuz I liked to go fast, but he'd always say, "Walk slow."

He was the boss, so I'd walk slow. But it went against my nature.

It was the same with workin. Every couple a hours he'd say, "It's time ta rest." An so we'd have ta sit for five, ten minutes ta rest. He was jest killin time, makin the job last. But I wasn't used ta that. I was used to *workin*. Time went better for me if I had a sweat on.

Next job we had was cuttin tall grass that'd grown up between the rails on the railroad track. Piddly little job. Twenty-seven cents a hour, that was our pay. An then they took out room an board.

We got off for the Fourth a July, an I asked Art Bus for a couple extra days becuz I had hay to make at home, for Gramma's cows. He was a little reluctant, but he said okay.

When I got back ta work, back ta camp, I heard that Hank Fau Fau was dead. They'd found his body in the Wisconsin River.

A Windfall Homestead

See, when Hank an me'd go to work, there was a big collie dog that would come along with us. Whether that was Hank's dog or the camp's dog I ain't sure ennymore, but they figgered Hank musta jumped off the bridge, into the river, cuz they found his coat on the bridge an that big collie dog was laying on the coat. Waiting, I guess, for Hank ta come back.

That's what gave'em the clue that Hank was drowned.

I think he liked ta drink a little, an there was a tavern jest acrost the river, right along 107. So people figgered booze probably had somethin ta do with his jumpin off the bridge. Maybe being an Indian in yer own country that ain't yer own country ennymore might've had somethin ta do with it. Easy for us ta say "Get used to it" when we're the grabbin ones. Might be a whole lot different way a lookin at it if we stood a while in Hank Fau Fau's shoes.

Ennyway, I didn't have a partner ennymore, an I ain't even sure what it was I did the next couple a weeks.

But I knew what I wanted to do. The rail line came right behind the cook shanty, an they had a smaller, different sort a steam engine parked out there. It was called a Lima. It was a little bugger, but it was spozed to be better in the woods—could go where the bigger ones couldn't. An there was a fella always workin on it, fartin around, maybe, I don't know, but I'd go visit with'em after supper.

I found out from him that they were gonna start cuttin logs later in the season, an I tried to get'em to help me get a job as a hooker on a loading crew. An he sez, "I'll put in a word fer you."

See, hookin on a loading crew was a job I knew how to do. I was good at it, an it was piecework. You worked yer ass off, but you could make money, a lot more'n twenty-seven cents a hour.

After dinner, all the men'd go back to the bunkhouse an wait for the boss ta come an roll'em out for the afternoon's work. I was one of'em, jest waitin. It was still summertime.

Almost all the men were sittin on benches in front a their bunks, two long rows a men facin each other acrost a walkway down the middle. Gabbin, ya know, visitin. Jest waitin. Killin time.

All of a sudden a man steps into the open doorway, an he jest stands there, lookin. I spoze he was lettin his eyes adjust to the dim light inside, but jest the way he stood there caught everybody's attention, an the gabbin jest sorta petered out.

Full a Little Tricks

He was a powerfully built man, jest like a wedge from his shoulders to his hips. He walked real slow, an he looked at every man, first on one side, then on the other, jest liked he owned the place or was a game warden an he'd come to pinch somebody—lookin for his man, ya might say.

Everybody is jest sittin there lookin at'em, wonderin Who the devil is this?

Well, he jest keeps comin down the walkway, slow an easy, lookin at every man, sizing'em up. I was sittin on the bench in front a my bunk, which was the last one, in the back, on the righthand side. An when he gets to me he stops an looks me over for a long time, an then he sez, "An what are *you* gonna do?" Well, I hardly knew what ta say to'em. Was he challenging me to a fight? So I sez to'em, "I'm gonna be hookin on the jammer."

He was jest standin there lookin at me. "Oh, no yer not," he sez.

Well, I was half aggravated an half fascinated, wonderin Who the hell are you to be telling me what I'll be doin or not doin? But I jest sat there starin at'em.

"You an me," he sez, "are gonna cut pulp together. An we're gonna make more money than all these other guys." An he kept right on talkin.

Well, it ain't long an I'm not only convinced, but eager, too.

"You'll have to get a saw," he sez. "A saw an a axe."

"I'll jest go to the saw filer's shack an get us a crosscut," I told'em.

"Oh, no!" he sez. "I got my own saw. We ain't gonna saw together."

Now I *was* puzzled. "Why ain't we gonna saw together?" I asked'em.

"Becuz we'd talk too much," he sez.

Well, you kin see for yerself how gabby we were. But not only that. Look how quick we went from total strangers ta not only solvin each of our problems, but getting ta be partners in the process. See, if we'd sawed together and got ta talkin too much, jest like my partner was anticipating, and if we'd solved every stinkin problem in the world as fast as we jest got done doin with our own, why we'd a had everything in the world taken care of in a matter a weeks. But then, what would there have been left ta do?

So I went to see the saw filer—that was Fred Bartelt, Seedy, who was yer Ma's uncle, though I didn't know yer Ma at the time—an Old Fred didn't have enny one-man saws, only crosscuts, so I had to pick out a couple a the shorter ones—two of'em, cuz every day you got one sharpened, and so ya had ta alternate yer saws.

Art Bus took Oscar an me—that strange new man was named Oscar Krause—took us into the woods an showed us our patch a hemlock. We weren't to cut ennything big enuff for saw logs, only pulp, an we'd be workin by the cord. An Oscar sez to me, "I'll work here an you work there, far enuff to be out a each other's way, close enuff to call if either of us needs help."

It took a while to get used ta cutting by myself with a two-man saw, but I figgered out how ta do it, an we cut pulp. I don't remember that either of us ever had ta call for help. We both knew what we were doin, an we were good at what we did.

We cut pulp for several months. Every Friday an Saturday we got a team a horses from the barn boss an we'd dray our piles a pulp out to the landing. I was the teamster. I always drove the horses. An we made two, three times what most a the men made, jest like Oscar said we would.

After we'd cut the pulp, we went ta cuttin logs. But then we had ta have a third man, a full-time teamster, an Art Bus gave us a man named Gunnar Anderson, who talked real broken. He was Swedish or Norwegian, but I can't remember which.

Gunnar was a poor teamster. He always drove the horses with a slack line, cursin at'em an hollerin. You could hear Gunnar all over the woods. An it didn't take long an he played out one a the horses.

See, you play out a horse an you can't get'em ta do ennything. They're jest done. They'll stand there with their head hanging down like they'd jest as soon be dead.

Oscar an me figgered we were done, too. But, another teamster had played out a horse that same morning. So Art Bus sez ta me, "You take Gunnar's good horse, an the good horse from those other guys, an you got yerself a team. Only *you* got ta drive'em. I'm puttin Gunnar on a saw."

So Gunnar had ta saw with Oscar. An Gunnar *was* a good lumberjack. He was just no good with horses.

All the rest a that winter, I was the teamster. I drove the horses with a *tight* line, and they *pulled*. There were lots a times I was hooked onta the log they hadn't even finished sawin off yet. That meant that when they'd cut'er off, I was gone with it. Saved'em lots a swampin. Kept things clear.

But Gunnar came ta work one Monday morning with a lumberjack-sized hangover an sat on a log holdin his head so it wouldn't explode. Oscar jest lit into'em. Called'em things nobody ought ta hear. But, except for that one time, Gunnar carried his weight, an we made money.

The only block a time I missed was a week, in the fall a '35, when I'd banged up my left wrist an those perty little red streaks started climbin up my arm. Blood poisoning.

Full a Little Tricks

So I had ta go home, go see a doctor, an I ended up with my arm in a sling for most of a week. This was before Gunnar joined us, so I found Oscar a temporary partner, in order to hold my place. I asked Daisy's husband, Jim Meier, ta fill in for me, an he did.

But while I was home, I saw that my well was gonna cave in unless I put some cement curbings down the well hole. So, with one arm in a sling, I made three, four curbings with some forms I'd got a hold of. I mixed all the cement with one hand. I didn't get those curbings *down* the well that week, but I got several of 'em *made*.

An then I went back ta Kinzel's an got my job back, sawin with Oscar Krause. An Oscar sez ta me, "I cudda done jest as much by myself." He meant Jim Meier wasn't a good lumberjack. But that was okay for me cuz that meant I could pick up where I'd left off—sawin with Oscar, makin some money.

Sometime in the winter a '36 we finished at Camp 41 an moved ta Camp 42, which was alongside the north end a what's now Frostbite Avenue. We cut logs there until the camp shut down for the spring breakup. I had saved two hunnerd an twenty-five dollars, an I took that money an went ta see Frank Kurth. I stood by his desk an counted it out for'em, an he jest looked at me. I don't think too many people were payin off their debts those days.

When I walked out a Frank's office, I *owned* my forty acres. I might a been broke again, or next to it, but that land was *mine*.

Well, I jest went home, got out my beaver traps, an went back ta Kelly Crick. That wudda been the spring a '36, an, before long., I had some hot hides ta bring ta Ray Trantow.

Everything seemed ta work out jest fine.

4

The Biggest Walleye I Ever Caught

It was in '36 when Pa an Ma an all a my sisters an brothers, except for Mary an Daisy, moved to the state a Washington. But I ain't told you that Batchelders, who lived next to the Boulder River, about a quarter-mile west a the log shack, but on the south side a the road, that they moved ta Jensen an that Dick an Tillie Hahn moved inta the Batchelders' house.

I think they made some sort a house swap, but I ain't sure about that.

Ennyway, Pa an Dick hunted together once in a while, an sometimes I'd come along. I still wasn't much of a deer hunter, always gettin the buck fever, an Pa wasn't much of a hunter, either. Not fer deer, ennyway. I think he only shot ten, twelve of 'em the entire time he lived in Wisconsin, all of 'em at a lick.

There were two times the three of us were out an a game warden come nosin around. One time we were up in what was then called the "Game Preserve," a patch a land south a Whiskey Bill Road. We were walkin along the road when I saw a car comin. I guessed who it was, so I lit out for the woods.

It was legal ta be there, if you had yer gun in a case, an both Pa an Dick had some kinda sack coverin up their guns. I was carryin some old shotgun, but I didn't have a case for it, an I hadn't bothered with a bag, so I knew it was illegal. That's why I lit out.

Well, it was Leo Gould. He stopped an talked to Pa an Dick, even felt Pa's gun inside the sack, an bawled 'em both out. Who did they think they were foolin, an that sort a thing. An he wanted to know who that third guy was an how come he ran away; but, a course, neither Pa nor Dick knew who I was or where I'd gone. Their memories jest weren't workin.

Well, I was layin back in the woods listenin. I was scared a gettin pinched, but I knew Leo'd never catch me. I was a young fella, an I could run. But he never came after me, an then he drove away.

Another time we were up in that same area an Dick shot a big doe. We were five, six miles from home, a long way ta drag a deer, especially when there ain't no snow, an so I told'em ta wait, I'd go home an get my car. An so I did. That's when I had that Model T. Ran most of the way.

They were waitin, alright, when I got back. But Dick told me that Ed Bosworth had stopped and jest sat lookin at him an Pa as they were sittin by the side a the road. An finally Old Bosworth sez, "Drag it out an I'll haul it down for ya."

Dick thanked'em, but sez, "We got somebody comin." An Ed Bosworth jest drove away.

See, I was with Dick once when he shot a deer at a lick with a shotgun that Ed Bosworth had loaned'em. (The first time Dick pulled the trigger, that shotgun jest went "click." I think I was jumpy enuff to have quit right there. But Dick jest pulled the hammer back once more—that deer was still standin there lookin—an "Boom!" that deer went down.) An Ed's son Walt kept bees at Dick's. I was there several times when Walt was workin on the hives. He wore a cap an a veil, but he'd walk right in with his sleeves rolled up an go messin with those bees. I'd jest stand out a the way an watch.

So Dick an Ed were some sort a friends. I offen thought that Ed must a recognized how desperate people were—kids ta feed, hardly enny jobs—an people still had ta eat. We mighta been a bunch a outlaws, but we weren't wasteful. We liked ta hunt, but there was a reason for it.

Oscar Wangen once said ta me, "When we started earnin a little more money, the deer started comin back." An that was true. Once we could afford ta eat a little beef, we weren't eatin so much venison.

I'd say the big change was the Second World War, or maybe jest after. Until then, huntin was part a what ya did ta make a livin. If only outlaws ate venison out a season, then almost everybody was a outlaw. That's jest how we lived.

A Windfall Homestead

Well, speakin a World War Two makes me think a John Rowe. John was a bachelor who lived at the end a Heatstroke Lane, jest west a Ed Zastrow's. When John got drafted, at the beginning of the war, he sold his place ta Quinten Ament, thinkin he maybe wouldn't be comin back from the fightin, but he did.

Ennyway, John was older'n me by a few years, an he was a husky brute. One spring—I think I mighta still been livin at home—John an Ed Zastrow an me, toward evening, rowed a boat up the Wisconsin from the mouth a the Boulder, up ta Bill Cross Rapids.

People were already fishin for suckers at the mouth. But that ain't what we had in mind.

Season wasn't open yet for game fish. But what did we care about that? We each had some sort a rod'n reel—I know mine was a cheap junker —an when we got there, maybe a mile upstream from the mouth, we put ashore on the west side a the river, spread out, an started castin.

Wasn't long an I caught a walleye. I ain't lyin if I tell ya that was the biggest walleye I ever caught. There was a place, under the back seat a the boat, which, if ya lifted it up, you could put yer fish in. When I laid that walleye in there, it reached from one side a the boat to the other. It was that big.

Couple a minutes later, John caught a big bass, an that fish went under the seat, too. Well, catch a couple big fish right off the bat an ya start ta get excited. Ed had gone farther upstream, John was in the middle, an I was farthermost downstream. All of us eager, ya know, castin away.

Well, excitement an those old castin reels don't mix too good, an perty soon I got me one hell of a backlash, a real bird's nest, an I'm kind a squatting down, sort a behind some big rocks, tryin ta untangle that mess, when out a the corner of my eye I see a man go by, upstream, on a trot.

It was Walt Bosworth, an I hunkered down even lower.

In jest a little while here comes Old Ed Bosworth, tryin ta trot, ya know, breathin hard, an I watch him go by, too. When both of 'em were past me, headed upstream, I dropped that rod'n reel, jumped inta the woods, and started runnin.

It was kind a stupid. I should a gathered up my line an took that whole mess with me, but I didn't. Might even been able ta jump in the boat an get away. But I didn't do that, either. I ran for it.

Ennyway, by then John an Ed heard the commotion an had jumped inta the brush, too. John told me later that Walt had run after 'em, an was catchin up to 'em, so he jest stopped an turned around an faced Walt. Well,

Walt, he said, stopped too, kinda looked'em over like he was sizin'em up, an shrugged, an jest turned around an walked back to his Pa.

I don't know if John was a fighter, but he was a husky guy, an Walt sort a had him cornered. But Walt had second thoughts about it, an he jest walked away.

So we all got away. Lost my rod'n reel. Ed an Walt Bosworth took the boat an found out it belonged ta Ed Zastrow's Pa, but Ed's Pa didn't have nothin ta do with us fishin, so he got the boat back.

The only people who got pinched were the fish. John's bass an my walleye. Biggest one I ever caught. I don't know if they put'em in jail, or what.

I ain't sure when I got the curbings put down the well. I know I didn't get'em all made when I was workin for Kinzel.

But it was Mary's husband, Otto Luedtke, who helped me put'em in. We cobbled together some kind of a contraption, with a crank on a cable, an lowered'em down, one at a time. Took longer ta make 'em than ta put'em in place.

The problem with that well was that it'd go dry on ya if ya pumped hard for twenty minutes. Later, with more cows, that wasn't good enuff. It was close ta twenty years before I solved the problem. Jest about the time Jack was born.

But we ain't up ta that yet.

By the spring a '36, Pa'd perty well given up on stayin in Wisconsin. He never did fit in an, especially with the Depression, he couldn't buy a job. So him an Clara's husband, Stub Lohff, took a train an went ta Washington.

Ma had some shirttail relation out there, so I guess that was the connection.

Ennyway, they went. Pa got a job right away, in the woods, but he didn't like it very much, so he got a job on a section crew, on a railroad, an he liked that a lot better.

But Ma got sick an had ta go to the hospital. I know she was bad enuff that no garden was put in on the flats that summer.

I can't tell ya what made'er sick. Change a life, maybe. There was lots a anger in'er about Minnie, about what happened ta Grampa an Gramma losin their place an all.

A Windfall Homestead

Ma had some sort a operation. They thought she was gonna kick the bucket. Pa even came back from Washington for a week or two. I remember he had a extra pair a shoes with'em, new ones he'd bought out in Washington. They fit me, so I bought'em from'em. An then he went back ta Washington—couldn't afford ta lose his job.

Well, I got hired again by the Universal Engineering Company. Had ta go to Mauston an drive a loco. My old Ford was petered out, so I bought a old Star from Mark Lemmer. Somebody'd made that car into a pickup, with a little box on the back. It was a junker, but it ran, an I drove it down ta Mauston.

Mary an Otto came out an stayed at the log shack an took care a Gramma's cows. Otto wasn't no farmer, so I spoze it was Mary who did the milkin.

It was perty routine at Mauston. But I was one a the few men who stayed over the weekend, an Old Frank Pierce almost always found something extra fer me ta do, like sprinkle water on the drying cement, an I saved every nickle I could get my hands on.

When the pavin was done an the crew moved out, Old Frank kept me an a man named Maynard on for a couple more weeks. I don't know what Maynard did—he was spozed ta be a mechanic—but my job was runnin the tar buggy an tarrin joints in the summer's pavin, about two miles worth.

Maynard an me bunked in the office, jest the two of us, an we ate in the cook shanty. I was the cook.

About the only entertainment in the last couple a weeks was when I set the tar buggy on fire, an then when Maynard showed up, while I was workin, handed me a .22, an told me a deer was in that patch a woods over there. A local fella who'd worked for Universal was on the other side a that patch a woods, waitin for me ta drive the deer out to'em.

Well, that was right up my alley. So Maynard dribbled tar in the cracks while I crept inta the woods an, by golly, that deer came out to the fella on the other side. One shot an he got'em.

Well, I had ta go back ta work, but that fella brought Maynard an me a whole mess a venison steaks, an were they ever good!

When I got home, middle a September, something like that, Ma was out a the hospital an everybody was all worked up, in the mood ta leave.

Gramma Coster came ta me, wantin ta sell me her cows an all the household stuff that was still in the log shack. She wanted forty dollars apiece for those two Jersey cows, an fifteen dollars for all the household stuff—stoves an chairs an whatnot—an so I jest peeled'er off ninety-five dollars.

Ma asked me ta come along ta Washington, practically begged me, but I told'er, "The log shack's the best home I ever had, an I ain't comin." So she asked me if I wanted her cows, an I said I did.

I didn't pay'er for'em until the day I took'em ta town ta catch the train. Things were kind a awkward. An Ma sez ta me, "I don't have enuff money ta buy the tickets." Well, that kind a pulled me out a my daze, an I remembered I hadn't paid'er for those cows. Maybe I didn't want ta pay'er for'em. Maybe I didn't want ta see her go.

But it was too late for all a that. So I jest reached inta my pocket an pulled out my money an paid'er one hundred an twenty dollars for her three cows. An she went into the depot an bought tickets for herself an all the kids.

Clara hadn't been able ta wait. She'd already gone ta be with Stub, her an her two kids.

Sayin goodbye ain't easy. It ain't easy ta do, period. But when there's a whole flock a excited kids an lunches an luggage an the next thing ya know yer watchin the train disappear down the railroad track, ya realize you really didn't say goodbye, an there's this feelin of "Hey! Wait a minute! We ain't talked about this! We ain't said goodbye yet!"

But it's too late for that.

Almost everybody left, except Little Hobo. But he had a log shack, a log barn, forty acres a land, an five cows. He might a been damn near broke again, but Little Hobo had a home.

The Little Hobo was a *farmer*.

5

A Peculiar Kind of Exercise

MY STAR WAS JEST about wore out. After the folks left, I went ta town an, on the east side, I saw a Model A roadster fer sale, about a hunnerd dollars. Since I'd spent all my money for cows—Gramma's two an Ma's three—I had ta finance that car. But then I had somethin fairly decent ta drive.

Now I was gettin ta be a better hunter, finally gettin past the buck fever. What seemed ta get me over the hump of always gettin buck fever was the time, past deer season, I was trackin a deer in the timber. I had borrowed Jack Young's .32 carbine. I'd take a step or two an look, examine everything, take another couple a steps an look.

An there, all of a sudden, was a bump on a tree. I looked at it real close an I figgered it was the side of a deer's belly, with the deer standin behind the tree. So I took a step or two sideways, ta get a better look, an that deer bolted like a streak a lightning. I never even got a shot.

That made me so mad I started ta run after the deer. I ran up a little rise, an there he was, standin, lookin back at me. He started ta run, I up an shot—I was still mad—an down he went.

So I ran up ta where he was layin on the ground, an I jumped on top of 'em, pulled out my huntin knife, an cut his throat. I jest laid on top of 'em till he was dead.

Then I had ta gut 'em, a course, an I looked to see where I'd hit 'em. It was a buck, but his horns were gone already. He throwed 'em. But all I could find were a couple bloody strings where his testicles ought ta be. I'd shot his nut bag off!

Well, that got me ta thinkin. If I hadn't jumped on'em, he might've got over the shock a havin his testicles shot off, got up an run away.

After that, my buck fever went away.

But huntin with Dick Hahn was good. He taught me a lot. He was a slow shooter, but he had a good aim. He even taught me ta *smell* deer.

When I told Ned Fox I could smell deer, Ned laughed right in my face. Well, we were friends, so I told'em, "You wait. Sometime we'll go hunting together an I'll show you I kin smell'em."

An it wasn't too long an we were up west a where George Bohman used ta live, though Donald Graap lives there now. There was a little snow an we were followin a pair a tracks headed east. But the wind was out a the north, an all of a sudden I smelled deer.

So, real quiet like, I sez ta Ned, "You kin keep followin these tracks to the east if you want to, but I smell deer an I'm going north, inta the wind." Ned jest looked at me, standin there an thinkin. Finally he shrugged an said, "Okay, I'll go with you."

Well, we hadn't gone north a couple hunnerd yards when up jump two deer and—bang!—I got one of 'em. The other one got away.

"Well," I sez ta Ned, "do ya believe I kin smell'em now?"

Being able ta smell deer helped me lots a times. The best time for it is a damp day. See, there's some kind a gland in the back joints on the back legs, an that scent carries on a damp day. Once you learn it, you never forget it.

Ya might say I learned ta hunt with Dick, but once Dick's boys were big enuff ta hunt with'em, Fidelis especially, cuz he was the oldest, I hunted more an more with Ned. Ned and Pete Horgan.

Once Dick wanted ta get out real early on the opening day a season, but I told'em I had ta milk my cows first, an do barn chores. See, his boys could do his chores, so he didn't have ta wait.

He told me where he'd be—he had a favorite stump near Averill Crick—an I told'em I'd come up, but that I was gonna sneak hunt all the way, so not to expect me till maybe mid-morning.

Well, I was in those up-and-down hills north a Doc Sievert's (though Doc wasn't in there yet), an I got one look at a buck. I threw up the gun, but I didn't get a shot. One jump an he was gone. But right behind that buck was a big doe. One shot an down she went.

A Windfall Homestead

I pulled the guts out a her (I was quick at that, ya know, five minutes an yer done), an I kept right on huntin, headed north. I was startin ta get perty close ta where I figgered Dick'd be when, all of a sudden, there was a buck comin through a grass swamp, like he'd been kicked out by somebody else. One shot an down he went.

So I gutted him, too, an dragged'em out a that swamp. I was closin in on the place where I expected ta find Dick, when two little ones jumped up an ran off to the side.

I didn't get a shot at either of 'em, but I went ta find Dick, an I told'em those little ones were in there yet. So he went to another place ta stand, an I looped around behind where I figgered those deer ought ta be, an, by golly, they came out by Dick an he got both of 'em.

One morning's huntin, an we had four deer!

Well, that was a lot a draggin. We pulled the buck over to the landing by Camp 30. Laverne Culver happened ta be there with a car, an he said he'd haul the buck fer me. But the doe an the two little ones weren't exactly legal, so we had ta drag those home ourselves.

Dick had made a rule about our huntin together: "Bucks we keep an does we wide." Dick had a hard time sayin "divide," so the word always came out as "wide."

We had lots a venison that year.

"Bucks we keep, an does we wide."

Ya know, Seedy, all this gets me ta thinkin about payin attention. I mean, when yer workin yer payin attention to what yer doin. But if it's kinda routine, yer mind kin be somewhere else, thinkin about whatever it's thinkin about.

But with huntin it's different. You got ta be on the ball all the time—payin attention. But it's a special sort of attention. Yer both focused an unfocused, all at the same time.

Do you know what I mean, Seedy? Are ya noddin yes or are ya jest noddin off?

What I mean is, when yer huntin yer lookin for what ain't there. Or if it's there, you don't know when or where you'll find it. So yer payin attention ta everything—not only ta how ya walk, where ya step, how hard yer breathing, but ta everything around that you can see or hear or smell. Yer waiting fer something ta really focus on, but until that happens, yer mind

A Peculiar Kind of Exercise

is taking in everything it can—all around, front, back, to the sides—a complete circle, really. It's like yer payin attention to everything and nothing, both of'em at the same time.

Yer waiting—ready—for somethin ta happen *in* that circle, but you have no idea when or where. I think it's that, Seedy, that makes huntin so special. It's a peculiar kind of exercise fer yer mind, somethin that's different than ordinary work.

I wish I could explain it better. But sittin here now, thinkin back on what huntin meant to me, I kin see it wasn't all about puttin meat on the table, important as that might have been. There was somethin else goin on, somethin harder ta talk about. It's like hunting was some sort a exercise for yer mind. It's like being a living core a consciousness drifting through the woods, focused an unfocused at the same time.

Damnit! I'd like ta talk more about this, but it kinda feels like chasin a ghost. I think this one's got me stumped.

Now I don't know if I owned my .303 already or if I was still borrowin it from Jim Meier, but I'm perty sure I hadn't shot a deer with it yet. An on this perticular time, I was huntin with Dick Hahn—I was his driver, as usual—an he had along with him his father-in-law, George Ament.

George was a old man already. He was tall an slender an very active. (He lived, ya know, ta be one hunnerd years old. He was Quinten Ament's Pa, an Quinten's the youngest a all George's kids, an Quinten's a month older'n I am. So George was old enuff ta be my Pa an then some.) So George was with us an right away I made a drive for Dick an George. Several deer came out by Dick an he shot all his shells an missed every shot.

When I came out by'em, he was perty perturbed. See, Dick was a slow shot but he was a good shot. He had that long-barreled .32 an he'd fill'er up with six, seven shells, an that's all he ever needed. He never took enny extra in his pocket. So there he sat like a dunce—way back in the woods, no deer, no shells, kinda disgusted with himself.

So I sez to'em, "Here, you take my gun. All I'm doin is drivin, ennyway. I'll carry yers." An that's what we did.

Next drive, up near Camp 30, a nice buck comes out by Dick. Two shots an he got'em. Well, he was happy as a lark. But I noticed that as Dick was field dressin that deer, with all our guns leanin up against trees, he would now an then look over at mine—all new an shiny, ya know—an I felt perty proud a that Savage. I didn't know what Dick was thinkin, but I could tell he was lookin at my gun.

When he was done an off to the side scrubbin blood off his hands in the snow, he sez ta me kinda quiet, "Would you mind if I gave that buck ta George?" Well, why should I mind? So I told'em ta do whatever he wanted. An when he told George "Put yer tag on'em," I think Old George was as happy as a kid in a candy store.

But every now an then I'd see Dick lookin at my gun.

In the winter a '36 an '37, I didn't go workin in the woods. I had five cows ta milk, did a little trappin, an I got to the woods fer huntin as much as I wanted.

I think the closest I got to a loggin crew that winter was standin in the woods, on the east side a the Boulder, up by Camp 30, watchin the Scheu brothers, Ed an Alvin, work their logging operation acrost the river.

They had bought a cat, an that's what they were usin ta pull sledloads a logs to the landing. But that cat was broke down half the time, an I think the Scheus kinda lost their ass that winter. Later, I was up there, jest pokin around, an I saw where the bobsleds had been heaped an burned, in order ta salvage the iron fer scrap. Now that's getting right down to the bottom a the barrel.

A course when I'd be there watchin'em, I had my new rifle with me. See, I'd borrowed Jack Young's .32 carbine off an on for a long time an, if I got somethin, I'd give Happy Jack a piece a meat. But that gun never quite fit me.

You'd think guns are all the same, same as you might think canthooks are all the same. But they ain't. Sometimes you find jest the one that *fits*, an that's the one ya want.

Well, the rifle that fit me was that .303 Savage lever-action, an I first got ta use it when Daisy's husband, Jim Meier, loaned it to me. Jim had gotten it through some sort a game a chance when he was a bartender. He got it brand new. An when he let me use it, it didn't take long ta realize *that* was the gun I liked.

So I offered ta buy it from'em, but he didn't want ta sell. Now I was bringin venison down ta him an Daisy, jest like I was bringin it down ta Mary an Otto, though Mary always canned a bunch an gave me half back. That way you kin eat venison all year long.

Ennyway, I told Jim, "You know I'm violating all the time. If I get pinched, I'm gonna lose *yer* rifle, but if it's mine, *I'm* the one who'll lose it."

Well, that kinda decided'em, so he sold it to me for twenty-five dollars—though I didn't have twenty-five dollars in my pocket, an I paid'em a little at a time out a my milk checks.

I'd never known ennything about peep sights till I'd worked in Mauston, for the Universal Engineering Company, an this young fella, a local guy, took a liking ta me an asked me ta come stay with'em one weekend. He lived on his folks' farm, an he had a wife an kid.

It was a nice place, big hills, with a small herd a Holstein cows that looked as big as elephants ta me. I offered ta help milk—they milked strictly by hand—but the old fella turned me down, said "Nope. The cows are used ta us, an we'll do it ourselves."

Well, on Sunday morning my friend gets out his .22 ta show me, an it's got a peep sight on it. He shot a few sparrows off the barn roof an, by golly, he could really hit'em. Sparrows ain't a big target, but he could do it.

An then a friend a his drove in the yard with a car he wanted help on. So he hands that .22 ta me, with a box a shells, an sez, "Here, you shoot some sparrows." Well, that's jest exactly what I did. One shot, ya know, an they all fly away. But give'em ten, fifteen minutes an they're back again.

It took'em longer than he figgered ta work on that car, so I had most a the morning ta shoot. An I *shot*. An by the time they were done futzin around with the car, I had fallen in love with a peep sight.

I still got the .303, an the peep sight I got from Ned Fox is still on it.

Soon as I was a bachelor I had ta do all my own cookin. Well, I ate lots a venison, had my own potatoes, but I'd buy pork'n beans an bacon squares an baker bread.

But I soon learned that I could eat half a loaf a baker bread at a meal. I was used ta homemade bread, an that baker stuff was jest a puff a wind.

So I went ta see Old Man Karban. He was livin by himself in his shack at the top a Karban Hill. I knew he made bread, an I asked'em how ta do it.

Seemed like he was kinda tickled to be asked, an he wrote it down for me, cuz he said he measured it all out when he baked. An so I did it the way he had written, an it worked, and from then on, once a week usually, I baked bread. Two, three loaves. Tried it once with milk, instead a water, but it was like a brick, so I didn't try that trick again.

A Windfall Homestead

Old Man Karban was, I think, Hungarian, an he talked real broken. His family had been in an out, lots a unsettledness there, his wife an kids all gone, an I think he was kinda bitter an lonely. Ya never knew if he'd be friendly or not.

I know once, when I was a big kid, there'd been a little snow, an I tracked a badger to a hole on Karban's forty, an I set a trap. Later I came ta check the trap an Old Man Karban saw me an called me over an wanted ta know what I was doin. When I told'em, he said, "Better move your trap." So I did.

Badgers, ya know, are kinda queer animals. They're low, short critters. Husky buggers. Tough, too. Fighters. I trapped a few of'em. If it was a fur badger, Ray Trantow'd give me four dollars for it. But he'd only give me a dollar or two for a hair badger.

Ray said a hair badger was no different than a fur badger except that he'd wore the fur off his back by livin in a tight hole in the ground. I think I only trapped one fur badger. The others all had that short hair on their backs. They weren't worth as much.

They were also hard ta catch. Badgers, I mean. All of'em. You could set a trap for'em, alright, but they might jest dig themselves a new hole an come out somewheres else. An dig! Man, oh man! One time Emil Oestreich an me tried ta dig a badger out of its hole. We dug for a couple a hours, dug hard, but we couldn't catch up ta that badger. We jest quit.

Maybe some a these memories are like badgers. You try an dig'em out, but they come out a some other hole than the one you figgered.

Ya know, Seedy, I was batchin it from the time the folks left, in the fall a '36, till yer Ma an me got married in the spring a '40. That's three an a half years a the freest time, probably, in my whole life—owned my land, had a log shack an a log barn, five cows, raised my own potatoes, trapped a few beaver an mink, ate a lot a venison, had a car so I could come an go as I wanted or needed to, an, except maybe for being a lonely bastard, I was happy as a lark, free as a bird.

I built a brick chimney in the log shack an, cuz the roof leaked, I put cedar shingles over the used roofing I had put down first.

See, when Grampa an Gramma moved in, I only had a stovepipe, an it went right through the roof. Sometimes, ya know, that stovepipe would

A Peculiar Kind of Exercise

get awful hot, even start ta glow cherry red, an burnin yer house down ain't no joke.

So I bought a batch a bricks an made a chimney. That chimney didn't go into the cellar, didn't even go all the way down to the log shack floor. About four, five feet above the floor, supported by some posts, I made a plank base, an the chimney went up from there.

I wasn't a bricklayer, but I did it. The smoke went out. That's what mattered.

The shingles started out as half a pig. I'd bought the pork from a fella—cost me seven cents a pound—an it was a whole lot more'n I needed. Then I happened ta run inta Ned Fox's brother Charlie, who lived in the Doering area, an when I told'em I had more pork then I knew what to do with, he said he had a batch a cedar shingles he didn't need, an so we traded.

It jest happened there was one a those February thaws, several days a warm, mild weather. So I got right at it an got almost all those shingles down before the weather changed. When the wind turned out a the west-northwest, I thought my hands were gonna freeze. But I kept right at'er an got'er done. An that roof didn't leak ennymore.

Now I can't tell ya for sure, but it must a been in '37 or '38 that I bought a pair a snowshoes. (Those are the ones, ya know, Steve Schulz asked me for, an I finally gave'em to'em.)

Ennyway, Ned Fox an me were huntin more an more up in Kinzel's timber, two, three miles north a where we lived, an sometimes the snow was awful deep. At first, each of us got hold of a pair a skis, an that was okay for getting up *to* the timber, but *in* the timber the snow was softer becuz the sun didn't get to it, an in that soft snow the skis'd jest sink in an were no damn good. We even tied hemlock boughs on the bottom of our skis to keep from sinkin in, but that was real clumsy an no fun.

So I went down ta Howland's Hardware Store, an Old Man Howland ordered me a pair a snowshoes. Michigan style. Said they'd cost seventeen dollars. A few days later they came in. An when I went ta get'em, I had a milk check with me for jest over seventeen dollars. So for that check I got a brand new pair a snowshoes an a little bit a change for my pocket.

Now Dorothy Lansbach had married Otis Winchester, an they lived jest east a the Copper School. Both of'em were teachers, an they took turns teachin at the Copper. But they had bought a tanned moose hide an they were makin moccasins on the side. So I had'em make me a pair.

I'll tell ya, ya put a insole in there, an a couple pair a good wool socks, an strap yerself inta those snowshoe sandals, an you feel like yer walkin on air. Long as the snow is cold an dry, you kin be out all day an yer feet'll stay toasty warm. I only used the moccasins for snowshoein, nothin else.

But one a the first times I was out with'em, I did what it seems like everybody's got ta do, at least once, an that is step one snowshoe on top a the other an take a header inta the snow. An it ain't funny. It's like bein upside down in the water with bags a air on yer feet.

Well, where I went down the snow was deep, but there were popple saplings comin up—big as yer wrist, maybe, big as yer arm—an finally I got hold a one an *climbed* my way up an out a the snow, hand over hand. After that, I was a lot more careful about where I put my feet.

One a those years, an I honestly can't tell ya which it was, I bought a trappin license an got legal. Along with that license, as I remember, I had ta buy tags for the hides. I bought half a dozen of'em, one for each beaver caught, an, when the hides were dry, Abey Block surprised me by comin out ta see me. He brought another fella with'em, an they both came inta the log shack an sat down.

Well, Abey did all the talkin. He looked my hides over an he offered me so much for'em, an I told'em no. See, there was a new system for measurin beaver hides, an it came out to a dollar a inch. I'd measured those hides, an I knew exactly what they were worth. But that ain't what Abey was offerin.

Abey talked an talked, tryin ta get me down, but I wouldn't budge. Abey, ya know, wasn't the only guy there was ta sell'em to. Finally, Abey looks at that other guy, who'd jest been sittin there the whole time, sayin nothin, an that guy nods ta Abey an Abey paid me what they were worth.

I think that other fella was the guy Abey sold his hides to. All of us probably made a little money that day. Except for the beaver. They were jest hides. An them I didn't even have ta take ta town.

It was probably about a year after the folks left that Daisy an Jim packed up an went ta Washington, too.

Jim could never find a good job. They jest gave up, an left.

6

A Cocky Little Wretch

THERE WERE FIVE YEARS in the '30s, five summers, when I worked for the Universal Engineering Company. Six in a row, I mean, an one I didn't. I think it was '37 when I didn't.

In that time somewhere I built a hay shed right next to the log barn, an I also built a silo, about ten feet in diameter an sixteen feet high.

Once I had the silo foundation built, I drove up ta Allard's sawmill, up toward Tomahawk, an bought some lumber. Some a that lumber was elm one-by-fours. When I got home, I took those elm boards into a swamp ta soak.

Otto Schnee lived on the Anderson Homestead an, after the elm boards were completely soaked, he made bands out of 'em. Most a the lumber was used for vertical boards, but the elm bands were horizontal, bent in a curve, an they held the whole thing together. It only took us a couple days ta build it. Otto was a carpenter. I never did put a roof on it.

I'd also made a power plant out a my Old Star car. I'd ripped the body off an had somebody weld a pulley onta the engine. So with that for power, I helped Otto fill silo in exchange for him helpin me.

Those years I cut all the corn I raised by hand. The only thing I had ta have engine power for was ta run the silo filler. Everything else could be done with muscles. The horses' an mine.

A Windfall Homestead

I can't remember my folks ever singin. But I liked ta sing. When I finally got around ta joining the choir at St. Stephens—that wudda been in the 1960s—the lady who directed the choir asked me how I sang, an I sez to'er, "Like a old crow." So she put me in the back row. But in the years when I was batchin it, I used ta sing even while pickin stones. I can't remember if the horses hummed along or not, but the neighbors heard me singin way acrost the field.

At least they told me they did. I don't know if they were happy about it or complainin. The horses didn't say nothin about it, one way or the other.

You asked, Seedy, whether I got the folks' horse, Old Jack. Well, I didn't. Mike Stevens got'em.

Jack was a tough old bugger. He never looked fat. But when Mike got'em, he turned'em out ta pasture. I came over once ta help Mike fill silo, an there was Jack, lookin good, maybe in the best shape I'd ever seen'em. Which shows ya what a little bit a good pasture kin do for a horse.

He was a rangy cuss, ennyway, but I think he never got enuff ta eat when the folks had'em. Always on a starvation diet.

I got a horse after the folks left, an she would sometimes jest start ta kick—for no reason at all, as far as I could tell.

I had a old slusher an was diggin a basement under the log house. I had a slanting hole dug under the log house, an I'd drag the slusher down an load it with a shovel. When I was done shovellin, I'd climb out an try'n get that horse ta pull—the slusher was hooked ta the horse's harness by a long chain—an one day she was jest standin there waitin an she started ta kick.

She kicked an kicked an kicked—there wasn't a thing ta do about it—until she'd kicked nearly all her harness off except for the collar an the hames. It took me a couple a days jest ta repair that mess.

I walked that horse ta town, took'er to the horse barn, an somebody bought'er for twenty-five dollars. I never saw'er again an was glad of it.

See, I'd had a partial cellar hole under the log shack, but it wasn't a full basement. So I hired Otto Schnee's son Warren, ta help me finish the diggin an then build a stone foundation.

I rented four jack screws from Old Dave Ament, an then Warren an me raised the log shack up an built that foundation. Took us about a month,

A Cocky Little Wretch

though when we'd get tired a workin, we'd go shoot the .22 a while. When we got the foundation finished, we lowered the log shack down onto it.

An then I took the jack screws back ta Old Dave's house. Dave's wife told me Dave was down at August Smite's tavern. Since I hadn't paid'em yet, I drove over ta give'em the five dollars I owed'em.

But Old Dave liked ta drink, an when I gave'em the money, he started buyin. By the time I got out a Smite's, I had drank about half a that five dollars, an I think I was carryin one a those jack screws inside a my head.

Somehow I made it home, though me an the Model T were turnin circles all the way.

When I broke a patch a land over along the west fence line, the dirt was black an damp an I planted mangle beets. Man, oh man! Did they ever grow! In the fall, I hauled wagonload after wagonload out a there an put'em down the cellar a the log house.

I got a choppin tool an a tub. The chopper was a S-shaped blade mounted on a wooden handle. In the winter, every day, I'd chop a big mess a those mangle beets an feed'em to the cows. An did they milk!

Ya got ta be careful, though, that you chop'em inta small enuff pieces. Otherwise a cow'll choke.

That winter there was one hell of a snowstorm. Blocked me in. I spent all a one Friday shovellin out the driveway, an the next mornin it was all plugged up again. I didn't go ennywhere that weekend.

Couple a days later the county sent out a man an a cat ta plow the road open. There was a huge drift across the road between the end a my driveway an Dick Hahn's. It took that cat several hours ta punch through the drift.

I put my snowshoes on an went out in my field ta watch'em work. An while I'm there, here comes a long line of horses an sleds from the west—a whole string a men from Berndts' loggin camp. They'd run out a food, an they were comin out. But they had ta wait until that cat had the road plowed open.

So one of'em—I think it was Walter Berndt—asked if all a those milk cans were mine, sittin there at the end a my driveway. I said they were. He couldn't believe I had that much milk from only five cows.

Well, the milk hauler was late, too, count a all the snow, but, even so, I told'em, "I feed those cows mangle beets, an they *milk*."

Those beets lasted all winter. The next summer I planted'em again. But they didn't grow so good, an I never fed mangle beets ta the cows again after that.

I had no idea that the Universal Engineering Company was workin in Jensen. So when I went ta town one summer's day in '38, I was totally surprised ta see some a their equipment on the road.

A course, I had ta smell around, an I found their office in the Sixth Ward up near Ollhoff's sawmill, an I jest went in ta see about a job. Frank Pierce was surprised ta see me, but he said, "I can't hire you cuz all the local men have ta be registered through the employment office."

Well, I was makin a livin off those five cows, so it wasn't like I didn't have ennything ta do, cuz I was busy clearin land an pickin stones. But I liked workin for Universal, an here they were, right in Jensen.

I jest stayed in the office a while, talkin with the boss, with Frank Pierce, an all of a sudden he sez ta me, "Oh, ya, I got somethin for you," an he told me I could move pipeline, for water, ahead a the paver.

An so that's what I did, for—maybe six weeks. Eight or nine-hour days, I forget.

See, they weren't runnin locos on this job, an the trucks were all hired. An since the streets were jest loaded with men lookin fer work, Old Frank had ta be careful where he put me. There were state inspectors all over the place, cuz this was state highway work, an they kept track a who was registered an who wasn't.

So Frank gave me a couple a young fellas ta work with, an mostly what I did that summer was move pipeline. Universal had four jobs in Jensen. Well, three in Jensen, an the big one was several miles a Highway 64 west a Jensen.

That's what those two fellas an me did—put pipe together an take it apart. It takes lots a water ta mix cement like that, an it's got ta be there when they need it. So it ain't no messin around kind a job. You got ta be on the ball.

I worked all those weeks without bein registered.

One day Frank Pierce asked me ta fill in for a man puddlin behind the paver. He even dug out a pair a knee boots for me ta wear. See, there were two puddlers behind the paver, each of'em had a short-handled spadelike shovel, an their job was ta fill wet cement in around the forms, ta make sure

A Cocky Little Wretch

there weren't enny air pockets in there. You had ta wade in wet cement all day long, an after a while it seemed like yer legs were made out a cement. That was a hard job.

But at the end a the day Old Frank sez ta me—an he was always smokin a cigar or a cigarette, "You can't work at this job ennymore. The inspector's already got his eye on you." But one day a that was enuff.

Another time, a man got sick whose job was unloadin bulk cement from a railroad car, an I filled in for'em a whole week. There was a inspector there, too; but that was such a dirty, wretched job that the inspector never got very close ta us.

Another guy an me had ta shovel loose, dry cement out of a boxcar with scoop shovels. I'd only been at it for a few minutes when I got a faceful a cement powder—right in the eyeballs. Man, oh man! Does that burn!

So I learned ta shovel that stuff real careful. But there ain't no way a keeping it from sinking inta every pore in yer body, so yer hands an face an clothes an hair an even inside a yer clothes jest gets caked with powdered grey cement.

I did that all one week. I was glad when the fella who'd been sick came back again. That was one miserable job. Maybe the most interesting thing that happened that summer was meetin up with a local Jensen guy, who was also workin on the crew, an we got ta talkin about fishin an game wardens, an he told me he'd gone with Ed Bosworth up ta Bill Cross Rapids the day after Bosworth an his son Walt had almost caught three guys they'd seen fishin. Well, not caught'em, exactly. Jest chased'em. An this fella I was talkin to said he'd found a rod an reel layin on the bank. It was a casting reel that had a messy bird's nest of a backlash still waitin ta be untangled. Said he got ta keep that rod an reel. Bosworth didn't want it.

When I told'em I was the guy who, when Ed an Walt came runnin, had dropped it an lit out for the woods, he said, "Oh! Well, I'll bring it back ta you tomorrow."

Well, next day he didn't bring ennything, an he said he'd forgot that he'd loaned that reel to another guy, an so he didn't have it ta give back. I figgered he was lyin, that he'd changed his mind, so I jest told'em ta forget about it, ta keep the whole damn thing.

But it was a good summer. I was makin forty-five cents a hour from Universal, an I was sellin milk from my five cows. I didn't get much land cleared, but I had some money in my pocket.

I had enuff ta buy me another rod an reel, if I'd wanted.

A Windfall Homestead

See, the '30s were rough. We were poor ta start with, then along comes the Depression, an in '33 was a drought, an, on top a that, there was the big fire.

There ain't no way a knowin enny a this for sure, but would the folks've left fer Washington if Pa cudda found a job? Or if Ma hadn't got so sick? I guess we'll never know.

Well, I told ya I bought Ma's three cows, but I didn't tell ya she had a dog, a white spitz, an she wanted ta take'em with'er to Washington. But there was lots a red tape about takin a dog on a train, an so I ended up with'em.

He was a cocky little wretch, with long hair. I had ta cuff'em up a couple a times ta get'em ta mind. Got so, when I'd go to the pasture ta get the cows, he'd walk right along behind me an, if a cow started ta wander away, all I had ta do was point at'er an that spitz'd zip over an nip'er on the leg an get'er over where I wanted. Then he'd come back an walk behind me again, jest like before. He was a sharp little bugger.

He also liked ta chase deer. He was fast. But he didn't have much of a nose—he wasn't no hound—an if he lost sight of'em, he'd come back.

Sometimes I'd take'em along hunting an sometimes I'd try'n make'em stay home. But he'd jest wait until I was out a sight, an then he'd come ennyway. One time he kicked out a doe an I got'er with one shot from the .22; an when he got ta where she was laying, he grabbed hold a one a her hind legs an started ta shake it like he was gonna show'er who's boss. Only she was dead, an he was such a little dog that all he was shakin was himself. I jest stood there an laughed.

Another time I was carryin pails a milk from the log barn up to the well, where I had a water tank the milk cans stood in ta cool. The spitz was sleepin near the hay shed. An a deer was standin by the hay shed lookin at the dog.

Well, when the deer saw me, it took off runnin inta the field, which had a nice crop a clover in it, almost up to yer knees. And a course that woke up the spitz, an he took off after the deer.

The deer, ya know, was makin long jumps through the field, no trouble at all, but the clover was thick, taller than the spitz, an he only went in a little ways before he quit an came back. It was jest too thick for'em.

I don't remember if it was the same year or not, but I had a wagon load of hay to put in the hay shed, and I had some sort a hook an carriage ta pull the hay in with, so I didn't have ta carry it all by hand, an I had a long rope that got hooked up to the horse.

A Cocky Little Wretch

Well, it was time for lunch, so I went in ta eat. When I came out, the spitz, who liked ta play with ropes, had got a hold a that hay rope an started ta roll with it, an he had rolled himself inta such a tangled mess that he couldn't get himself out. There he was layin, all wrapped up in the rope. I had ta stand an laugh at'em. An then I had ta roll'em over an over jest ta get'em out a that mess.

I musta had him three, four years, ennyway. But he was a male dog, an one time somebody's female came down the road, with a whole string a males behind'er, and a course my spitz had ta go join the parade. I called for'em ta come back, but his ears weren't workin good that day, an that's the last time I ever saw'em.

Next day I went askin around for'em, but a course nobody'd seen'em. Which meant somebody'd shot'em. I figgered I knew who had done it, but I'd shot other people's dogs, too, for bein where they weren't spozed ta be, so I had ta keep my mouth shut.

He was a cocky little wretch, but I liked'em.

After the big fire had burned everything off, the prairie chickens moved in. There hadn't been none of'em before the fire, but once the area had been burned, here they were. Where they came from I do not know.

I shot quite a few of'em—they're two, three times heavier than a partridge—an by 1940 or so there were hardly enny left. Maybe it was the brush an woods comin back. Maybe we jest shot'em all.

It wasn't unusual fer me ta take a gun along when I went ta get the cows from the pasture. This perticular time I had the slide-action shotgun that'd belonged ta Grampa Coster, an the spitz dog was right behind me, when up jumps a small flock a chickens.

I got a shot an one went down. But I noticed there'd been a second bird right in line, an I watched it coast for a long ways ta the northeast, until it dropped into that little meadow we always called Foster's Clearing. So I picked up the first bird an walked over with the spitz. I can't remember if I found that second prairie chicken or if the spitz did.

That was the only time in my life when I got two birds with one shot.

One spring—an this was when Grampa Coster was still alive, though he might not a been getting out a bed ennymore—I got ta see a prairie chicken dance off ta the northwest a the log house. Two mornings in a row they were out there in the field, kinda hoppin an cooin an dancin in a circle, an makin a funny sort a boomin sound.

Another time—this musta been late in the summer or early in the fall—I was going past the place where we lived when we first came out from Jensen, in '22, an Clarence Schneider owned that field an he had a nice crop a buckwheat in there, an a whole flock a prairie chickens was in there, too, cooin, talkin, eatin that buckwheat.

I guess prairie chickens are jest bughouse over buckwheat.

There was a time I had a cow in heat, but I didn't have a bull. Fidelis Hahn did have one, so I put a halter on my cow an walked her over. But she didn't know nothin about bein led, an when I got'er as far as Fidelis's driveway, she jest laid down an wouldn't get up. I mean, she *would not* get up.

So finally I figgered there was somethin wrong with'er. I walked home an hitched the horses to the stoneboat an came back, rolled'er onta the stoneboat, an pulled'er back home. I thought she was a goner.

Well, I got'er home an she got up an switched'er tail an walked away. I cudda killed that cow.

Maybe she jest had a low opinion a blind dates.

In the summer a '33, when I was workin at Lyndon Station, I'd send Ma five dollars every payday. An once she sent a brand new shirt she'd jest made for me.

I learned ta knit by watchin her. I never did learn how ta do heels an toes, but she let me knit part of a pair a socks once, an then she finished'em. Only I'd knit'em way too tight, so I could hardly get'em on when they were done. But she wouldn't take'em apart an do'em over. I had ta live with'em.

I could always tell which pair a socks I'd worked on. Those were the ones I could hardly get on my feet.

I learned ta do my own darning, too. But ennybody kin do that. All ya got ta do is weave some yarn in an out. Dumber'n a post an you kin still darn a sock.

A Cocky Little Wretch

When the farm was at its fullest size (I ain't talkin here about enny rented land, or the woods forty I bought later), it was three forties big, kind of in the shape of a blocky L. I already told ya about how I got that first forty from Al Batchelder, though it was really Frank Kurth who owned it. That was in 1931. And how it was becuz a my girlfriend Gladys that I got interested in that forty in the first place.

It was '36 or '37, jest about the time the folks moved ta Washington, that Ned Fox came ta me an said so-an-so is sayin Hank Buckberry is gonna have trouble makin his farm bigger if somebody buys that forty jest ta the north a his.

Well, a course, that was the kind a idea that gets inside yer head an won't let ya alone. So I went down ta the court house ta find out who owned that land. Well, it belonged ta Kinzel. But once Kinzel took the logs off it, he hadn't bothered ta pay taxes ennymore. I think lots a lumber barons forgot about taxes, once they'd taken what they wanted off the land. So for twenty-five dollars an sixty cents I got ta own that forty. That's how much the county had against it for back taxes. Twenty-five dollars an sixty cents.

Now a fella named Albert Forester lived in a shack over along Frostbite Avenue, about a half a mile due east a the back pasture, east a my forty, an he was buyin a couple a those forties from Frank Kurth. He had a couple a cows an he was tryin ta make some clearings.[1]

But Albert didn't have enny fences. So I went to 'em an told 'em I'd bought the forty to his west, an that I intended ta put a fence up. An since a quarter-mile a that fence would be on a line between our forties, an since I already had the fence posts an was willing ta put up the fence, I asked him ta buy the wire.

"Well," he sez, "why do you want ta put up a fence? I only got a couple a cows, an you only got a few. So what if they wander back an forth? You chase mine home, an I'll chase yers."

But that didn't suit me at all. I didn't want ta waste my time chasin cows, or lookin for 'em. An so we had some hot words.

I think he was trying ta dodge payin for the wire, an maybe he didn't have enny money ta buy it. But it wasn't long an Albert got in touch with Frank Kurth, an Frank brought me out a couple rolls a wire.

---

1. There is a long-standing discrepancy regarding names involving Albert Forester's clearings. I grew up hearing "Foster's Clearing," which is the name my family used. This might be the result of careless or slurred speech. But Albert Forester made "Foster's" Clearing. S. B.

A Windfall Homestead

So I put the fence up, an then I had a full forty acres a rough pasture for the cows an horses. It wasn't much of a pasture—nothin cleared, only brush an swamps—but it was a place for the cows ta go an try'n find somethin ta eat. A place ta hide. A place ta lay down. A place ta get their tits all scratched up by blackberry brush.

Eventually I cleared a few acres a that forty, a long, skinny strip about in the middle, an I planted a crop a rye. That name stuck. That field's been the Rye Field ever since.

The fences have perty much fallen down. Steve Schulz owns all a that land for hunting now—Foster's Clearing, the back pasture, an a whole lot a woods land to the north.

But the Rye Field's still the Rye Field, so I spoze that jest goes ta show that words don't rot as fast as fence posts or rust as quick as wire.

7

Orange Pajamas

JEST SITTIN HERE IN my easy chair, Seedy, when it's twenty below zero outside, an the house is toasty warm from the woodburnin furnace in the cellar, I start ta think back ta those years batchin it in the log shack.

I know yer tryin ta herd these cats in a direction that more or less follows the calendar, but a cat is a cat, an they don't always go where you want'em to. I ain't sure that cats have ever really learned their minutes an months.

But I'm thinkin of the times, after Grampa died, an after Gramma went ta Jensen ta live with Daisy, that my brothers John an Bill would come up an stay with me in the log shack—three in a bed, jest like we used ta do at home. For them, I think, it was a lot a fun, kind of a picnic.

I remember we woke up one winter morning an the potbellied stove was out cold. It had snowed in the night, with some wind with it, an the window by the bed opened on top (it wasn't very tight, ennyway), an there was snow on top of our covers.

Well, we were plenty warm underneath, but that was a big joke to my brothers—wakin up in Henry's shack, with snow on the bed.

I used ta buy boxes a shells an let those boys shoot my .22. That was a lot a fun for me as much as for them. An Bill got it inta his head that he wanted ta shoot a rabbit. He was seven, eight years old, maybe, I don't know, an I had a couple a brushpiles where I was clearin land, so I took'em

A Windfall Homestead

back there—he had my .22 and I had the shotgun—an I told'em, "Maybe there's one in there. You stay here an I'll go around the other side."

Well, by golly, there was one in there, an out he came. Bill threw up his gun an he's aimin and aimin an that rabbit is goin an goin, an I figgered that rabbit's gonna be by the river by the time Bill gets around ta pullin the trigger, so I up an shoot an down goes the rabbit.

Turns out that we each musta shot at the same time, cuz when that rabbit went down, Bill hollered, "I got'em!" He was all excited.

When we went ta get'em an clean'em, Bill was puzzled cuz all he could find were two BBs in the rabbit's head. But we hadn't heard each other shoot, so he didn't know I'd shot it with the shotgun, an I never told'em.

Well, I told'em about it years later, when I went out ta visit'em in Washington. He remembered the brushpile an that rabbit. We both got a good laugh out a that.

Those years a batchin it was when I *really* hunted. Oh, I worked hard, too—clearin land an makin a farm—but when I got tired a workin, I jest grabbed my gun an went to the woods. Wasn't nobody ta tell me I couldn't.

You shouldn't be writin all a this down, Seedy, cuz most a that huntin was, ya know, under the table. Sometimes I couldn't make it ta town ta buy a license, an sometimes the season wasn't open when I wanted it ta be, an I had ta open my own season. So if the FBI or the DNR or one a those guys with the big badges comes ta take me away, it's gonna be yer fault. I'm already getting free room an board, so I don't need ta spend the rest a my life in somebody else's crowbar hotel, wearin a pair a those orange pajamas. I don't mind shootin off my mouth jest sittin here in my own easy chair, but you don't need ta be tellin the whole damn world what a violator yer Old Man's been.

Jest remember what I'm tellin you—if those guys in the creased shirts come ta get me, it's yer damn fault.

Ennyway, I really learned ta hunt from Old Dick Hahn. He was a expert hunter, an I'm grateful ta have had such a good teacher. After his boys got big enuff ta hunt with'em, I either hunted on my own or with fellas like Ned Fox or Clarence Samuelson.

I already told ya about learnin ta smell deer. Dick Hahn taught me that, an then I proved ta Ned Fox I could do it.

Orange Pajamas

I offen wondered what's the use a those glands on a deer's leg. I'm kinda jumpin ahead here, but that first fall I had the little tractor, that wudda been, I think, 1950, I was plowin in the field north a the barn, an it was a grey damp day, but I was in my glory becuz I could jest sit on my ass on the tractor seat, I didn't have ta be hangin onta plow handles behind horses, an that little Farmall had single-bottom reversible plows, one furrow up, turn around, one furrow back, never getting tired, an it got ta be late in the afternoon, damp enuff ta be wearin a raincoat, an all of a sudden there's four deer in a patch of the field that ain't been plowed yet, an when I turn around an come back they're still there, a buck, a doe, an two little ones, all of 'em eatin.

Well, one more trip back to the barn an I got my .22 an, still wearin the raincoat, I made a big loop on foot around to the east an north till I got up by the gate to the back pasture, an I found a place in the weeds ta sit down. I waited. I wanted that buck.

He wasn't a big one, but that was alright. He was meat. An perty soon here comes one a the little ones. It comes acrost a corner of the field, turns by the fence line, goes up a ways, an jumps over. I jest watched it. Perty soon here comes the other little one. Same thing. It comes acrost the field, up along the fence, jumps over. Same spot. Then along comes the doe. She was a big one. Same thing as those two little ones—acrost the field, turns along the fence, an—but I'm lookin behind'er. Where's the buck? I don't see'em.

Oh, oh, I thought. Maybe he ain't comin. So I turned my head back toward the doe, an she's jest getting ready ta jump the fence. Up she goes an I pull the trigger an she falls in a heap on the other side.

I got ta my feet real fast an looked for that buck, but he was nowhere to be seen. Those bucks are sneaky buggers. I think he jest evaporated.

But what I want ta tell ya is that I thought a lot about those first three deer. Two of 'em followed *exactly* where that first one'd gone. Now why would that be? They weren't followin tracks. There wasn't no rutted deer trail. The only thing I can figger is they were followin a odor. How do you explain how those critters kin find each other so easy in the woods? They can't see through brush an trees. They got ta be able ta *smell* each other. An I think the little glands on the back a their legs has got somethin ta do with that. If I could smell'em with my little nose, why couldn't they smell each other with their big ones?

Ennyway, that was a lesson ta me, an I never forgot it.

A Windfall Homestead

Once I got past the buck fever, an I had my own rifle, with a peep sight on it, I really learned ta shoot. Seems like I could almost jest point the gun at a deer an I'd get'em. It got ta be easy.

So yer askin for a few hunting stories, Seedy. Jest remember you ain't spozed ta be writin'em down. You don't seem ta be worried about the law, but they aren't *yer* stories, are they? It ain't *you* that might get pinched, is it?

But, what the hell, what are they gonna do with a ninety-five year-old man? Lock'em up for bein a dangerous criminal? I'm damn near blind in my right eye, an can't hardly see out a my left, an I ain't even shot a gun for years—so do you really think I ain't got nothin ta worry about, Seedy?

Grin all you want to, but if they come after me, you better tell'em some a yer own stories, so you kin come an keep me company.

I never did like orange pajamas.

Ennyway. Alright. I'll tell ya a couple stories.

First I'll tell ya about a time—it might a been the only time—I hunted with Eber Lansbach. He was a tall, skinny guy, kind of a jittery fella, a lonesome cuss, an I made a drive for'em north a Mail Route Road, back a Frank Gleason's. There was a big, open grass swamp in there, an Eber was watchin in the woods on the far side a that swamp, an I was makin a drive for'em.

Well, I was almost up ta where Eber was standin, or where he was spozed ta be, ennyway, an up jumps a deer. Bang! One shot an I got'em. Down she went.

Well, Eber got all riled up. He started shoutin, "You shot at me, Henry!"

So I took'em ta where the deer was layin an I said to'em, "Look here, Eber! It's a deer. I wasn't shootin at you."

Well, that sort a calmed'em down. But I think he'd been daydreamin or somethin, cuz I'd seen where he'd been buildin a fire, jest fartin around. He might a been havin fun in the woods, but he wasn't *huntin*. Ennybody could see that.

After yer mother an me were married, I got ta know a whole lot a the Oestreichs, especially Emil an Martin an Paul. Yer mother was a Berndt, an a lot a those Berndt women married Oestreich men, an so all of a sudden they were family. An there were lots a times when one or another of'em would come over, usually on a Sunday morning, seven-thirty, eight o'clock. The women'd visit an us men'd grab our .22s an go look for a deer.

Those Oestreich men were all hunters, an I think Emil was the best a the lot.

It was one a those Sunday mornings when both Emil an Martin came over. (Was Paul with'em? I can't remember.) Ennyway, we grabbed our guns an went back by the river, behind the back pasture, ta do a little sneak huntin, an Emil got a doe, first thing.

We cleaned that one an we're jest startin ta hunt again an out comes a doe an two fawns, an we got'em all. We were back at the log shack by ten o'clock, an we had four deer. Everybody had meat.

But the two fellas I enjoyed huntin with, when I was batchin, were Ned Fox an Clarence Samuelson. I jest liked both of'em.

Clarence'd come over, almost every season. Sometimes he'd come by himself, an sometimes he'd bring along some a his wife's relations, from east a Jensen, from Pine River. Now Clarence wasn't a good hunter—he always wore overalls, an they'd freeze at the cuffs, an you could always hear'em walkin in the woods—scrape, scrape, scrape—so you always knew where Clarence was, an I expect every deer did, too. But he was a real good scout. He was jest fun ta be with, full a corny jokes, jest a nice guy.

Once he brought a bunch a guys, jest showed up with'em, an they didn't know nothin about this area, but I did, knew it like a book, an so I figured out a drive—Clarence an one a the guys he brought with'em would be the drivers—an I took the rest of'em around to where they'd be watchin.

Well, you give yerself only so much time ta be in place, an it was getting late—I was on the end of the line for watchin, an I wasn't to my spot yet—so I started runnin. I was headed down a neck of land into a swamp, an there's a buck comin down that neck toward me, runnin like a bat out a hell. He was a dandy. Beautiful rack a horns. The drivers'd already kicked'em out.

Well, I stopped an threw up the gun an lit into'em—three shots—missed every time. He jest kept runnin right at me. I froze. But when he was headed away from me, I up an gave'em three more shots, an down he went.

Well, that was the first drive. Second drive Clarence took most a the fellas ta watch, but one of'em—his name was Dave Van Slate—stayed with me, ta drive. We were spaced out, back a Foster's Clearing, waiting till the watchers'd get ta where they were spozed ta be. The brush wasn't high—still comin back, ya know, from after the '33 fire—an I kin see Dave. An all of a sudden I see'em pointing his rifle in a big swing from north ta south.

Well, I was standin in the middle a that swing, due east of'em, an my heart was in my throat, wishin I was about as big as a mouse, but that pointin went right past me, on south, an perty soon Dave shoots. See, there was a brushy hollow between us, an there was a deer headed south in that hollow. Dave could see'em, but I couldn't.

But once he shot, I was all eyes, an it ain't long I kin see that deer crossin a swamp an headed up a deer trail inta what's now yer pine woods, Seedy, two hunnerd an fifty yards away, maybe. He wasn't goin real fast, cuz Dave had hit'em. But he was goin.

Well, I up an lit into'em. Two, three shots an I knocked'em down. Jest about wrecked the gun barrel, ya know, it was such a long shot. Strained it. Dave put his tag on that deer.

Two drives, two bucks. But we hunted all the rest a that day an nobody saw a tail. Ya jest never know.

Another time Clarence came over with five guys. Well, first drive I got a nice doe. Second drive, I was one a the watchers, an four deer came out an I got all of'em.

That's all we got that day. But they came back another day, an I got one more.

Six guys, six deer. An I shot every one of'em. Everybody got a deer ta take home.

Ned Fox was a kind a carefree cuss, always had a joke ta tell. We got ta be friends perty fast. It was him I showed that I could smell deer. But I think I told ya that already.

Him an his wife Martha had a flock a kids, poor as rats, an I think he was always broke. But he always came up with some kinda gun, some pumpkin slinger, an this time he showed up with a old automatic.

We went up in the timber, west a George Bohman's, sneak huntin, walkin real slow in the same direction, maybe fifty yards apart, an I heard Ned shoot. Well, a course, I went over ta see what he'd got.

Well, he'd got nothin. He'd missed. But his junker of a gun had jammed after the first shot, an by the time I got to'em, he was poundin the barrel against a tree.

"What the hell are ya doin, Ned?" I asked'em.

"This damn gun don't work," he said.

I jest stood an laughed at'em.

Another time—I think it was the last day a deer season—Ned an me went out an Pete Horgan went along with us an so did Ned's oldest boy Eugene. We were up west a Schnee's, west a the old Anderson Homestead, an when it got ta be about ten o'clock in the mornin, Pete said he had ta go to town. So he left. Ned an Eugene went with'em.

They all said they'd be back at two o'clock, so for several hours I hunted that whole area, jest sneakin, an I never jumped a thing. Well, I knew where we were spozed ta meet, so I headed there, jest before two o' clock, when up jumps a small buck. One shot an I knocked'em down. I jest got ta cleanin it when here comes Ned an Pete an Eugene.

"We thought you'd made a call shot," Ned said.

"Well," I sez to'em, "here's my call shot." I was cleanin that buck.

We hunted a while an saw nothin. Startin ta get toward the end a the day, so we crossed Frostbite Avenue, over to the east side, spread out, an slowly headed south.

I always liked ta be on the end, so I was farthest to the east, the farthest away from the road. I was on a deer trail, goin slow, when I saw a brown spot up ahead. I knew it was a deer, but all I could see was that patch a brown. I didn't know what part, so I didn't shoot. I decided to jest stand there an wait. An then it disappeared.

Well, I didn't know where that deer had gone. I'm lookin an lookin, an all of a sudden here he comes on the same deer trail I'm standin on, comin right at me, a medium-sized buck, head down, an I jest froze. A few feet from me, he swung off the trail an went right by me. I think I cudda jabbed'em with the end a the gun barrel. I know I shot at'em as he went by, don't know if I even had the gun ta my shoulder, missed'em, an he swung back to the deer trail, headin north in a hurry.

I got one more shot at'em, an I hit'em, too, but I didn't kill'em. A course those other guys came right over. We talked about it quick, cuz the light was startin ta go, an the three of'em made a big loop to the north an spread out ta watch.

After I'd waited a while, I followed the blood trail, an it wasn't long before I found a bed where he'd laid down, which meant he was hit perty hard, an then, a minute later, I heard all those guys cut loose. They shot an shot an shot, an they got'em.

When I got up to'em, they were standin around the buck. Somebody asked, "What are we gonna do with'em?"

Well, our rule a thumb was whoever wounds'em gets'em. But I already had a buck, so I sez, "Eugene never got a buck before. Let him put his tag on it."

An, so, that's what happened. I think that mighta been Eugene's first buck. Last day a season. I think he was perty happy.

8

Married Two Days an Broke

Potosi an Lancaster are way down in the southwestern corner of the state, not all that far from Dubuque, Iowa, actually. It was down there where I got called ta work by the Universal Engineering Company. That was in the summer a 1939.

Now I was a lonesome cuss, but I liked ta dance. So that winter or spring, before I went ta Potosi, I'd go ta dances at the Corning Pavilion. That's where I met yer mother, Seedy. We met dancin.

The first time I met'er, though we danced a lot, there was hardly a word spoken. A few weeks later, she was back again, an then we started ta talk a little. By the time I left for Potosi, I'd never even took'er home yet. But we wrote back an forth a couple times in the summer.

Well, when I got ta Potosi, I learned they weren't using locos ennymore, jest trucks, an I got a job as a cement finisher. As a loco driver, I'd made forty-five cents a hour, but as a finisher, I was makin seventy, which was ta me like money from heaven.

It was a hard job, a fussy job. There were two of us, both husky brutes, an our job was ta do the final finishing on the newly poured cement, workin right behind the mechanical bullfloat. We had a hand-held bullfloat, with a pair a somethin like handplow handles on each end, an the state inspector was right there.

A Windfall Homestead

If a spot was too low, one of us had ta jab in a little green cement an bring'er up. If it was too high, we had ta cut'er down. Oh, that inspector was lookin all the time, an you had ta be on the ball.

You do that eight, nine hours a day, an you know you've done somethin, especially when yer workin on hills becuz, ya know, green cement wants ta sag, head downhill, an that road's always got ta be brought up ta snuff.

While I was gone, Mary an Otto an their kids—I think they had three or four of 'em by then—stayed at the log house an took care a my cows. Otto was only getting a couple days a week at the factory, in Jensen. An since I was makin good money in Potosi, I jest told 'em that they should keep the milk checks. An they did.

I think Mary did all the milkin. Otto wasn't a farmer. In fact, Mary told me later—she told me, not him—that Otto'd harnessed up the horses one day, figgerin ta do some plowing for me, but he couldn't get those horses ta pull. So he jest took the harnesses off of 'em an turned 'em back into the pasture. That was the end a his plowin.

Those horses had a easy summer.

When I got back in the fall, yer mother an me started goin together. I went ta see'er real offen. I had a '30 Model A roadster.

So I saw'er two, three times a week, sometimes. She an her mother an her sisters an her brother lived in Jensen. See, yer mother's older sister was Mayme, then yer Ma, then Myrtle an Florence. Their brother—Martin—was in there somewheres, but I ain't sure, exactly, where he fit.

Florence was too young ta have a job, but all the others worked, except for their Ma, who kept house. Yer mother worked at the shoe factory. I think she an Mayme an Myrtle kept 'em a goin. Martin, I think, spent most a his money in the tavern.

See, their Pa was dead. He died somewheres around 1930. I never knew 'em. He spozedly had a drinkin problem, an I think Martin did, too. An so those older sisters kept that family a goin. But they musta always been behind in the rent, cuz I think they lived in three different houses over that winter a '39 an '40.

I know yer mother asked me if I had firewood ta sell, an I knew about a patch a popple trees the fire had killed, burned 'em out at the roots, an they'd tipped over, an I got load after load a those trees. Hauled 'em home on the bobsled behind the horses, cut 'em up on my sawrig run off a that old Star engine, an I took 'em trailerload after trailerload a that wood.

Married Two Days an Broke

I think she paid me a dollar a load, which might a paid for my gas, I don't know.

We never went a lot a places. We didn't have enny money. Everything between us was perty straight an businesslike. She wasn't the kind ta fall all over a guy. An she wasn't a kid. She was twenty-five years old when we got married.

But in the early spring a '40, before we got married, she wanted ta come out an see the log house. So one mornin I went ta get'er, brought'er out, an after we'd looked things over, I told'er, "I got work ta do. I'll be back at noon."

When I came in, she had dinner on the table, an though I probably stayed in longer than I usually did, I went back out ta work after we ate. When I came in for supper, she had that ready, too. After supper, I took'er home.

She'd kept herself busy all day, don't ask me doin what. Women kin always find some dust ta chase. But I think she was checkin out whether she wanted ta live in that shack.

We got married in the spring a '40. See, she'd been raised a Protestant, so we got married at the Evangelical an Reformed church in Jensen, St. Stephens. The preacher was a old fart, about ready to retire. It was a small affair, about as cheap an simple as we could make it.

Lorinda wanted ta have a feed, so she made a meal at her mother's house. I remember I gave'er five dollars ta help pay for the groceries. Maybe a dozen people, mostly her friends an a few of her relatives.

A couple a nights later, five, six guys—I knew all of'em, Ned Fox, Pete Horgan, an a few other guys—walked up the driveway singin an hollerin an beatin on a washtub an givin us a real shivaree. Well, when fellas do that, ya know, they ain't gonna quit until you give'em somethin. I dug around an found two dollars, an I went out an gave'em that. You could buy a pony a beer for two dollars.

When I came in, I told Lorinda that was my last two dollars. An she told me that she didn't have enny money at all, either.

Married two days an we were both flat broke! We got a good laugh out a that.

A Windfall Homestead

Right away she wanted ta help me milk the cows, but at first I told'er no. Those cows were used ta me. But, a course, sayin no didn't last long. Perty soon she was milkin, too.

She never complained about livin in the log house, except she wanted a window put in on the west side. So we got her mother's brother, Fred Bartelt—she called'em Uncle Fritz—ta put a window in. Took'em all day. He kind a grumbled about it, said he thought the log house was jest a shack, which it was, but he got'er done.

A few years later, after Birdy an you were born, Seedy, yer mother wanted ta make the kitchen bigger. So I did that. Put a room on the east side. You boys both lived in that log shack.

But in the early summer a 1940, yer mother an me were both out in the yard, doin somethin, an in drives Old Gus Wasserman. He was Frank Pierce's foreman, an he'd come from Antigo ta say Universal had a job for me, in Eau Claire, operating a mechanical bullfloat.

I talked nice to'em, but I told'em no. I had jest got married, an I had a farm, an I wasn't gonna go. See, I'd seen other men who worked for Universal who'd brought their wives an their families with'em for the summer, an it was perty clear ta me that by the time they'd paid rent, an movin back an forth, they'd perty well spent all their money. I couldn't see enny advantage ta doin that.

I was a married man an a farmer. An I was stayin put.

But when I'd been workin in Potosi, there'd been a lot a excitement about Germany an war. The price of a couple things had gone up by a couple cents, an everybody thought, "Oh, no! Here she comes!"

By the time I'd been married, I had ta register for the draft. But I got deferment becuz I was a farmer an becuz I was married. So I never got called up, never had ta go to war.

John Rowe got drafted, an he had ta go. He lived at the end a Heatstroke Lane. Quinten Ament bought John's place—I guess John figgered maybe he wasn't comin back, but he did—an Quinten lives there to this day.

One of us is a month older'n the other—I think Quinten's the one that's older—an once he borrowed my Star engine ta fill silo, but he couldn't get it ta start, so he jest brought it back.

Well, I looked it over, an I saw that two a the spark plug wires were in the wrong place. When I put'em where they belonged, she started right up.

Married Two Days an Broke

Mary an Otto came out almost every Sunday, an they always had their kids with'em. Those boys loved ta piddle with engines, an I figgered it was them who'd got those spark plug wires crossed.

They always came out hungry, an Lorinda always fed'em. Those were some good years.

If there was a extra job ta pick up ennywhere in the neighborhood, I'd do it. I know I was helpin load pulp on railroad cars, up at the Camp 30 landing, when I came home an Lorinda had been ta town an had seen a nice winter coat.

A course, she wanted me ta see it, an after a while I went ta town with'er, an she went ta try it on. It was a nice coat. Had a fur collar. She was turnin this way an that, lookin at herself in the mirror an showin me, an, well, once yer in yer hooked.

So, five dollars down and five dollars a month. It *was* a nice coat. She was really proud of it. A course, we had ta pay for it on time. But we did it. We got'er done.

One day Lorinda's Uncle Ferdinand an cousin Walter came walkin up the driveway—wasn't night, wasn't dark—an they were perty loaded. Ferdinand especially.

They'd been in the woods an were comin out. They'd been drinkin, an their car'd gone off the road, hit a tree, an the fender was rubbin up against a tire.

Ferdinand jest leaned up against the log house an kept mutterin, "I lost my cap. I lost my cap."

I looked at'em an said, "It's on yer head, Ferdinand. Yer cap's on yer head." An, by golly, it was.

So I got a bar an pried the fender away from the tire. They thanked me, got in their car, an drove away. I ain't sure if Ferdinand knew even then where his cap was.

A Windfall Homestead

I think I told ya, Seedy, that after yer mother an me were married, a bunch a the Oestreichs used ta come over. The women'd visit, or do whatever women do, an us men'd grab our .22s an go huntin.

But I didn't tell you yet that, when your mother an me were gonna get married, I didn't have a .22, cuz the last one I'd had I gave ta John Oestreich for helpin me make hay—I didn't have enny money ta pay'em ennything, but I knew he didn't have a .22, so I offered it to'em, an he took it. It was one I'd bought from one a my sisters—I think it might a been Melva—when the family went ta Washington, in the fall a '36. It was a single-shot bolt action, an I never did like it very much.

Ennyway, I think I've told ya that I'd got a .22 from Orin Sommers when I was fifteen, sixteen years old, got it for twelve dollars—a slide-action Remington—but it'd only shoot shorts, an I traded it ta George Eberhardt for a torpedo body Model T. It was a junker, but it ran. For a while.

I knew I liked a slide-action Remington, an I figgered that once I got married I wasn't gonna be able ta buy one, so I looked in the Sears-Roebuck catalogue, an they had exactly what I wanted for twenty-one, twenty-two dollars, somethin like that. Well, ya had ta send in a down payment an give a couple a references an they'd send you the gun an you could make payments. So that's what I did.

But that gun didn't come an didn't come. An I started ta get perturbed. One day I had ta go to the bank, an when I went in the president saw me an motioned me over, an he asked me, "What's this about a gun?" So I told'em I'd ordered one from Sears-Roebuck, an I'd listed the Lincoln County Bank as one a my references.

"Well," he sez, "I already wrote back to'em. I told'em ta send that gun."

Couple a days later I got it. An it wasn't long after that I put a peep sight on it. Slipped it in ahead a gettin married. An it's that gun I took huntin with the Oestreichs.

I shot more deer with that .22 than most guys've shot with a rifle. I spoze I'm braggin, but I knew how ta shoot. I could almost get'em with my eyes closed. Almost. Not quite.

Some things I did weren't so smart. Jest sittin here in my chair, with nothin else ta do, I kin remember some a those not-so-smart things, too.

I had this knife that Dan Young had given ta me, after I'd cooked a couple batches a booze for'em, an I really liked it. Well, the blade wouldn't hold much of a edge, but it had a bone handle, an it was kinda like my pet.

Once—I was still batchin—I was down the cellar a the log shack, it was night already, an somebody got ta poundin on the door. I was skinnin a deer, an that deer wasn't exactly legal. Got me perty scared.

Well, I came up through the trapdoor ta see who it was, an it was only Ned Fox, an when I went back down the cellar I gathered up all the deer legs, brought'em up wrapped in a wad a newspaper, an stuck'em in the cookstove ta burn.

Next mornin I looked an looked for that knife. Couldn't find it. Finally I got ta pokin around in the ashes of the cookstove, an there was the blade, all black an warped.

I guess I'd had that knife inside that bundle a deer legs, an inta the stove it went. Burned up that beautiful bone handle.

Makes ya kind a mad at yerself for not payin attention. I really liked that knife.

Lorinda took over the gardening after we were married. Before that I'd always kept a little garden—had ta grow potatoes, ya know.

When I was batchin it, I'd usually boil up a mess a potatoes at supper time an jest let'em cool till the next day. Then I'd slip the skins off, slice'em real thin, an fry'em up in bacon fat. Oh, they were good!

Regular bacon was too expensive fer me, so I'd buy what they called bacon squares, which were smoked pig jowls. But that was jest fine by me becuz what I really wanted was the fat for fryin, an there was more a that in jowls than there was in the regular bacon.

Fry up a mess a potatoes in bacon fat, open a can a pork'n beans, maybe fry up a few venison steaks, slice some a yer own homemade bread—that's a meal a man kin go ta work on.

I was never much interested in cookies, but I always had coffee.

I remember, though, one a those years—this wudda been after Dan Young died, an Helen married Mark Lemmer—an Mark had brought up eight, ten Brown Swiss heifers from his brother's farm in Marathon County. At that point, Mark had perty poor fences, an there wasn't much grass, so those heifers wandered all over the place lookin for somethin ta eat.

A Windfall Homestead

Well, I got up one mornin an there they were in my garden, eatin and tramplin. They jest about wrecked it.

I chased 'em out, a course, but I got perty mad about it, an I told Mark what I thought about his heifers getting inta my garden.

A couple a days later he brought me a basket full a cucumbers—kinda makin up, I guess, for what his heifers did—but what good was a basket a cucumbers ta me? I gave most of 'em to my sister Mary.

When Gramma Coster left the log house, I got rid a the chickens. I didn't have time ta piddle with 'em. But Lorinda wanted chickens, so we got a couple a old cluck hens, an perty soon she was raisin chickens.

We ate a lot a chicken. Oh, I'd have ta chop their heads off, scald 'em, pull their feathers off an take their guts out, but that was okay. We liked chicken.

It wasn't long an Lorinda's sisters'd come out an stay at the log shack, sometimes two, three days at a time. It got ta be routine.

We didn't see so much of her brother Martin, though.

Martin was a smart guy. He got ta be a lumber scaler for Ritter an Hass sawmill, an you got ta be able ta do a lot a quick figgerin in yer head ta do a job like that. He wasn't dumb. It's jest that he couldn't leave the booze alone.

But once he said he wanted ta go huntin with me. Well, he meant shinin, at a lick. So we walked up ta Camp 30—I knew right where the lick was—an there was a sort of half-assed blind ta sit in.

So we sat there an waited, an it started ta get dark.

After a while a deer came in an it smelled us an it started ta snort an stamp its feet on the ground. It made a big loop around us, always out a sight, snortin an stampin.

I thought that man was gonna die. He was scared ta death. I jest sat there an laughed. An when that deer finally left, we got up an walked home.

But, ya know, if ya don't know what it is, or if somethin takes you by surprise in the night, it's real easy ta get scared.

When the folks were still here, an I was livin at home, I used ta come visit Dan Young in the evenings sometimes, an he'd tell deer stories. Well, one night I was headed home, late, pitch dark, no moon—an ya gotta remember there was no electricity those days, no yardlights or ennything like that—an I was headed down Karban Hill, walkin on the edge where the road met the grassy ditch, jest feelin my way with my feet, an all of a sudden—"Woof!"

Well, there musta been a dog on the road, an I musta took'em by surprise, an so he woofed at me.

I think if blood was yellow, I was shot.

Another time, I was jest a big kid, I went ta Eberhardts' ta listen to their new radio. An, a course, I stayed till it was late, an then I had ta walk the railroad track for about a mile ta get home.

There was a big moon, so I could see real good. But at the 27 landing, near where the track crossed the county road, there was a big pile a logs, an all at once, somewhere ahead a me but behind that pile a logs, a brush wolf started ta beller. Howlin, ya know. First one an then a whole string of 'em. Yippity, yippity, yow, yow, yow.

Well, I had ta go towards'em ta get to the road. Half scared ta death, jest pussy-footin along on the ties, tryin not ta make a sound, sneakin toward the road—an when I finally reached it, I turned ta the north an I *ran*. No, I didn't run. I *flew*. All the way home.

I don't know if those coyotes cudda caught me, I was runnin so fast. Or maybe they couldn't a caught me becuz they were too busy rolling on the ground laughin.

Yippity, yippity, yow, yow, yow.

Oh! I was scared!

9

When Enuff's Enuff

I worked lots a times helpin Mike Stevens fill silo. He'd come over an ask me ta help'em, an I'd go. He never paid me nothin, but I'd get fed.

But those farmers would work the ass right off a kid. Usually, with Mike, I had the job a throwin corn bundles on the wagon, out in the field. Me an horses an wagons, so that meant you'd get one wagon loaded an there's another one waitin, empty. So you had ta *work*.

Maybe it was becuz I was such a husky brute, but it was kind of the same with Lawrence Walencyzk. He had the biggest farm in the Town a Boulder, about half a mile north a the Copper School on Mail Route Road. An he'd ask me ta come help'em fill silo. I did that lots a times. Only Lawrence'd always give me the job a throwin bundles a corn off the wagons, feedin the silo filler.

He had a big silo, an it was in a spot that was kinda hard ta get in to, where only one person could work at unloadin, an the sun'd jest beat in on you an jest about cook yer brains.

Everything, ya know, was horses an wagons, except that Fred Schulz's brother Harry always brought his big iron-wheeled tractor ta supply power ta run the silo filler. An Harry never threw bundles. He jest stayed by his tractor ta see that everything worked right, I spoze. Maybe that's as hard as he wanted ta work, I don't know.

Ennyway, one day I started ta feel like I couldn't take it ennymore, so I decided I was gonna get a break by pluggin the silo filler—feed'er more'n

When Enuff's Enuff

she could handle, ya know, an plug'er up tight. So I started ta throw in bundles like a wild man, an perty soon Harry's tractor starts ta grunt. Ain't long now, I figgered.

But there was Harry, leanin up against one a his tractor wheels, an he jest reached up a hand and gave'er a couple more notches on the throttle. That tractor had too much power for me. I jest could not plug that silo filler.

But all a that experience gives you a feelin a when enuff's enuff.

For instance, some years later I was workin in the woods when Lawrence Walencyzk was havin a auction. I knew he had a reversible riding plow, so I gave Fidelis Hahn some money an asked'em ta buy that plow for me, an he did.

Well, I was real happy about it, cuz instead a holdin the handles of the handplow, with the lines draped around my neck, now I was gonna be able ta sit on my ass an hold the lines in my hands.

So when I was ready ta plow, I hitched up the team, an got on the seat, an let the plowshare down, an right away I saw those horses were luggin ta beat hell.

Well, I couldn't stand that. I don't think I made one full furrow before I got off that plow seat. *Then* they could pull it alright.

It was a good plow, an it did a nice job a plowin. But put a hunnerd an eighty pound man on the seat, an it was jest too much for the horses.

I always said, if *I* got ta work, the *horses* got ta work, too. But the opposite a that was also true. If *they* had ta work, it wasn't right for *me* ta sit on my ass an make *them* work even harder than they had to.

I never rode that plow again.

Those horses had stalls in the log barn an, like I told ya, if *I* had ta work, *they* had ta work, an so I fed'em good.

Now I kept the log house perty clean, so I didn't have many mice ta deal with in there. But in the barn you got hay an you got oats, so you got mice, especially in the wintertime.

I didn't monkey around tryin ta *trap* mice, but I did try'n *shoot*'em. An I did some a that with a single-shot .22 pistol, but I don't think I've told you how I'd come ta have it.

By the time yer mother an me were married, Seedy, I had four guns. I had Grampa Coster's shotgun. I had the .303 rifle from Jim Meier. I had the

.22 from Sears'n Roebuck. But I also had that single-shot pistol, which later got stolen. But that's another story.

Ennyway, I got that pistol when I was workin for Universal Engineering, down at Mauston. I can't remember if I told ya that Old Frank Pierce used ta send me out on odd little jobs, after supper, sometimes on the weekend, an sometimes—like cleanin sand out a new culverts after a rain—he'd send a couple a local guys, little fellas, ta go with me.

I liked both of'em. They were quick as weasels an feisty as a couple a roosters, an sometimes they'd be standin face ta face jawin like they were about ta kill each other, an I'd jest stand there an laugh at'em.

Good workers, both of'em. They could get inside the clogged culverts, but I couldn't, an we had a scoop-shovel type a thing, with a rope on both ends, an we'd get that rope through the culver, with one a the little guys pullin the empty shovel in, one of'em *in* the culvert getting the shovel full, an I was usually the guy pullin the loaded shovel out.

Hour here, hour there, but I was savin every penny.

Ennyway, one a those little guys seemed ta take ta me, an he invited me ta come home with'em one weekend. He lived on a farm with his parents, eight, ten miles out a Mauston, big hills, rough country. I really liked it. He was married. Him an his wife had a kid.

I think I told you he was the one who introduced me ta using a peep sight. Shootin sparrows with his .22 rifle while he was helpin a guy fix a car.

When they were done, he showed me that stupid pistol, an, a course, I was a gun nut an I was interested.

Well, some time later he brought that pistol ta camp. He was showin it ta somebody, wantin ta sell it, had his eye on a new automatic, but he couldn't afford it, so he was tryin ta sell that single-shot. Wanted six dollars for it.

An, a course, it ain't jest *lookin* at it, it's also *shootin* it. Got some empty cans set up, an guys are takin turns, an, a course, I had ta take a turn, too.

Well, I had the six dollars, so I bought it from'em. An that's the gun I used ta shoot mice in the log barn. Or shoot at'em, ennyway.

I used ta walk up the railroad track, north a where Fidelis Hahn now lives, an I'd shoot chipmunks. Got ta be perty good at it.

But Warren Schnee was the guy who could really shoot a pistol. He was the fella who helped me put the foundation under the log house. Worked about a month. Paid'em a dollar a day an fed'em.

When Enuff's Enuff

But we were more like pals than workmen. We'd get tired a workin an go shoot a while. He was a better shot with a pistol than I was.

But one time I was up at his place—the old Anderson Homestead, ya know, up off a Frostbite Avenue—an I had my pistol, an Warren's Pa an Ma were out with me by their well, by the pump, an a sparrow came an sat on the peak a the old log barn, an I pulled out my pistol an I shot it. Warren's Ma turned ta Otto an said to'em, "I told you Hank could shoot better'n Warren."

Well, that made me feel good, even if it wasn't true. I think I'd jest made a lucky shot.

One time—this was when I was still livin at home—Grampa Coster came out with a nephew a his who'd come up from Kentucky. Or Ohio. Or wherever it was. An they were both gun nuts. An this nephew—his name was John Mantz—had a slide-action .22 an somebody tore a corner off a playin card an stuck it on a stump, sixty, seventy yards away. An Grampa Coster got ta shoot first.

Well, he up an shot, an he hit the corner a that card. An then everybody else had ta try, ya know, some a my sisters, too, but nobody could hit it. An then John wanted Grampa ta try again, but Grampa said no, he wouldn't do it, he'd already showed what kind a shot he was, an he didn't need ta prove ennything more ta ennybody.

I think we all sort a thought he'd made a lucky shot, too. But how ya gonna prove a thing like that?

I pulled some foolish tricks, though. Some of 'em you realize real quick what a dumbass thing it was ta do, an you don't do *that* ennymore.

I think I told you about borrowin that Model T tractor from Dan Young. That's the time, in the spring a '33, when Daisy drove it an I held the handles on the walkin plow, on my first patch a field. That's where I planted those ten bushels a potatoes.

Well, when Dan Young died, Mark Lemmer married Dan's widow, Helen, an I bought that tractor from Mark. It had lots a power alright, but it jest had little wheels, an so long as you were workin level ground everything was fine, but try'n go uphill an she'd jest sit an spin.

So I was out in the field with'er one time an two guys were goin by in a car. They stopped an came over ta where I was workin, an before they left I'd sold'em that tractor for thirty-five dollars. An then I bought a horse. That

A Windfall Homestead

might a been the one that kicked an kicked and kicked the harness all ta pieces, so I don't think I came out ahead on that deal.

Ennyway, when I had the Model T tractor I had ta have gas. So I had a fifty-gallon drum sittin right outside the log shack. An I had a empty bean can sittin on top a that gas barrel.

One mornin I was comin in from the log barn—I had ta carry the pistol ta milk the cows, ya know—an I spotted that can an I up an shot at it, sittin right on top a that gas drum. "Oh, oh," I thought, "if I missed I could punch a hole in that barrel."

Well, as it turned out I didn't hit the barrel, but I sure didn't try'n shoot enny cans off the top ennymore.

Some things jest ain't too smart.

I think I got one more thing ta tell ya about that Model T tractor.

Before he went ta Washington with the folks, in the fall a '36, my brother John helped me plow. He was a perty big lad, not exactly a real good driver, but I got'em ta steer that tractor while I was walkin behind plowin.

We were workin northwest a the log shack, me walkin along holding onto the plow handles, when all of a sudden the tractor stopped. Well, the engine didn't stop. The frame broke. Front an back were up in the air, an the middle was layin on the ground. John was sittin there at the bottom a that V.

But we went down ta home an dug out Pa's old Model T pickup, which was nothin but junk, stripped'er down to the frame, took that frame out by my Model T tractor, an put all the workin parts on the pickup frame.

Couple days work an we were back ta plowin.

Wasn't long after that when those guys stopped an bought it off a me, for thirty-five dollars. An then I went an got that horse that'd kick the hat off yer head.

That was farmin.

10

Gettin Over That Flirtin Business

Now some a this, maybe, ain't gonna fit together like one a those big jigsaw puzzles that's got a thousand pieces. Yer getting a rough fit, rough carpentry, nothin exactly square or plumb, pieces missin. We're talkin about a farm, after all, a barn. We ain't talkin about a church or a courthouse. There are things that slip through the cracks. I got lots a those cracks in my head.

See, the Town a Boulder was growin by leaps an bounds. Oscar Wangen, Pete Horgan, Ned Fox, Earl Bennett, the Culver brothers, Clarence Samuelson, John Oestreich, Ed Meyer—all of'em clearin land, milkin more an more cows. Most of'em livin in shacks an buildin their barns first.

See, makin a livin comes out a the barn. It doesn't come out a the house. Maybe that's the difference between then an now. Oh, ya had ta have some kinda shack ta crawl into. But that was perty basic. Nothin fancy. But once you had a place ta come in out a the rain an cold, a cookstove an a bed, you worked on yer farm—on clearing land, on gettin yer barn built, on milkin a few more cows. A nicer house came later.

So I don't know what ta tell ya, Seedy. Ya see, once I got married I got over that flirtin business. Once yer married yer mind ain't on jest goin ta bed ennymore. That first thrill is past, it kind a tapers off, yer mind comes back to yer work. An, in my case, that meant thinkin about the farm, more clearing, more cows.

Now I already had the log barn, had the five cows. Those cows had calves an some of'em were heifers, an so what are ya gonna do with'em?

A Windfall Homestead

From the beginning, when Grampa an Gramma first came out, I never had enuff hay for those cows, always had ta buy more, so I was always clearin land. Always thinkin more an more an more.

An I found out real quick you can't put yer hay up in outside stacks. Too much rain. Too wet. Gets moldy. Ya needed a barn ta put it in. I'd already added onto the log barn, but it was kind of a shabby deal. Well, I needed a new barn, a bigger barn, a better barn. I was thirty, thirty-one years old. I had ambition stickin out a my ears.

So I went to the Lincoln County Bank an I told'em what I wanted ta do. Told'em I wanted a barn sixty feet long by thirty feet wide, a hip-roofed barn for more cows, for hay an straw.

The fella there—it was either Talbot or Meyer—said, "That ain't big enuff," but I told'em I only had eighty acres, an a lot a that was swamp, so I figgered a barn that size was about as big as I could handle. An the bank loaned me some money.

Now I had a used slusher, one that'd belonged to the town, jest about wore out. But I dug the hole for the barn foundation with that slusher an the team a horses. Now the back part, the north part, got down ta clay an hardpan, hard ta dig, so I went ta town an bought some dynamite an loosened up that stuff—I'd learned ta be a dynamite man from Tony Zillman, years ago—an *then* I moved the dirt.

Seems stupid, but the first thing ya do when you got yer hole dug is practically fill it back up with stones. Wagonload after wagonload of 'em—took'em from the stonepiles—till you think you got enuff, which you probably ain't. Takes *lots* a stones ta build a foundation, an you got ta sort out the face stones, the ones that got at least one flat surface.

On the west side an on a perty good-sized piece a the north side, the foundation was gonna get built into a rise, into a little hill. But on the east an south, I had ta dig down another four feet ta get below the frostline. I did all a that by hand, by myself. Lots a work.

An when I was ready—this wudda been in the summer a '42—I hired a older man, he was jest about old enuff ta retire, an he stayed with us for a whole week. I mixed mud for'em an lifted stones, an he got the west wall up an a start on the end walls, but he was always grumblin an at the end a the week he quit. I think it was jest too much for'em. Liftin stones is hard work, more like work for young men. But I had ta pay the old guy. Can't remember what it was.

Well, now what was I gonna do?

Gettin Over That Flirtin Business

I heard that E. O. Culver an his son LaVerne were good at stone masonry, an so was Martin Oestreich. So I hired LaVerne an Martin. I think LaVerne was about a month younger'n me. Martin was, I don't know, six, seven, eight years older.

They were good workers, both of'em, fast. One of'em worked on the inside, one on the outside, right acrost from each other. See, some guys work together that way an some like ta work by themselves. When I helped Fidelis Hahn build his foundation, I worked for'em about a week an all I did was mix mud an carry stones, an the guy I was mud monkey for was always singin. Workin like that is fun. I sang right along with'em.

Ennyway, I worked my ass off, mixin mud for LaVerne an Martin an keepin'em in stones. There cudda been a hunnerd wagonloads a stones in that foundation. I don't know. I never counted'em. I ain't sure my arithmetic went that high. All muscles, ya know, no brains.

I think I paid LaVerne an Martin forty cents a hour for their work.

Now I had a perty good-sized bunch a black ash logs ready for makin the floor beams. Those I got from a guy who said he owned a forty up off a Whiskey Bill Road. He said he'd sell me all I needed for five dollars, an I didn't waste enny time givin'em the money.

I cut all I needed with the crosscut saw. They were nice straight trees, not big enuff for veneer, I guess, so maybe that's why nobody'd cut'em before. I hauled some of'em home with the horses an the wagon—took all day ta go up an back—an I hauled some of'em on a trailer behind the car.

When the fella who'd sold'em to me saw how many I was haulin home, he said, "If I'd a knowed you wanted so many I'd a charged you more." But we'd made a deal, an I never paid'em another nickel.

On one a those trips I had the trailer loaded, ready ta come home, still daylight but getting late, an somebody had my road blocked. I could see'em, ya know, maybe a eighth of a mile down the way. So I waited an waited, but nobody was movin. I mean, I could see a couple a cars down there, an some men, an finally I walked down ta see what was goin on, an here's two game wardens, one of'em layin on his back, lookin with a flashlight under a guy's dash, while the other one's searchin the man whose car it was.

Well, I saw right away what they were doin, but I never did learn what they figgered they had on the guy.

I didn't hang around there very long. I never had much use for'em, ya know. Wardens, I mean. They were *bad* men.

A Windfall Homestead

Ennyway, I may've cut an hauled all those black ash by myself, but Lorinda rounded up a crew a the Berndts ta help me put'em all in place. Paul an Frank an Harold an Elmer. Took us all day.

I used one horse ta drag the logs over as we needed'em, an those guys got ta work with saw an axes. When the beams were all in place, they even helped nail down the first layer a lumber floor—or ceiling, I spoze, dependin on how yer lookin at it—an I never paid'em a nickel. But there was a lot a work exchange those days. I did have a pony a beer, though, enuff ta keep everybody's whistle wet.

Well, I put tarpaper over the top a that floor, an that was the roof a the barn over the winter a '42 and '43. It leaked, ya know, but Lorinda an me put the cows in there, an by then we had—I don't know—seven or eight of 'em.

Everything was jest like magic. Everything fell into place.

Before the cows went in, though, I had ta make a cement floor in the barn, with gutters an mangers an all that sort a thing. Yer askin me, Seedy, whether that was done *before* the black ash beams were up or *after*, an, ya know, yer askin me ta dig stuff out a my head that's buried in places I don't even know where ta look. I don't know where it's stored in there or if it maybe got lost or throwed out with a lot a other garbage.

There ain't room in there for *everything*, ya know. Somethin's got ta go.

Well, one day John Oestreich showed up, jest like that. He sez ta me, "I want ta show you where there's some trees might work for you for barn lumber."

John'd walked over from his place off Forks Road—he'd come kiddy-corner through the woods—an then we walked west a where Wolf Crick crosses the county road, back into the woods a half-mile or so—this was huntin land for John—an he took me to a ridge with a whole lot a standin dead hemlock trees on it, big ones, a whole ridge a giant scarecrows, an then he turned south an walked home through the woods.

Well, I walked home, too, but the next day I went back with my axe, an I went to the backside a every one a those dead hemlock trees, the side you couldn't see from the loggin road, an I sliced off a piece a every tree. The bark was still on'em, an under the bark there was punk, but under the punk the wood was perfectly solid.

That land an those trees belonged ta Menzner Lumber Company, out a Marathon City, an Menzner was practically givin it away ta get rid of it. See,

Gettin Over That Flirtin Business

it'd been logged, but the loggers hadn't wanted those dead hemlock. So they left 'em, a whole ridge of 'em. Scarecrows—though I ain't sure if the crows were scared of 'em or not.

First I went to the bank. There were two forties for sale, but I only wanted one of 'em, turned out that Dick Hahn wanted the other one. Seventy-five dollars a forty, so I borrowed enuff money ta buy both of 'em, one for me, one for Dick.

An then I went ta Menzner's an bought both of 'em. I think I bought 'em from right under Jul Krause's nose, cuz he was loggin in there that winter, an I figgered he had his eye on 'em too, though he never held it against me for getting 'em first.

In fact, when I'd cut all those hemlock with the crosscut an had 'em skidded to the loggin road—very little snow that winter—Jul let me use his jammer ta load those logs for haulin. In fact, it was Jul that hauled three, four loads a my logs ta Ritter an Hass, each log marked for what I wanted cut out of it.

See, I'd already been ta see Joe Berger about what I needed. It had been, I don't know, a year or two before I'd helped Emil Wegner put up his barn. Jest one day I'd helped, but that was the day I met Joe Berger.

Joe ran a tavern halfway ta Marshfield, jest where 97 an 29 cross, only what Joe really did was build barns. Him an his sons. An so I went ta see 'em, told 'em what kind a barn I wanted, how big an all that, an he made me a list a everything I needed—so many two-by-eights, so many two-by-tens, all that sort a thing.

So all those logs that got hauled ta Ritter an Hass were marked on both ends. The sawyer could see jest what I wanted.

Jul Krause hauled most a those logs. Hank Krause hauled a couple a loads.

When the logs were sawed, I had ta go stack the lumber myself. Somebody helped me, but I can't remember who it was. Maybe it was Martin Berndt, yer mother's brother. I ain't sure.

In the summer a '43, that barn went up.

First Joe Berger sent three, four men over. It took 'em two days ta frame all those hip-roofed trusses. On the third day, Joe came ta be the boss.

Lorinda had spread the word an somethin like forty men showed up, plus she had somebody ta help 'er with the cookin. This was July, an Albert was born on the twenty-eighth, so she was carryin a big baby in her belly.

77

A Windfall Homestead

Joe climbed up on somethin an he gave a little speech. He told the men ta keep it down, no jokin, no talkin except for what ya needed ta say. He said this is dangerous work an everybody's got ta pay attention ta what's goin on. He didn't want ennybody ta get hurt.

An he was the boss—not sharp, but he watched everything real close. By noon a that day, all the trusses were up. Joe had a little perch—I jest happened ta see this—an he wanted a board cut at a certain angle. He told the fella on the ground what he wanted.

Joe was sitting up there in his roost an he says to the guy on the ground, "You got yer square laid on wrong, turn it so-an-so." An, by golly, that fella did what Joe told'em ta do, an it came out exactly right.

Oh! He didn't miss nothin!

End a the day he left with his men. "Now," he sez ta me, "you got ta finish yer own barn."

We had scaffold up all around. But before the cedar shingles got nailed down, we hung the hay track in the peak—that way you can be on the roof but reachin through.

I was fifteen hunnerd feet short a drop siding, so that I had ta buy from Ritter an Hass. An I wanted good green-cut hemlock plank for the second layer of the haybarn floor—I was jest a little skeptical about usin plank from those scarecrow hemlocks—so I bought all I needed from Herman Berndt. I tried ta get'em ta come down on the price, but he wanted thirty-five dollars for the mess of it, an he wouldn't budge. It was good lumber. So I paid'em what he wanted.

But before the barn was finished, before the hay went in, I got pushed by some a the men who'd helped pound nails ta have a barn dance. "Got ta have a barn dance, Hank."

So, okay. Yer Ma was big as a pumpkin. Birdy wasn't born yet. I got a couple half-barrels a beer, an somebody brought an accordian, an we had a barn dance.

Barn dances brought people like flies to a gut wagon. People'd show up an ya didn't even know who they were. A little free beer'll do that.

We had some lanterns strung up in the barn—no electric lights in there yet—an well into the party who should show up but Old Fred Schulz. Fred liked his booze. I was kinda surprised ta see'em, but he handed me a couple a dollars an told me ta go get a bottle.

Gettin Over That Flirtin Business

So somebody drove me over to a bar on Highway 64 somewhere, an I bought a fifth a booze. Before we got back, it started ta rain. Perty hard, too.

Now the shingles weren't all on the barn roof yet, an so by the time we got that booze bottle passed around there was a puddle a water on one end a the barn floor an some a the younger people who, ya know, had got enuff beer in'em ta loosen up were runnin through that puddle an splashin each other. People were jest a howlin, havin a good time.

It wasn't a good floor ta dance on. But after you've had a few beers, an maybe a swig or two out a the booze bottle, an uneven floor don't make no difference. I don't think ennybody got really drunk, but those who wanted beer got plenty. I think they might've invented a new dance that night—The Splash Puddle Polka.

I was a couple a weeks late gettin hay made that summer. But, when I got it cut an dried, it went right inta the new hay mow.

Albert was born on July 28, 1943, in the hospital right in Jensen. There were two women in that room, an both of'em had brand new babies. One was Lorinda an the other was Len Donohue's wife. Len was married to Doc Kelly's daughter. Len was kind of a big shot, only his wife had a daughter an my wife had a son.

I knew Len Donohue becuz we used ta sell'em eggs. A couple a times I even sold'em big Christmas trees, an on one a those times he invited me inta his "den" ta give me a drink. By the time I got out a there I was perty well loaded. I don't think I'd ever seen ennybody have as many bottles a booze as Len Donohue did.

Ennyway, he took me aside in the hospital an said, "Let's trade." He meant babies. I think he was jokin, but with Len you never knew for sure.

When Lorinda was in the hospital, when Birdy was born, I was home alone an it was rainin. All of a sudden here comes John Oestreich an he sez, "Let's go fishin."

"Well, man," I sez, "it's *rainin*." An he sez, "A course it's rainin. That's the best time ta go."

So we got ready an went down to the crick back a where Dan Young used ta live, down inta that mess a alder brush, an we got soakin wet. But ya

A Windfall Homestead

know what? It was rainin, the crick was risin, an—jest like John said—the fish were bitin.

We were down there maybe an hour, maybe an hour an a half, but we came back with thirteen nice trout. That's the best trout fishin I ever did. On Birdy's birthday. Or close to it.

I kin tell, Seedy, that this three-steps ahead an four-steps back ain't exactly what you got in mind. But you got ta realize it's all back ta me. So if my mind is slidin back seventy years, say, how ya gonna keep it from stoppin at something interesting at sixty-seven or maybe seventy-four? My mind ain't like a measurin tape. It ain't all laid out in inches an feet, or in years where everything is neat an numbered. My mind, ya might say, has got a mind of its own, an there ain't nothin to be done about it.

So, ennyway, you asked me the other day about gettin electric power. Well, I never lived in a house that had electricity until the power company brought it out to the Town a Boulder sometime after yer Ma an me were married. It cudda still been 1940.

My folks, a course, never had electricity in their bunkhouse shack down by the river, an neither did Grampa an Gramma Coster in their big brick house down by Devil's Crick, on South Foster Street. (An, a course, they didn't have it when they lived with me in the log shack, either.)

Ennyway, when people out here heard that the power company was gonna set poles an string wire, a lot of us men went out an cut brush alongside the road ta make it easier an quicker for'em ta work. We were excited. We were gonna get *power*.

An perty soon, ya know, we had a couple a bare bulbs hangin in the log shack an, when it was built, in the new barn. We thought that was jest the cat's meow. We were getting *modern*.

Like I told ya, the new barn went up in July a '43—the top part, the lumber part—the same month Birdy was born. But when the foundation was built, I'd left a doorway on the north end a the west wall. That doorway was gonna open into a small silo room, an beyond that was gonna be the silo.

But I didn't have the money ta build that silo until about 1945, in the spring of the year. Yer Ma's old Uncle Paul, who was jest like a Dad ta me, said he knew a silo builder who could do the job. An he took me over ta

Gettin Over That Flirtin Business

meet that silo builder early in the winter, which musta been late in '44. An when that man an his crew came (I jest can't seem ta remember his name), they brought metal forms an scaffolding an some kind a hoist run by a gasoline engine. I mixed all the mud for'em, an help'em run it up the hoist for'em to dump in the forms. It took'em four days, I think it was, ta do the job. Only so many feet a day. I think it was about eight feet a day.

An, a course, once the silo was up, they put a domed cement roof over it, with a little window lookin to the west. There were U-shaped metal rods embedded in the exterior west wall, so we could, when we had to, climb up an stick the nose a the silo filler pipe through that window, or, when the silage was so high ya couldn't climb up the inside metal rungs from the silo room ennymore, you could climb inta the silo through that little window, headfirst. I don't think enny of us was exactly tickled to do that little trick, but we did it when we had to.

An when the silo was done, I built the silo room all by myself—cement floor, cement walls, an a little wooden room above for storage that, later, Jack an me made into a bin, built out a used hardwood flooring, for storing ground grain feed for the cows, an we made a hole in the silo room ceiling, with a sliding door, so the grain would fall right into the grain cart, which was a big improvement over liftin hunnerd-pound gunny sacks a grain that the mice'd already chewed holes in.

So this was beginnin ta be a real farm, ya see. Every year I'd clear a little more land. There was more hay ta put in the barn, corn for the new silo (I gave the old wooden silo ta Quinten Ament), always some oats ta binder an shock an thresh an get ground inta cow feed. An the barn was built—mangers an gutters an stanchions an calf pens an horse stalls. Even enuff chaff an litter here an there for the cats ta scratch up an do their job in.

Ten years after the family went ta Washington an I was a real farmer.

Yer Ma had lots a relatives. One a her aunts was married to a man by the name a Harry Henrichs, an Harry Henrichs was a businessman. He owned a little hardware store in Little Chicago.

Now I been ta Chicago, or at least I been *through* it, an *Little* Chicago ain't no *Chicago*. *Little* Chicago had maybe half-a-dozen houses in it, an if you looked the wrong way as you drove past you might've missed it entirely.

But Harry an his wife were a couple a those relatives yer Ma would invite over for a meal. Once when they came, an after we had eaten, Harry an me had ta go outside an find somethin ta do. Probably a Sunday. So I sez to'em, "I'll get my .22, an let's go for a walk." But Harry sez "Wait a minute" an walks to his car an when he comes back he's got *his* .22. So off we went, walkin acrost the field.

Well, we hadn't gone all that far an there's a rooster pheasant sneakin away—on the ground, ya know, runnin. I up an—plink—an down he went, an so we ain't gone but a few minutes an back we come with a nice plump pheasant.

By the time I had that bird cleaned, it was gettin a little late ta head out again. So we went inta the barn ta look things over. I had six or seven cows by then, an Harry sez, "You need a milking machine."

That thought had never occurred ta me before. I need a milking machine?!

A few days later here comes Harry Henrichs with a whole milking machine setup—vacuum pump, little motor, vacuum lines, rubber hoses, an two complete milking machines run off that vacuum line. I'm still tryin ta get it inta my head that I *need* a milking machine.

But Harry was determined, an he worked all day settin up that whole contraption, till finally he had ta go call somebody ta come out an help get it ta work right.

I hadn't even asked for it. But there it was. An I paid'em a little at a time, as I could afford it, an he never crowded me for the money.

When that outfit petered out many years later, somebody else sold me a Surge. An those were the only milking machines I ever owned.

Sometimes ya don't know what ya need, I guess, until somebody sells it to ya. Funny how that works.

I think I told ya yer Ma's Uncle Paul was like a Dad ta me. Oh, he was a Dutchman, an when all those Dutchmen got together, they talked *Plattdeutsch*, that growly Low German, an I couldn't understand hardly enny of it. But Uncle Paul was always good ta me—better, maybe, or jest closer, than to his own sons.

When I was gettin ready ta build the barn foundation, Uncle Paul came over with a platform truck an hauled enuff sand from the pit Oscar Weaver an me had opened back in 1931, enuff for all the stone masonry. An once (he already had some sort a tractor), he sent his son Harold over

Gettin Over That Flirtin Business

with that tractor ta plow a field west a the log shack, becuz, for one reason or another, I was too busy ta get it done with the horses.

A course I'd got ta know a whole crowd a yer Ma's relations, startin already before we were married. Some a that was becuz I was a deer hunter an, since I had nothin ta spend on her, I'd come ta visit with a chunk a meat, an they liked it. Word a that got around.

An after we were married, I'd go with'er over to the little church, kiddy-corner from the tavern her folks had run in the Town a Corning, and a whole flock a her relatives went ta that church, too. An she'd invite some of 'em over for a meal, an so I kinda became one of 'em, one a the Dutchmen.

Of all her relatives, I think Uncle Paul and Aunt Rica were her favorites. They were tops. I know Uncle Paul was tops fer me.

Ennyway, one winter after the barn was built, I saw right away I was gonna be short a hay. I figgered about ten tons short. So I smelled around an found that Ray Kurth, who was the son a Frank Kurth, the man I'd bought my first forty from, had sold his cows but still had a barn full a hay. He lived north a Jensen.

I didn't have enny money, so I borrowed two hunnerd an fifty dollars from a finance company, an I bought ten tons a hay from Ray Kurth, though I only paid 'em for one load at a time.

Well, how was I gonna haul that hay? I had ta go ta work sawin logs for Rib Lake Lumber Company in order ta earn enuff money ta pay the hay debt, and so, besides barn chores, I went to the woods six days a week an cut trees. That left Sunday for a day in the hay.

Now Uncle Paul still had that platform truck, an he sez ta me, "You drive the truck, an I'll come with you ta haul yer hay." An so every Sunday, that's what we'd do. I'd drive my '34 Chevy over ta Uncle Paul's, we'd get in his truck—an he always made me do the drivin—an we'd go haul a load a that hay from Ray Kurth's barn over ta mine. That would take us most of the day, an Uncle Paul wouldn't even take enny money for gas.

When I paid Ray Kurth for the last load, he handed me a small bottle a booze. It wasn't big, but it was good. We didn't get drunk, but by the time Uncle Paul an me were done unloading that hay, the bottle was empty, an Uncle Paul was standin there with a nice little smile on his face, lickin his lips.

He was a friend ta me, an he lived ta be ninety years old.

11

Life's Little Accidents

It mighta been the summer a '44, I can't remember fer sure, but I was married an I think the barn was built. But one a those summers we had rain, man oh! man, an there was water everywhere. The entire road between the bridges, down where the folks used ta live, was under water. An the bridge up here, to the west, had water over it, and the current had washed away the dirt an gravel around both ends. Plus, ennywhere there was a low spot in the road (like between the log shack an Ned Fox's place, which is where Dan Young used ta live), there was a foot or more a water.

So the county came out an wanted ta know if ennybody out here'd help'em patch up the roads, ya know, help'em fill in the washouts.

They brought out two old dump trucks an asked me if I'd drive one of'em. I said, "Sure, I kin drive it." Only it didn't have enny brakes.

Well, the main pit was at the bottom a Karban Hill, the pit Oscar Weaver'n me had opened somewheres in the early 1930s, an so ta go down that hill, not ta speak of turning inta the pit without tippin the truck over, I had ta shift'er down, ya know, before I got to the hill, an jest kind of crawl down.

All the loadin was done by hand, with shovels.

Ennyway, once I missed'er shiftin down an went shootin down the hill in neutral, which meant no brakes an no compression, an I ended up between the bridges, bouncin up an down over ruts an washouts, but the engine stayed runnin. So when the truck finally stopped, I jest put'er in reverse an backed'er up to the pit. (Another time, in that low spot near Ned's place, I hit'er way too fast an water splashed up an killed the engine. Somebody had ta come an help me get'er started again. My foot was jest too heavy, I guess.)

At the bridge up here, I had ta turn around in Dick Hahn's driveway an back down loaded to the bridge. But I didn't have enny brakes, an I sure didn't want ta back that truck right inta the washout. So, right away, I looked around an found a old log ta use for a wheel blocker, so when I backed up I had somethin ta bump up against, ta stop the truck.

When the washout on the east end was filled, we still had the hole on the west end ta fill. The county boss thought that backin truckloads a gravel acrost the bridge—it was a little kiddy-wampus from all the water pressure—was jest too ticklish ta try. So, instead, he got a lot of us men ta fill wheelbarrows an push'em from the little pit that's now on Bill Pittman's land (then it was Ned Fox's), push'em loaded over to the washout on the west end a the bridge. Push an dump. Push an dump. We had maybe a hunnerd yards a pushin ta do, each way.

It takes a lot a wheelbarrow loads a dirt ta fill a hole like that.

So I'd been pushin a wheelbarrow a couple days, it was noon, I'd been at it all morning, an I jest let go a the handles an said to the boss, "That's it. I'm done. I'm goin home. I got my own work ta do." I walked to the log shack an never went back.

Fidelis Hahn, Dick's oldest son, was pushin wheelbarrow, too, but he stayed on. In fact, he worked for the county right up to the day he retired. But I couldn't do that. I wanted ta be my own boss, an I wanted ta be a farmer. An that's exactly what I went home ta do.

There was a washout on the west side a the bridge one spring, jest past Dick Hahn's place, an I was down there with two, three other guys fillin in the hole, an somebody sez (don't ask me how he knew), "The suckers are runnin." Then one a those guys jest happened ta have a fishnet in the truck of his car, an somebody else had a gunny sack, so what do ya think we had ta do?

We went up the Boulder close ta half a mile—over a quarter of a mile, ennyway—where there's a whole string a riffles, an in that fast, shallow water you could see the suckers, females jest a little bit ahead a the males, sometimes with their top fin stickin out a the water, an she's kind a half-layin on her side an squirtin out a mess a eggs an he's jest behind squirtin out his milky-lookin stuff on top of 'em. Everywhere ya looked you could see'em. Fish everywhere.

A Windfall Homestead

Well, we're all lookin, ya know, fascinated, but we got work ta do, too. So a couple of us waded down below the riffles with that big fishnet, an somebody broke off a long stick, an the guy with the stick went inta the water above the riffles an started splashin an smackin the water with the stick.

Well, those fish, a course, turned an hightailed it downstream. Not far, though, cuz we were waitin for'em with the fishnet. An it ain't long an we got that gunny sack a quarter full a suckers.

Now that might not sound like much, but that's a lot a fish, an fish are *heavy*.

But, how'd it happen that somebody jest happened ta have a fishnet in the trunk of his car? Jest one a life's little accidents, I guess ya might say. Jest a mystery.

Well, that reminds me that when what's now Boulder Road was bein made into a road fer cars, I was up there with a few other men helpin ta dig out the rotted railroad ties. (The rails, ya see, had already been taken out by Kinzel or Rib Lake or whoever it was owned that logging line.) I was only a laborer. Had my car. Drove home every night.

But there were a couple guys who had teams a horses, an those horses stayed. An, a course, somebody had ta stay in a little shack an take care a those horses.

Well, the person who was stayin was Harry Eberhardt, an he sez ta me, "I got my rifle along. You come back tonight with a light an we'll get us a deer."

So I drove back later an there's Harry, waitin. He knows jest where he wants ta go—some lick in there close by—an my job is ta hold the light.

Everything happened real quick. We ain't there long an here comes a nice buck. Harry up an shoots an down goes that buck. Well, he's down but he ain't dead. I started ta run toward'em, but Harry sez, "Step aside. I'm gonna shoot'em again." An he did.

So it ain't long an that deer's in the back a my car, an I'm goin bumpity-bump down Boulder Road, all pocked up with those rotted ties missin, on my way ta Harry's place, down by the Wisconsin River.

But how'd Harry jest happen ta accidentally have his rifle with'em on that road job? Maybe his horses made'em bring it. Ya jest never know.

That story I jest told ya, about Harry an the buck, happened when I was still livin at home, with the folks. But this one I'm about ta tell ya happened later, when I was first startin ta hunt with Dick Hahn. By that time I was already livin in the log shack.

The lick I went to with Harry was a good mile up Boulder Road. But the one I went to with Dick was maybe a quarter-mile north a Whiskey Bill Road, on the east side a Boulder Road. It was old Camp 24, an about all that was left of it was a little clearing an a roothouse. A course, in that clearing was a lick.

The roothouse had been built above the ground. So it was hardly more'n a pile a dirt with a room inside. When I got there with Dick (my job, ya know, was ta hold the light), he sez ta me, "We won't go in the roothouse. Too many people know about it, an ya never know who's gonna show up." So we went away from it, laid in the grass, an waited. It was jest startin ta get dark.

We weren't layin there long when two guys showed up an went right inta the roothouse. We saw them, but they didn't see us. We'd walked all the way from home—five, six miles—so there wasn't enny car ta give us away.

In a little while Dick whispers ta me, "No use of us stayin here ennymore. Let's sneak out." So we did. But when we were a hunnerd an fifty yards away, maybe, Dick suddenly started ta talk real loud, sayin things like "There are two men in that roothouse. We'll get'em." An then we jest walked home.

Dick was workin a couple days a week at a factory in Jensen. The next time he went ta work, there were a couple guys all excited, tellin how they'd almost got caught by the game warden, up at Camp 24. They said they'd run so fast they even left their guns behind.

Dick said he never told'em he was the "game warden." He laughed about it when he told me his loud talking had scart the ass right off those guys. "Why," he sez ta me, "we cudda even had their guns, if we'd gone back an looked." An then he really did laugh.

I don't remember if this was the summer when we got so much rain, but rain makes me think of it, an it was in that neighborhood a time, ennyway, when this thing happened. It was the first or second year after the barn was built.

I was in the barn, an it was rainin ta beat the ban. I could hear a airplane buzzin, real low. The clouds were thick. I went an stood in the doorway ta listen an watch. All of a sudden I got a glimpse of a small plane landing in the field jest west a the log shack. I grabbed a couple a raincoats an ran toward it.

A Windfall Homestead

The pilot was a young man. He climbed out on a wing when I got over to'em. "I'm lost," he said. "Where the hell am I?" He'd taken off from Manitowish Waters, headed to Milwaukee, but he'd gotten confused in the clouds. He had a map, so I showed'em where he was.

"Well," he sez, "I guess I'll have ta call Wausau, take the wings off the plane, an have'er hauled to the airport there."

That seemed like a lot a monkeyin around ta me. So I sez to'em, "Why don't you fly'er out?"

Well, a course he wanted ta know how I thought that could be done, so I took'em in my '34 Chevy down to the corner an up Frostbite Avenue about half a mile, in that area where, maybe fifteen years earlier, I'd helped Tony Zillman blast stumps. See, once yer past that little crick bottom, Frostbite goes uphill to the north.

So we stood there, lookin south, all downhill to the crick bottom, where the popple trees were jest gettin high enuff, big enuff, ta cause'em some concern. But I convinced'em it could be done.

So back we came to the farm. I hooked a rope or a chain (I can't remember which) onto his plane, an I pulled'em down to the corner an on up Frostbite Avenue. By then we were attracting a crowd, ya know. All kinds a people were standin an watchin down at the corner. Obergs lived right about where we stopped an turned around—which was easy ta do—jest grab the tailend a the plane an walk'er around. An so there was a small crowd gathered around us, too.

The pilot was still a little leery a those popples. "What about those trees?" he kept askin. "You got ta be up an over those trees," I told'em, "an you got time ta do it."

I don't know what made me so confident he could do it, but I was.

Well, he got in the plane an started'er up. But before he took off, he reached out an handed me a twenty-dollar bill. When he gave'er the throttle, I jumped in the car, thinkin ta follow'em in case he cracked up, an help'em if I could. (Maybe I wasn't as confident as I thought I was.) A course, a whole load a people had ta jump in the car with me. Everybody wanted in on the excitement. But I never even got the Chevy inta high gear before that plane was in the air. People at the corner were scatterin like a flock a chickens.

Up he went, right over top a those popples, over the people, headin south. But then he made a circle, flew right over us, tipped his wings, an headed off toward Milwaukee.

He never even told me his name.

Life's Little Accidents

After yer mother an me were married, I put that '34 Chevy ta work haulin kids ta school. Once I was married, all a that kind a stuff—haulin kids, being elected to the school board, gettin ta be town treasurer—jest seemed ta happen on its own. I guess bein single means you ain't quite reliable, too much of a lone wolf. But bein married means yer gonna buckle down an take responsibility—that yer trustworthy, I suppose.

At first I jest hauled kids to the Boulder School, not to the Copper. See, now ya got zoning that sez you can't live up in the brush, back in the woods. But back then people lived wherever they wanted. An they did, too. So I had ta make a big loop up an around the county road an come down Frostbite Avenue. There were kids up Conservation Road almost ta where Joe Smitty lived—first the Wards an then, when the Wards left, a family by the name a Kellogg. There were a couple a Sprafke kids on Whiskey Bill Road, kids by the old fur farm along Averill Crick (Willis Klemme had a little sawmill there), an even some kids by the name a Hessel up Camp Road, not too far from where I used ta work with old Hank Fau Fau.

An the roads weren't nowhere so good as now. Lots a potholes. I even laid planks over some sinkholes on Frostbite Avenue, jest ta keep from gettin stuck. Once on the county road, ya know, in the spring, during breakup, I was headed north toward Whiskey Bill an—plop!—down I went. The frost had gone out from under a culvert, the culvert had dropped, an the front wheels a the car plopped right in. There I sat like a dunce, with both front wheels kinda splayed out.

Well, I jacked'er up an rolled'er back—got out okay. But what was I gonna do about those splayed wheels? I always had a few tools along, an one of 'em was a axe. So I chopped down a small tree an, using a piece a that tree as a lever, I put the razz on those bent tie rods an got'em straight enuff ta drive. Finished my route, dropped the kids off at school, an went right down ta Johnson's garage in the sixth ward, in Jensen. Old Johnson hoisted'er up, looked at those tie rods, an said, "There ain't nothin crooked about'em. I can't make'em enny straighter than they are already."

Imagine that! With that stinkin green pole I'd managed ta straighten those tie rods jest right!

A Windfall Homestead

I think I was fifteen years on the Town a Boulder school board. I also collected taxes for eighteen years an drove school bus for twelve. But those two jobs came later.

Yer askin me, Seedy, what was my "educational philosophy"? I think yer kinda makin fun a me, maybe even bein a little mean. I was, ya know, only a dumb shit out a the eighth grade. I never was taught ennything about "educational philosophy." Maybe that's for people who wear white shirts and got no dirt on their hands, no cow manure on their shoes. Bein clerk a the school board jest meant seein to it the school buildings were in decent shape, that a teacher got hired who could do the job, that the furnace worked, that the kids who lived too far to walk got hauled.[1]

[1]. These one-room schools for all eight grades, including the Copper and the Boulder, were phased out in favor of consolidation by the early 1960s. I went to both the Boulder (for five years) and the Copper (for three). Neither school had running water or flush toilets. Sometimes our teachers were fresh out of the county Normal School, twenty years old with no classroom experience. One of these teachers, at the Boulder (even now I don't think I should give her name), we really liked but terribly abused.

I was in the fourth grade, maybe the fifth, almost old enough to be one of the Big Boys. We had taken—or the Big Boys had taken—all the door knobs off the internal doors, so the only way to go from room to room was by means of a certain type of scissors, which could be inserted into the door-opening mechanism, and all of which, of course, the Big Boys had appropriated. You were on track to becoming a Big Boy if you could come into possession of such a scissors.

One spring day, warm and balmy, a couple of us younger boys were out pumping water. The handpump was just below the library window. The window was open and some of the Big Boys were in the library, joyously throwing books down at us. The area around the pump was totally littered with thrown books. It was a mess.

Suddenly into the driveway drove Mr. Brace, the tall, greying, dignified Assistant Superintendent of Schools. We all knew Mr. Brace. He got out of his car and just stood staring at this incredible scene. We did our best to act invisible, nervously stooping to pick up the flapping books, as if they'd accidentally come up the well with the water. He stalked right past us, stomped up the stairs, and (one of the Big Boys had the wit to beat him to the upper school door with a scissors) stunned our poor unsuspecting teacher with a sudden appearance. All who were in the building—except, of course, Teacher—were told to "Go outside and wait"—though it was more like GO OUTSIDE AND WAIT. Everybody did exactly that. Quickly. Very quickly. We all took shallow breaths, hardly spoke, and waited in fear for the end of the world.

After what seemed an eternity, Mr. Brace came out, glanced at us cowering children with utter unmentionable contempt, said not a single word, got in his car, and drove away.

We stood there, stunned and anxious, for several minutes. And then, drawn by the gravitational silence, we crept slowly in, up the stairs (trying hard not to make them creak), and peeked through the door into the main school room. Teacher was sitting at her desk, up front, her face buried in her arms, her lovely dark hair jiggling in sympathy with her awful sobs. We slowly crept up to her and, in great distress and embarrassment, surrounded her desk.

Ya know, Seedy, I have ta say I didn't remember yer story about Harley

"Teacher," somebody finally said, "we're sorry. We really are. We'll behave. We promise. We'll never do it again." We really meant it. We actually loved our Teacher. And then she really wailed.

Another time, a few years earlier, one of the badest of the Big Boys, Harley Garler, decided to give Teacher a bouquet of spring flowers. We were all outside, at recess. Harley walked up to Mrs. Mitbauer with his bouquet and said, "Here, Teacher, I got some flowers for you."

I can still remember the sudden softening of Mrs. Mitbauer's face as she registered first surprise and then gratitude at this unprecedented gesture. But as she reached to take the bouquet she was also examining Harley's offering. She pulled her hand back without taking the bouquet and said, "Harley, there's poison ivy in there."

"Oh, no," said Harley. "There's no poison ivy in here," as he held the flowers a little higher.

"Oh, yes, there is," said Mrs. Mitbauer, the softening no longer visible in her face.

"I know poison ivy when I see it," said Harley, who was something of a bully, "and there ain't none in here." He was now shaking his bouquet as if it were an item up for sale at an auction.

"Well, so do I know poison ivy when I see it," replied Mrs. Mitbauer, "and there is some in that bouquet."

"No, there ain't," said Harley.

"Yes, there is," said Mrs. Mitbauer.

By now Harley, who wasn't the brightest bulb in the chandelier, was getting aggravated and reckless. His clever scheme wasn't working as he'd planned. We little kids (who had no forewarning of this stunt) were all eyes and ears. Harley was being humiliated by tiny Mrs. Mitbauer, and his pride began to kick in as the little audience began to giggle and smirk.

"There ain't no poison ivy in here," Harley said loudly, with just a hint of pleading in his voice. (Was he secretly asking Mrs. Mitbauer to go along with the gag or offer some way to get him off the hook?) He obviously didn't like the way his prank was backfiring.

Mrs. Mitbauer just stared at him, a look of disgust on her face. A prank, I think, she could have gone with; but this was a bouquet, spring flowers, something that had briefly touched her heart; this was just too wicked.

"Teacher," Harley began. "Look," he said, "I'll show you there ain't no poison ivy in here." And he rubbed that bouquet on his bare left arm, transferred it to his left hand and rubbed it on his right arm, transferred it back to his right and rubbed it all over his face. "See," he said. And, then, with a look of injured pride and scorned dignity, he walked to the edge of the school yard and threw the bouquet over the fence into the ditch.

Mrs. Mitbauer watched him with a look that seemed to say, "I think I've now seen everything."

Harley Garler was out of school for at least two weeks.

I mention these two events to indicate that these backwoods schools were no bed of roses for teachers, and that being on the school board (with or without any "educational philosophy," and for almost no pay) was an exercise in frustration. And, when the Boulder was closed and, a year later, the building and the acre on which it sat reverted to the original owner because of a buried clause in the ignored land contract, my father was verbally tarred and feathered at a public meeting for letting the school building and its acre "get away."

"I didn't know nothin about it," he told me. "I spoze I should a known, but I didn't. Two fellas raked me over the coals until there was nothin left but a little patch a burnt hide. All a that for the fabulous pay a fifteen dollars a year. Some people must be nuts." S. B.

A Windfall Homestead

an that bouquet a flowers fer Lulu Mitbauer. Well, maybe I knew about it at the time an jest fergot about it. But it brings ta mind another story that's got Harley actin kind a dumb, although it ain't so bad as rubbing poison ivy in yer own face.

One winter I got a job from Otto Oestreich cuttin dead an windfall cedar out of a swamp downstream from Grandfather Falls, on the west side a the Wisconsin River. Otto owned a bunch a land near there; but this was close to the river, an it was owned by Wisconsin Public Service Corporation—one a their blocks a land along the river, ya know, becuz a their dams an backwaters.

Ta get there, I had ta drive about three miles up Frostbite Avenue, then quite a ways east on one a Otto's woods roads, though that perticular road used ta be Kinzel's Camp 42 branch line. Then there was a steep hill goin down before ya got to the swamp. I always parked on top.

Well, one day I was in there cuttin cedar an here comes Harley drivin some junker of a pickup he'd jest bought. I ain't sure he was even old enuff ta have a driver's license, but there he was, happy as a lark, proud as a peacock, wantin ta show me his truck. A course, he had come right down the hill with it.

After I'd looked it over I said to'em, "Easy enuff fer you ta drive'er down the hill, but how are ya gonna get'er back up?"

"Oh, I'll get'er out," he sez ta me. "You jest watch."

So he gets in an guns'er an tries, but all that truck'd do is get up a little ways an sit an spin. So he had ta back'er down. Then he got out, all excited. "What am I gonna do now? How am I ever gonna get out a here?"

I loaded'em down with a big bunch a cedar posts (I was cuttin all a that stuff fer fencing), an then he did make it up. I gave'em two dollars ta drive that load home fer me. But, ya know, without weight in the back end, he never wudda got that truck up the hill. Harley had a reputation fer not thinkin very far ahead.

Once I hired a man named Allard ta put new cedar shingles on the Copper School. A course that meant he had ta tear the old shingles off. One day I drove past an he's workin on the roof an there's a heap a old shingles layin on the ground below the eaves, an so I stopped ta gather up a bunch ta take home ta use for kindling.

Life's Little Accidents

Now Allard had a sawmill up toward Tomahawk, an he did odds an ends a carpentry on the side. He was a older man. Not a kid ennymore. An right away he calls down ta me an asks what I think I'm doin. So I sez to'em, "I'm jest gettin some a these old shingles for kindling."

"Oh, no, you ain't," he sez. "The last time I had a job like this people started ta argue an fight over them stupid old shingles. When these shingles are all off, I'm gonna throw'em in a big pile right here in the schoolyard an burn the whole batch of 'em. I ain't puttin up with no more fightin over used shingles."

Well, I'd hired'em, but he was boss a the job, so what was I gonna say to'em? Nothin, that's what. I couldn't very well tell'em he was wrong, even if I did hate ta see all those good used shingles goin ta waste. An he did exactly what he said he was gonna do—heaped'em and burned'em. The whole stinkin batch.

Another time—this was during the Second World War—the school board decided ta be patriotic an bought a goverment savings bond. Cost us thirty-seven dollars an fifty cents. An every year I had ta take our books down an have'em checked by the Superintendent a Schools. Her name was Nellie Evjue, an I was scared ta death a that woman.

Twice she had me come down to her office. We were missin thirty-seven dollars an fifty cents, an she was demanding ta know where that money went. I was in a real sweat. I could not figger out how come we were short a that money. I thought about it all the time, an I jest could not figger it out.

An then it came ta me: that goverment savings bond! So I went right down ta see Nellie Evjue, an when I told'er where that money had gone, she was all smiles. I can't begin ta tell you what a relief it was ta get out from under the hooks a Nellie Evjue. All becuz of a stupid goverment savings bond that cost thirty-seven dollars an fifty cents.

The first time I was ever elected ta ennything was when some people urged me ta run against Tony Zillman for assessor. I did an I beat'em. But I only lasted one year, an then I quit. At the Board a Review, two fellas came in an said they didn't have the livestock I said they did. Well, I'd counted'em. One had sheep. The other had a batch a heifers. But both of 'em came to the Board an said they didn't have what I said they had, an the Board agreed with'em. I knew they were lyin. I couldn't take that. So I quit.

A Windfall Homestead

But while I was assessor I had ta go snoop inta everybody's business. That's how I got my anvil. See, there was two old guys, brothers, Ira an Hiram Chadeen, who'd come up from southern Wisconsin somewhere, an they'd moved into a shack on old Camp 26, up off Conservation Road. They said they were gonna make a farm, but they never did. They were too old. Wasn't long an Ira died.

Ennyway, I had ta go do an assessment a Hiram's place. All he had was a shack. When I went into his shack, all there was ta sit on was one chair, an Hiram was sittin in it. The only other thing ta sit on was a big old anvil, which was sittin in the middle a the floor. So I sat on that. Well, it didn't take long ta do an assessment a nothin, or next ta nothin.

But I didn't have an anvil, an I wanted one, so when I got up I asked Hiram if he'd sell that anvil. He said he would, an I asked'em how much, an he said five dollars.

Well, I didn't have five dollars cash on me, but by then I had a checking account, an I had my checkbook with me. So I wrote him out a check.

I didn't want ta leave that anvil sittin there, an my car was parked out on the road, maybe a eighth of a mile away, so I got Hiram ta give me a burlap sack. I put the anvil in that sack, got it up on my back, an that's how I carried my new anvil.

Next time my cancelled checks were returned from the bank, the one ta Hiram wasn't in there. So I went up ta see'em. "Oh," he said, "I haven't been ta town yet."

"Well," I said, "I'll cash it for you right now." So I gave'em a five-dollar bill an he gave me back the check I'd wrote him. That's how I learned ta be a banker. Ennybody kin do it. Ya jest need ta start out with a five-dollar anvil.

12

Caught His Limit

I THINK I TOLD ya about the time my Ma an us kids netted a three-pound trout with a piece a chickenwire (we knew it was three pounds becuz Ma weighed it on her butter scale), an then she took it ta town with old Jack an the buckboard an gave it to her Ma an Pa an to Grampa Buckberry, who was stayin with her folks a while in the big brick house on South Foster Street. An I told you about catchin a mess a trout one day when it was rainin, with John Oestreich, right in that neck a time when Birdy was born.

See, I knew there was trout in the Boulder from the time I was a kid. It wasn't only becuz a that trout we netted. When we first moved inta the old bunkhouse, there was a man by the name a Ignace Obermeyer who lived in town. Everybody called'em "Nick." He was a bachelor, a older man, an he used ta drive out an park his car in our yard an walk up the Boulder, goin trout fishin.

Twice when he came back he showed me creels a trout he'd caught. My eyes jest bugged out, ya know.

He said this was the best trout fishin in the whole country, but he never took me with'em an he never showed me how ta do it. All I knew at the time was net an spear. Later, I got ta do a little trout fishin with a stick, a string, a hook, an a gob a worms. But when I was a kid, ketchin trout seemed like a miracle, an I wasn't holy enuff fer that.

A trout, ya know, is a very shy animal. They like cold water. An they'll scoot under a log if they're disturbed. Then you won't ketch'em.

A Windfall Homestead

Well, I had jest caught a trout from under a log, in the crick back a Dan Young's, an I saw another trout make a dive right past me. I saw'em zip under a log that was layin in the water, an he didn't come out. I knew he was there. So I very carefully looked an I could jest see his nose stickin out from under that log—not his eyes, jest the tip of his lower jaw. I dropped a worm in front of'em, but he would not bite. (Well, jaw, nose—on a fish they're jest about the same.) Ennyway, I took the worm off that hook, wound up the line, an cut a slit in the end a my fishin stick. Then I stuck the hook in that slit—made it real snug—an very slowly lowered that hook under his jaw. He never moved. When I jerked up I had that fish by hookin'em right under the jaw. That fish was awful careful, but he wasn't careful enuff. Maybe if he'd had a decent nose, he cudda smelled what was comin.

Ya know, lots a yer mother's relatives would come out ta visit an, if they were women, I'd have ta go find myself somethin ta do. I never knew people as sociable as those old Dutchmen. Ennyway, this time two women came out, one of'em yer mother's aunt an the other a cousin, an so I had ta go fishin. When I got back, those two women were jest about ready ta leave. But I'd caught a couple dandy trout—twelve, thirteen inches, both of'em. And, a course, they had ta look at'em an ooh-an-aah over'em. They didn't *say* they wanted'em. They didn't have ta *say* ennything. So I jest gave'em those trout. They cudda been a couple a grandfathers or a couple a grandmothers, or maybe one a each. It's hard ta tell'em apart.

Another time I went fishin with somebody (I think it might a been Art Wais, who was married to yer mother's sister Myrtle) an we were down at that same crick. Perty soon I caught a trout. But I also saw that a fish had zipped into a bunch a weeds next to the bank—you kin see the V-shaped ripples they make as they're scootin. Now the other guy (I think it was Art) was standin on the far bank, an I sez to'em, "Stand still!"

That bunch a weeds was on his side a the crick. So I waded in real slow, bent over with my hands out in front a me, an when I was close enuff I scooped with my hands in those weeds an out came a mess a weeds right by Art's feet, an in that mess a weeds was a nice trout. That's the only time I ever caught a trout with my hands. Though I guess you could say I didn't exactly "ketch" it. His legs were short, an he jest could not run away fast enuff.

An John Oestreich died fishin. He was maybe seventy years old by then. He was way up on Averill Crick. His wife was waitin in the car. She waited an waited an John didn't come. Finally she went for help.

They found John sittin up against a clump a tag alders, dead as a doornail. He had his fishin pole tucked under his arm, an in his creel he had eight trout. He had eight kids, an in his creel he had eight trout. I guess he'd caught his limit.

Lots a people moved into the Town a Boulder in the Depression. People were poor as rats. Floyd Peterson was one of 'em, an he lived with his family in a shack next ta Wolf Crick, about two miles northwest a where we're sittin now.

Floyd had several kids, an him an his wife even took in kids from Welfare. I spoze they got a little money fer doin that. Everybody was lookin ta survive. Ennyway, we sold 'em milk. One a the kids—I think it might a been Floyd Junior who did it most offen—would walk down to the farm for milk. An somehow they'd caught a little fawn. A course, after a month or two or three, that fawn was like a puppy dog, jest followin the kids everywhere. So when Floydy walked down fer milk, that fawn walked with 'em.

Well, that was a big thrill, ya know. Everybody wants ta pet the fawn. But when it's time for Floydy ta head home, the fawn ain't interested in goin with 'em. He ain't done visitin at the farm. So, after a while, I sez ta Floydy, "I'll drive ya home." But the fawn wouldn't get in the car. So Lorinda got a slice a bread, an when the fawn got a taste a that he was ready ta follow Floydy ennywhere. We had 'em in the back seat a the car in no time.

So Floydy's in the back seat with the fawn, feedin 'em little bits a bread. But we had a good half-mile ta go when Floydy ran out a bread. An then that fawn wanted out. Well, the kid tried ta hang onto 'em, but that deer began ta jab me an pound me with his front feet. Finally, he smacked me so hard on the head it knocked my cap off. "That's it," I hollered. An I pulled the car over, got out an said, "Git that deer out a here!"

Well, Floydy was almost home, so he didn't have all that far ta walk. But you can't drive with a deer that wants out. It jest can't be done. I never gave that fawn another ride in the car, I'll tell ya that.

13

Mark My Words

THERE WAS A SHORTAGE a men during the Second World War. Jobs were easy ta come by, compared ta what it had been in the thirties. I was a young man, fit an strong, an in the winter I didn't always have enuff ta do. Half a dozen cows ain't enuff ta keep a young man busy. So I went up ta talk ta somebody in the office of the Rib Lake Lumber Company, which was cuttin logs back a Sprafkes', way west a Whiskey Bill Road.

Rib Lake was a big outfit with their own loggin trains, haulin everything west to the town a Rib Lake, where they had a huge sawmill.

Well, I got hired all right, but they put me ta work making skidways, which I didn't want ta do. There was money to be made sawin logs, cuz that was piecework, but I was told "When we get a man ta be yer partner, then we'll put you ta sawin."

I worked a week an a half, two weeks maybe, makin those stupid skidways, and then I told'em, "I'm gonna quit." Well, they gave me a old guy real quick for a sawin partner, but it only took a week an he was wore out. He said he was sick, but I think he jest couldn't take it. I don't mean ta criticize'em. He worked as hard as he could. But I was twenty, thirty years younger than he was, an he jest couldn't keep up.

Well, now what? I went ta town an bought a one-man saw from Howland's Hardware Store. That old guy an me had been usin a crosscut, an I knew I could use a crosscut by myself (becuz I'd done it before, when I cut hemlock pulp with Oscar Krause), but I wanted ta work. I wanted ta make some money, an I didn't want ennything ta slow me down. So I took a chance they'd let me work alone, an I went ta Howland's. Old Man Howland had one saw left.

Now I'd sawed enuff ta know I wanted a lance-tooth saw, which has four cutting teeth an then a raker an then four cutting teeth an another raker—from one end of the blade to the other. But Howland only had a diamond-tooth, which has two cutting teeth an a raker an then another two cutting teeth. The lance-tooth is more touchy ta file (an that was a job I wasn't very good at), so it was probably a good thing Old Howland only had a diamond-tooth for sale. I paid'em about five dollars for that saw.

I think it was on a Saturday night when I went ta town an bought it. On Sunday I filed it. On Monday I took it with me to the woods.

I can't remember if it was that day or the next I thought I was done with the strip a trees the old guy an me had been workin on. Now you don't jest go an cut wherever you want to, ya know. Yer assigned a area, a strip ta cut, an that's where you work until yer done. Then you'll get another strip. So I told the boss I was done.

"What about those four big hard maples?" he asked.

"Well," I told'em, "I can't cut those trees by myself. They're too much for one man."

"No," he said. "You got ta cut those trees first. Then I'll let you have a new strip."

Oh, they were bruisers! Not only were they big, but this was winter an they were frozen solid. It was like cuttin inta a rock or a hunk a iron. I worked a couple a days jest ta take care a those four maple trees, and I wasn't too happy about havin ta do it, ta tell you the truth.

But then the boss, jest like he said he would, gave me a new strip a trees, an quite a few of'em were tall, straight white pines. Man oh! man, did I cut the timber! I was makin money hand over fist. One day I made somethin like thirteen dollars—which might seem like next ta nothin now, but back then it was really rakin in the dough.

Now on Saturday afternoon it wasn't unusual for some a the men ta quit a little early an, ya know, it's always temptin ta do that, too. But everything was goin so good, I thought, what the hell, I'm gonna cut one more tree. So I did.

I was always careful. Soon as that tree was cut an started ta go, I stepped behind another tree jest ta be sure ta be out a the way. What I hadn't noticed was that the tree I'd cut had a crooked branch, way up, an that branch had grown beyond the tree I'd stepped behind—grown beyond it, hooked around it, an when I'd cut the tree and it began ta fall, the branch broke off an came down on the back side a the tree I was standin behind.

Nobody wore hardhats in the woods those days. I jest had on my wool lumberjack cap, but even so I think that cap saved my life. That branch came down butt-end first an smacked me right on top the head an knocked me right onta my ass, though when I realized where I was, what had happened, I was sittin on a stump, with blood runnin down my face.

When my head cleared, I got up an tried ta work. I wanted ta finish that tree I'd cut down. But I was jest too shaky. So I went to the office ta check out. Well, when the boss saw me, he acted like he was mad an he started shoutin, "What the hell are you doin out in the woods by yerself? You got ta have a partner or you can't saw logs here ennymore!" Ta tell ya the truth, I think he was more scared than mad, but lots a people act mad when they're scared.

But that put me in a pickle. Who was I gonna find ta be my partner? I think it was yer mother, Seedy, who came up with Emil Oestreich.

Now Emil was, I don't know, eight, ten, twelve years older'n me, an he had some piddleass farm down by the Copper River, an his wife was yer mother's cousin. But he was a lumberjack. So I went ta see'em, ta ask if he'd work with me, an he said okay. So on Monday morning I went back ta work with Emil, an we sawed logs.

We used a Rib Lake crosscut ta saw with, but Emil was a good filer (a lot better'n me) and every day he'd touch up our saw right in the woods. Ya need a saw holder ta do that, so we always did what a lot a lumberjacks used ta do, an that was cut right straight down into a stump, an inch an a half or two inches deep, an that slit was what Emil used ta hold the saw, with the teeth pointed up. He always carried a couple little saw wedges with'em, an they'd get tapped in alongside the saw ta hold'er tight. He could file a saw in twenty minutes or so.

We never stayed in the bunkhouse, and I don't think we ever ate in the cook shanty. Lunch was always brought out to us. Some guy with a horse an sled would show up, jest about noon, an we'd break ta eat. Nobody was in the mood ta waste a minute.

Emil was my partner all the rest a that winter, until breakup, and we made money.

I think I told you that Jul Krause was a gypo, always gettin loggin jobs, hirin guys ta cut an haul. Otto Engel was one of his drivers. People called'em Ted. Ted Engel. Later he went inta business for himself.

Ennyway, Jul was a active man. He didn't miss nothin. He could be loggin, but he would be trappin, too. An once he caught a bobcat. He knocked that bobcat on the head an put'em in the truck Ted Engel was drivin, an he asked Ted ta take it to the game warden an collect the bounty that was on'em. So Ted drove off with the bobcat.

Only thing, that bobcat wasn't dead. An perty soon he starts ta prowl around the cab. Well, Ted couldn't stand that. So he stopped an got his hand on somethin—a tire iron, maybe—an then that bobcat did get dead.

But people laughed about Ted Engel taking Jul Krause's live bobcat for a visit ta the game warden. I suspect there was a minute when it wasn't very funny ta Ted.

There was that coppery eclipse a the moon last night, an you say, Seedy, it was twenty-six below this morning?

It'll be eighty-six years tomorrow I walked in the snow behind Old Man Lucier's team a horses an bobsled, out to the Town a Boulder. The twenty-second day a February, 1922. That'll be eighty-six years fer me out here in the brush, Seedy. Eighty-six years! Man oh! man, has there been the changes in eighty-six years!

I don't remember ennything about eclipse a the moon way back then—maybe there wasn't no such a thing in those days—but it cudda jest as well been twenty-six below. Oh! those were cold winters. Ten years old an walkin eight, nine miles in ankle-high shoes, followin behind a bobsled and a team a horses, on my way to a cold, vacant shack of a house in the month a February. Washington's birthday!

If there wudda been a cherry tree ta cut down, I probably wudda done it—an put it right inta the stove ta burn, cherry pits an all.

As long as I'm cold jest thinkin about bein cold, I'll tell ya one that might seem funny now, but it sure wasn't funny then.

My folks lived in this house on the edge a Dawson, North Dakota, an there was a shack of a barn maybe a hunnerd feet away from the house. In that barn, Pa kept Shorty an Bell, gelding an mare, his team a white horses, and (I ain't sure) six, seven, eight head a cows. An, a course, us older kids had chores ta do. So for one reason or another, we were back an forth between the house an barn.

Now in the winter we had blizzards. The wind'd blow that snow an heap it up. I even saw my Pa drive Shorty an Bell, with a bobsled hooked behind, up an over a drift a snow. That's how hard it would pack. (Pa was on his way ta get some stacked slough hay from out by Uncle Hugo's place.)

Ennyway, my older sister Clara an me were goin to the barn, an we had ta walk over a drift a snow three, four feet high. No problem. But Pa had a piece a heavy old iron—a old axle from a mower—propped up against the barn door ta keep it closed. It was a perty tall piece a metal, an it had a hole or an indentation in the top end. An in that hole was a spot a frost or snow. I can't remember which. An, without thinkin, I stuck my tongue in that hole ta lick out that nice spot a snow.

Well, it was easy ta stick my tongue in, but it froze to the iron before I could pull it out. An then I started squealin an hollerin. Clara wasn't no wallflower. She did stuff. She jest grabbed hold a my head an gave a jerk an part a my tongue stayed stuck in that frosty hole.

I had a sore tongue for a long time after, Seedy, but I never went lickin on frost again, I kin tell ya that for sure.

I spoze you kin explain it lots a ways, an maybe it ain't nothin more than thinkin yer own time a life is special, but it seems ta me there were more interesting characters back in those years before everything got so—whataya call it?—"normal," maybe. Before every single last stinkin kid had ta go ta school fer thirty years an watch TV fer seventy.

Go ahead an grin all ya want, Seedy, but I think it ain't no accident or coincidence that every last kid havin ta go to high school, and a lot of 'em to college, happened at exactly the same time as the little farms all died. Yer an example a what I mean.

But I ain't talkin about coincidences, in perticular. I'm thinkin about how people lived. Ya know, guys like Joe Smitty in his shack, with his cows an horses livin in the cellar. (Did I tell ya there was a "Lumberjack Days" in Jensen once—all kinds a stuff, like a log-loading contest—and Joe Smitty won the fiddlin contest? He wasn't the best fiddler by enny means, but he had a homemade fiddle made out of a cigarbox, an when he played *Turkey in the Straw* the crowd jest went wild, so they had ta give'em first prize.)

Mark My Words

Now Hank Becker was another one a those backwoods, solitary cusses. He lived in the Town a Corning somewheres, up off a Wegner Road, north of the Copper River, in Rib Lake's slashing. Him an his horse lived in the same shack—part of it for Hank Becker, part for the horse, with some sort a poles in-between ta keep'em from steppin on each other's toes. Kept the horse from eatin off a Hank Becker's plate, maybe.

Hank did some loggin—enuff, I guess, ta keep'em alive. I kin remember seein'em at Lamberti's in '34 an '35. He had long, dark hair an he wore a straw hat, even in the winter. Sometimes I'd see'em walkin by the log house, on his way ta town.

When Lorinda an me got electricity at the log house, I needed a couple a yardlight poles. I wanted cedar. Hank Becker got'em for me. I think he charged me twenty dollars.

He wasn't a bad man or a ornery man. He jest lived with his horse. He was different. Nobody got their nose all bent out a shape an called Social Services, becuz there wasn't enny Social Services. At least, not that I knew of.

I ain't sayin everything was always fine an dandy, cuz it wasn't. There was a story in the neighborhood—I ain't sayin enny names—about a couple a people who tried ta cheat a old lady out a her property. There was a fella with sticky fingers who spent a year in prison. There was another fella, a regular wild ass of a man, whose marriage lasted exactly one day. An there was a woman who was carryin a baby that wasn't her husband's, an she killed herself tryin ta do a homemade abortion.

So there were bad things that happened. But—I don't know, things are hard ta figger out—it seems ta me people were more acceptin of each other. You may not a liked somethin somebody said or did, but you lived with'em. You didn't shut'em out. They might not a been yer friend, exactly, but you didn't shun'em. You didn't treat'em like they weren't there.

See, when yer poor, when *everybody's* poor, when you ain't got radio or television or telephone or (whataya call them stupid little gizmos?) "video games," when you actually might need yer neighbor, an when everybody's livin close ta Mother Earth, you jest can't walk around with yer nose stuck up in the air.

That doesn't mean there wasn't gossip or backbitin or all a that sort a thing. There was, maybe even more than now. But people reached out to each other, too. Ya know what I'm sayin? It's rough when nobody's got enuff, but maybe it's even worse when everybody's got too much.

Now we don't know who lives acrost the road. Amazing!

A Windfall Homestead

I think I'd get a big thrill ta see Hank Becker walkin by with his straw hat on. I'd send you out, Seedy, to invite 'em in for a cup a coffee. I'd like ta ask 'em what kind a pancakes his horse ate for breakfast.[1]

Lots a things happened in the '40s, but it seems like even more things happened toward the tailend a the '40s than at the beginning. The war was over by '45, an it seemed like the Depression had got knocked in the head.

You say, Seedy, that federal spending fer war was what pulled the whole country out a the Depression? I guess that jest might be true.

But look at what we got now. I read in the newspapers that this country's got a bigger military budget than all the rest a the world put together!

It's like I told you before—it's rough when nobody's got enuff, but it jest might be worse when everybody's got too much. An what's that big military budget tell ya but that we got way too much, an also that we aim with our tanks an guns an bombs ta keep it that way? That ain't good. It's selfish an greedy an it can't last. Seems like we're in one war after the other, an we're either gonna start losin 'em or we're gonna go broke tryin ta win 'em. Or maybe some a each.

We ain't ever figgered out what it means ta live within our means. Maybe none of us ever learned when ta quit, when ta say "That's enuff." I look around an see all these little farms goin ta pot, all those little barns fallin in on themselves, an that tells me somethin ain't right. Somethin bad's gonna happen. Maybe it's gonna be worse than the Great Depression,

---

1. My father's thoughts remind me, in an odd sort of way, of my experience in St. Louis in 1967. Through a rather goofy connection, I landed a summer job encouraging youth recreation in poor, black neighborhoods. (It was absolutely ridiculous for me, a white kid from a northern Wisconsin farm, to have that job, but that's another story.) Lyndon Johnson's War on Poverty was kicking in, along with the practical consequences of the civil rights legislation of 1964 and 1965, which finally outlawed—a century after the Civil War!—racial discrimination.

One of the older black neighborhoods in St. Louis was called Yateman. What was happening, as an unintended consequence of the civil rights laws, was that the black professionals, prevented previously by segregation from living elsewhere, began to move to "nicer" neighborhoods, mostly white.

That meant Yateman lost its intelligensia, its professional class, the educated folks who provided a certain stability in the neighborhood. And then things really did begin to fall apart.

Segregation, like poverty, can provide social cohesion. That's not to argue in behalf of either poverty or segregation. But, like my father says, maybe it's worse when everybody's got too much. That's a problem we have yet to either face up to or resolve. S. B.

though nobody wants ta listen ta that kind a talk. People think they're so smart. They think they got'er all figgered out. We got computers now, an all we got ta do is punch a few buttons an the right answer'll pop up. We ain't gonna let no Depression ketch us with our pants down. We think we got'er licked.

We ain't got nothin licked. I think it's gonna be worse than it was in the Great Depression, Seedy. Bad as it was then—an it was bad, I tell you—at least people knew how ta hoe potatoes an milk a cow. Now kids kin play video games an cook frozen pizza in the microwave, an that's about it.

Mark my words, Seedy. Things are gonna get worse. I might not live ta see it, but things are gonna be worse'n they were in the 1930s. Mark my words.

14

These Bits an Pieces

IF YER DRIVIN UP the county road, up north a Wolf Crick about a mile, you'll see a big rock perched on a little knob alongside the road. That rock was in the way when the road was gettin built, an that's why the road's got a goofy little curve in it at jest that spot. The rock was too big ta move.

It was in that area that Lorinda's uncle, Robert Koepke, had eighty acres a land. He was a married man, but no kids, an he used ta come borrow a horse, walk on up to his eighty, do a little putzin around, an walk that horse back to the farm. It was about an hour up an a hour back, so you kin figger he didn't get a lot done. But he always found somethin ta fart around with up in the woods. I think he liked it.

One time he found a real big white pine tree, all covered with moss, layin in a grass swamp. With a one-man saw, he managed ta cut four twelve-foot logs out a that tree—good wood under the moss and under a rotten skin a punk. An then he asked me ta come with the team an skid those logs out a that swamp. So I did. But it was a big job, I tell you.

When I had 'em out where he could get 'em hauled, I asked 'em, "Now what are ya gonna do with 'em?"

"Sell 'em ta you," he sez.

So I bought all four a those logs from Bob Koepke. I paid 'em forty dollars. An there they sat.

Now there was another guy by the name a Ed Schmidtke who had land behind Bob Koepke's. An Schmidtke asked me ta skid some firewood poles for'em—skid'em with the horses. So I did. I didn't charge'em ennything an he didn't offer ennything. I jest did it.

Now in this same neck a time, in the wintertime, I happened ta be on the road with my team, with a sled hangin behind, up by where Benny Mootz later came ta live, which is about halfway between the farm an Wolf Crick. I could hear a loggin truck comin round the bend, up by where Old Doc Sievert later put his driveway in, an that truck was jest a snortin.

See, that hill by Benny's is steeper'n it looks, an before the county kinda stretched it out, it was even steeper than it is now. So those guys drivin trucks that were loaded with logs, once they got around Doc's corner, they jest made those trucks beller. They threw'er down in some in-between gear an tried ta put their foot right through the floor boards.

I heard one of'em comin, so I jest had the horses move off to the side a the road. We jest stood there, waitin. It was one a Hank Krause's trucks, though it wasn't Hank drivin. That man bellered up the hill an jest about had'er crowned when his engine blew. So there he sat. He was almost over, but not quite. I hitched the team to the front of his truck an tried ta pull'em, but the horses couldn't budge'em a inch. Those horses could pull, but they couldn't move that truck loaded with logs.

The driver figgered it'd be better—he wouldn't be blockin the road so much—if he let gravity take his truck backwards down the hill. So he started ta ease'er down. He got'er almost ta the bottom a the hill when she jackknifed on'em. An there he sat like a dunce, with the road completely blocked.

Well, it wasn't a terribly busy road (it's the only county road that still ain't paved, so that tells ya somethin), but there were other trucks haulin, so there wasn't enny time ta sit an cry about it. The driver didn't even have a canthook with'em, but I did. He climbed up on the load, I handed'em the canthook, an he started ta roll logs off the truck an onta the road. With the horses an a skidding chain, I pulled all those logs off the road, an then I hooked onta the back end of his truck an managed ta scoot'em over to the side.

We were jest in time. I jest had'em pulled out a the way when here comes another truck, loaded an bellerin around Old Doc's corner.

Nobody paid me a nickle fer my work, an I ain't even sure if ennybody said "Thanks." It was jest part of a day's work.

A Windfall Homestead

I'm tellin you these bits an pieces, Seedy, but perty soon you'll start ta see how they all fit together, maybe.

But, ya know, that business about "bits an pieces" reminds me of another story, which I might jest as well tell ya first. You got the time? That's all I got.

Ennyway, there was this old spinster lady that died, kind of a solitary cuss, an people had ta go inta her house after she was dead an sort through her stuff. Like lots a old spinster ladies, I guess, she had been awful neat an extra fussy, so everything was organized jest so.

Well, these people had ta work their way through the whole house, a course, and finally up in the attic they came acrost a whole set a boxes with all kinds a useless stuff inside, all of it labelled neat an nice. An in the last box they found all these itzy-bitzy pieces a string, all bundled up neat an perfect, an the label on the box said "Ends Too Short To Use."

Sometimes I think all a these little pieces a stories are kind a like that old lady's box a strings—ends too short ta use.

Ennyway, one day Hank Krause stopped by the log house. He sez, "Come along with me, Hank. I got somethin ta show ya." So I got in his truck an off we went.

He drove us up toward the big rock, an he took me back inta the woods next ta the land that Bob Koepke an Ed Schmidtke owned. He showed me a whole bunch a windfall hemlocks, stuff layin down that the loggers hadn't messed with, an he sez ta me, "I own this land. You kin go in here an cut all the windfall logs you want."

He was thankin me for helpin his driver with that truckload a logs that jackknifed on Benny Mootz's hill.

Well, Hank Krause's land was jest south a Schmidtke's, an I didn't waste enny time gettin in there with my one-man saw. I worked like a bulldog, an when I had those logs cut, I brought in my team a horses an skidded those logs up the hill, next to the heap a firewood poles I'd skidded for Ed Schmidtke. I had several thousand board feet a logs layin there, jest waitin ta be hauled.

Now here's another one a them ends too short ta use. I'm tellin you these stories, Seedy, an they do all fit together, jest don't ask me ta pin 'em into a calendar, becuz I can't. All this stuff happened over sixty years ago, when things were a lot different than they are now, an I wasn't in the business a keepin enny records. The only record I got is the one inside my head, an you kin come to yer own conclusion about how reliable that is.

Ennyway, I think I told you about John Oestreich showin me those scarecrow hemlocks I used ta build the barn, an how I bought that scarecrow forty from Menzner Lumber Company, right under Jul Krause's nose. Now I ain't exactly sure when this was—but by then I owned that scarecrow forty, an I think the barn was built—an I was up there cuttin an haulin wood, an there was a grass swamp dry enuff I could drive acrost with the horses.

It wasn't a real big grass swamp, but in the middle of it there was a hump, an it got ta be a nuisance goin over it. So I decided ta see what that hump was made of. It was a old tree an, like that tree Bob Koepke found, this one was also covered with moss. When I shaved it with my axe, I found that it was a oak—not as big as Bob Koepke's white pine, but big enuff ta cut several logs out of it. Which is exactly what I went an did.

Now I ain't tellin you that Ed Schmidtke hauled those oak logs for me, becuz I don't think he did. Ta tell you the truth, I don't remember who hauled the oak.

But one day in the summertime, Schmidtke showed up at the farm. It was a Sunday morning. He drove in with a county truck. See, he worked in the county garage. He didn't explain nothin ta me, an I didn't ask'em enny questions. All he sez was, "I'm gonna haul yer logs for you."

So up we went ta where I had those windfall hemlock logs all stacked next ta Schmidtke's firewood poles. We put on a load a logs by hand an took'em up ta Klemme's sawmill, up by Averill Crick.

We did one load every Sunday until we had'em all hauled. I never paid'em a nickle. He was thankin me for skiddin his firewood. I offen wondered how he got use a that truck, but I never asked'em. Some things work out better if ya jest keep yer mouth shut.

We were goin to that same church we got married in—St. Stephens—an I was kinda friends with the preacher. He owned a bunch a land up by Averill Crick. Somebody'd sold'em that land. It was supposed ta have lots a Christmas trees growin on it. So he hired me an another guy ta go in there an cut Christmas trees for'em. So we did. Took us about a week. An then

A Windfall Homestead

the preacher hired a guy with a truck ta haul those trees ta Illinois or Ohio or someplace, an he damn near lost his ass.

See, whoever'd owned that land before had taken out almost all the good trees. Then he sold the preacher the garbage, which is what we had left ta cut. Nobody wanted ta buy that crap, an that's why he lost his ass.

But, a course, when I was cuttin those Christmas trees I was also keepin my eyes open, lookin around. An right acrost from the mouth a Averill Crick, along the Boulder, there was a low spot with a pocket a hemlock. (That pocket was not too far from where that busted-up shack used ta be—the one I took lumber from an rafted it down the river an used in the building of the log shack.) An when I mentioned that pocket a trees to the preacher, he right away wanted ta sell me the logs.

Now it was a hell of a hole, which is why the loggers had left it. There was no easy way ta get those logs out a there. But I looked it over very carefully. An I figgered it could be done. So I paid the preacher thirty-five or thirty-seven dollars for the standing timber, an then I went in there with my one-man saw an cut logs.

The stumps were so thick I couldn't get a team a horses in for skidding. So I jest used my best horse, the big brown one, an made a go-devil sort a dray out of a crotch a wood, an I skidded one log at a time nearly all the way to the county road.

It was a lot a work, but I had somethin in mind. An when yer a young man an you got yer mind set on somethin, you jest go ahead an get'er done. Maybe that go-devil was inside a me.

After I had all those hemlock logs skidded out a that hole on the preacher's land, I hired Dick Nissen ta haul'em down ta Ritter an Hass, ta get'em sawed. Every log was marked on the end, so the sawyer would know what size lumber I wanted out a each perticular log. That took some figgerin.

Well, it wasn't Dick Nissen who drove the truck. It was one a his hired men. See, Dick had got himself inta the truckin business—by then he was haulin our cans a milk, too—an he also had a platform truck with a hoist on it. That made loadin a lot easier. We didn't have ta roll each log by hand up a set a skids.

Lorinda an I were goin ta town one day an she asked me, "Why are you gettin all those logs sawed?" An I said to'er, "I'm thinkin about a new house."

"Well," she sez, "you ain't even got the barn paid for yet."

So I told'er, "I know that. But you got ta think ahead."

See, it took me a couple a years ta gather all those logs. I figgered Lorinda would like a better house. In fact, I *was* surprised that she even had been willing ta come an live in the log shack in 1940. An here it was—end a the Second World War, new barn, more cows, another baby on the way (that was you, Seedy), makin perty steady money. It jest felt like it was time for a better house, a new house.

I used the horses an slusher ta dig the new basement hole. Lots a work.

There was some guy in Jensen makin cement blocks, eight-inchers. He was doin it in some kinda backyard set-up. So I went ta talk to'em, an I bought enuff blocks from'em ta make a foundation. It seems ta me that John Oestreich an one a the Culvers had a hand in layin those blocks. But I did almost all the framing by myself.

I hired a guy ta do the plumbing. I can't seem ta remember his name. He had a shop where Mill Street an Main come together, an I remember the first time I went in ta see'em. I walked in the door an here comes a skunk walkin up ta me. Scart the hell right out a me. The fella whose shop it was jest stood there, laughin an laughin.

It was his pet skunk, see, an it wasn't afraid a ennybody. Whoever'd walk in, that skunk'd come up to'em an sniff his feet. I guess he'd been deodorized, or whatever ya call it, cuz he never stunk like skunk.

Now yer mother insisted on a couple a things. One of'em was a fireplace, which was expensive but nice. An the other was that the house should look modern an not have enny eaves, which wasn't very smart becuz then the water would jest run down the side a the house, an it wasn't too many years before I had ta replace one a the windows becuz it had rotted out. You think maybe yer savin a couple dollars on eave boards, but it jest makes a headache in other ways. (Twenty, twenty-five years later, when I reshingled the house, I added eaves, an that solved the problem.)

There was a retired guy in Jensen—I think his name was Tommy Thompson—an he agreed ta build the chimney, the fireplace, an also do the plastering. His wife was dead an he didn't have a car, so he jest lived with us while he did the work.

A course, yer mother got all excited about the new house, an she started movin stuff in before it was ready. Ain't long an we're livin in a unfinished house. I even had ta nail a piece a canvas over the west kitchen window hole becuz we hadn't got the window in yet. But when a woman gets somethin in her head, you *can't* change it.

A Windfall Homestead

I had ta borrow a hunnerd dollars ta pay Tommy Thompson for his work—he was a little slow, but he was good—an when I paid'em with that big bill, he looked at it an he looked at me an he sez, "Ain't you got somethin smaller?" I don't think enny of us was exactly used ta one-hunnerd dollar bills.

After we moved inta the new house, the log shack jest seemed ta start ta fall apart. It doesn't seem ta take long for that ta happen. It was made out a tamarack poles, ya know. I think I told ya that. From up back a Benny Mootz's. So I took a log at a time an cut it up for firewood. We burned the log shack piece by piece ta keep warm in the new house.

Those pine logs from Bob Koepke got sawn inta five-quarter boards, which later I had resawn into beveled siding—enuff ta side the whole house. An those oak logs (the best of'em, ennyway) went into the staircase going upstairs.

It jest seemed like everything kinda fell inta place. A lot a things happened in the 1940s—got married, built a new barn, had two sons, built a new house. But that ain't all. Next thing we did was buy a new car.

We bought a new car the same year you were born, Seedy—1946. (An like Birdy, an Jack later, you were born in the hospital in Jensen. Seems like havin babies at home with midwives an that sort a thing was jest kinda fadin away.)

Well, we got that new Chevy in '46, an then again we didn't. See, I was in Old Man Nohr's car shop an he told me they were startin up car production again. Ya know, *after* the war. Nobody could buy a new car *during* the war. An for fifty dollars as a down payment, he'd put me on his waiting list. So I paid'em the fifty bucks. Our old '34 Chevy was jest about wore out.

But it took about a year before my turn came. By then Old Man Nohr wasn't in the shop ennymore. But his son was, an he notified me. An he told me the price had raised a hunnerd dollars. I had ta pay'em fourteen hunnerd an ninety-five bucks.

I jest reached inta my pocket, pulled out a wad a money, an started countin it out for'em.

"Wait a minute," he sez. "You kin make time payments, ya know. You don't have ta pay me all at once."

"Why would I want ta do that?" I asked'em.

That had'em stumped fer a minute. An then he sez, "Well, if you paid on time, I could make another twenty dollars on finance charges."

"Oh, no," I told'em. "I'm payin you right now." An I counted'em out the money an drove the car home.

Well, I put that car ta use right away—haulin kids ta school. I figgered I could make two dollars a day clear, so I did it. Those back road were hard on the car—ruts an potholes an lots a dirt an dust—but that car had ta earn its keep. An it did.

About half a year later I saw young Nohr again. He sez ta me, "I'll give you two hunnerd dollars on the deal." See, prices were set on new cars, but he could charge whatever he could get on used ones. Funny as it sounds now, used cars sometimes sold for more than the new ones.

An so I sez back to'em, "I'll tell ya what I'll do. I need ta finish out the school year—haulin kids—an *then* I'll trade ya even up for a new one."

"No," he sez, "I can't do that." But I could see he was tempted. Kinda tickled me ta think I almost got a brand new car by tradin one that was almost a year old.

I think that was the car we drove out to the state a Washington in 1957. Some years later, I sold it to one a my sister's boys—one a Mary's boys. I think it might a been Don. Her boys were kinda hard on cars, so I ain't sure how long it lasted.

15

The Most Worthless Piece a Land

I think I told ya that by the time I got married I owned two forties, one behind the other. (A course, I eventually bought that woods forty, up by Wolf Crick, in order ta cut logs out a those scarecrow hemlock trees John Oestreich put me on to, in order to build the barn, I mean.)

But in the year after you were born, Seedy, I bought the third forty that ended up becoming part a the farm. That forty belonged ta Emil Gruetzmacher. An, ta tell the truth, it wasn't a piece a land I particularly wanted. But I'll tell ya how I came ta buy it.

Maybe, ta kinda illustrate the point a why I wasn't very interested, I'll tell ya about a deer I saw one evening jest before deer season opened. See, ta the southeast of the old log shack, I made a little field. An acre maybe, at the most. That little field was in the extreme southeastern corner of my first forty, an the property line on the east side was the line I shared with Emil Gruetzmacher.

In order ta make that little field, I had ta clear it a stones—an it was jest plastered with stones, I tell you. Man oh! man, it was nearly all stones. So I began ta clear'em off, carryin'em over ta where the line was between Gruetzmacher an me. Carry an carry. Lots a carryin.

Well, eventually I got enuff of'em off so I could plow it with the horses. A course, plowin only turned up more stones needin ta be carried off. Eventually I had a little field, but I also had a perty good-sized stonepile from that little patch a ground.

The Most Worthless Piece a Land

So it was the evening before deer season. An, a course, I'm startin ta feel a little itchy about goin to the woods. An I look out the door a the log shack, an there's a deer standin *on top* a that stonepile! Well, I started ta reach for my gun—I had one a those licenses where you could start the season early, if ya had to—but I thought: Nope, I got all deer season ta get me a deer, so I ain't gonna bother with this one now. An ya know what? I went all deer season an I ain't sure I even saw a tail.

That's sort a like what buyin Emil Greutzmacher's forty amounted to. It had to have been the most worthless piece a land in the whole country. A course, that's where my new house ended up gettin built—I'm talkin about the one I built in the 1970s, the one we're sittin in right now—an, come ta think of it, where first yer shack an then yer log house got built, Seedy. So I guess people kin come to their own conclusions about how all those pieces fit together, about what that worthless piece a land is worth. Maybe this land jest attracts characters of a certain type. Whataya think, Seedy? Do we represent that remark?

Ennyway, Emil Greutzmacher lived in Wausau, but he had bought *his* forty before Al Batchelder talked me inta buyin *my* first forty. An Emil put up a shack, which was jest a little kiddy-corner from where this house is sittin. Emil liked bird huntin. Sometimes his wife'd come along with'em over a weekend. They stayed in that shack.

One year, jest before season, Emil asked if he could come deer huntin with me. Now Warren Schnee an me'd already agreed ta hunt together, but I told Emil "Sure, you kin come along." But I also told'em, "This is a big country back here. You ain't afraid a gettin lost?"

Well, he puffed right up an said he'd been huntin all over this country, an he wasn't gonna get lost. So, okay, first mornin the three of us are sneak huntin in a spread-out sort a way, up the other side a Kelly Crick, an—bang!—Warren an me got a deer, jest like that. Well, that got Emil all hepped up. We spread out in a line again, headed up towards those hills back a Doc Sievert's, an that's the last we saw a Emil Greutzmacher.

That evening, Warren helped me milk the cows an do barn chores, but there was no sign a Emil at his shack. So we hiked in back a Doc's—no snow, but the moon was bright—an we fired two or three call shots. Well, couple a minutes later there's shots bein fired in all directions. We figgered other hunters had heard us shoot an figgered *we* were lost, so they were answerin *our* call shots with the idea a helping *us* out. So there was no use ta our stayin there ennymore.

A Windfall Homestead

Sometime the next mornin, we found Emil back at his shack. He was kinda wild. Almost dark, he'd stumbled acrost a woods shack west a where Alfred Graap used ta live, an he crawled in there for the night. He was done huntin. He went back ta Wausau.

Wasn't too long after that he found out about a lakefront property somewheres between Tomahawk an Rhinelander, an he came ta me, wantin ta sell me his forty. He was askin two hunnerd an fifty dollars.

Well, I didn't want it an I told'em so. I sez to'em, "First you got a long alder swamp cuttin the forty in two, an on yer side a that swamp it's mostly pockets a swamp, an on my side it's the rockiest, most humpy piece a land in the whole country. There ain't enny of it fit ta be cleared. An I ain't sure it'd even be worth a nickle as pasture."[1]

But Emil wouldn't let me alone. He kept comin back, an I kept turning him down. Finally I told'em I'd give'em two hunnerd an twenty-five dollars for it, an that made'em mad. "Hank," he sez, "I got ta get at least what I paid for it." But I wouldn't budge an he finally gave in an sold that forty ta me for two hunnerd an twenty-five dollars. That was in 1947.

Right away I hired Pete Hessel an his boys ta come an cut trees on my side a that long alder swamp. Mostly popple, those trees had come up since the forest fire a '33, an they were only three, four, five inches on the stump. So I ended up with a piece of really rough pasture—humps an rocks an swamps. All becuz I took Emil Greutzmacher along huntin an he got lost.

I think I told ya there was a period a time when I hunted perty regular with Clarence Samuelson, Earl Geiger (who was some kind a shirttail relation ta Clarence), an Ed Meyer. During that time, Earl an Clarence each got a couple a bucks, but I ain't sure if Ed ever fired his gun.

They weren't the best a hunters. Clarence always wore farmer overalls. The cuffs'd freeze, an you could hear'em walkin—scrape, scrape, scrape—half a mile away. But he was a jolly cuss. They all were good guys, an we always had a good time. It jest made ya feel good ta be with'em.

Ennyway, this perticular hunting season we were in the woods west a where George Bohman lived (though it's Donald Graap who lives there now), an the snow was up ta yer knees. I always knew the area better'n the rest

---

1. The humpy land appears to be the result of huge trees upended in ancient windstorms—a rather impressive corrugation of decayed root humps. S. B.

The Most Worthless Piece a Land

of 'em, so I sent those guys on a loop ahead a me, told'em where ta stand, an then I'd come through, sneak huntin, but makin a drive for'em, too.

So I waited a while. Ya got ta do that, in order for the watchers ta get where they're goin, an then I started ta sneak in their direction. Well, I didn't go very far an up jumps a deer—bang!—an down he goes. I field dressed'em real quick an kept on goin.

A while later my sneakin took me past a big old pine stump, an I noticed that somethin had been scratchin on it. It looked ta me like fresh scratchin. I jest stood there lookin at it, wonderin what cudda done that. So, very careful, I pussyfooted around that stump, lookin everything over. On one side a that stump there was a hole, not very big, an in that hole I could see somethin black.

Well, all of a sudden it came ta me: that's a bear in there! He was already hibernatin, gone ta sleep for the winter. So I put the barrel a my rifle right inta that hole an pulled the trigger. I knew I hit'em, but I couldn't tell where.

Perty soon here comes Clarence an Earl an Ed, wantin ta know what I'd got. So I showed'em the hole. But the bear was still in there, nothin was happening, an the excitement started ta kind a wear off. We're jest standin there talkin when one of 'em sez ta me, "I think you better shoot'em again, Hank." I turned around an there's that bear with his head stickin out a the hole.

I up an shot'em once more, an then he *was* dead.

We managed ta get a rope around his neck, an we dragged'em up an out a that stump hole. Now we were all excited again. Somebody got a bear!

It wasn't a big bear—hunnerd an fifty, two hunnerd pounds, maybe. But the snow was deep an we had that bear an a deer ta drag, so there was lots a work ta do.

Well, we got'em home an it seems like everybody in the country knew about it right away an had ta come over an see that bear. They even took it ta Dirty Dan's tavern, an people made all kinds a wild guesses about how much that bear weighed. When they brought'em back they had ta put'em on my feed scale, a course, ta see who was the best guesser. Almost everybody, ya know, thought that bear was four, five times bigger'n he was, an so everybody was kinda let down, disappointed and even a little disgusted when that bear wasn't as big as he was spozed ta be. Maybe he was shy. Maybe he'd been on a diet. Maybe he'd jest kinda shrunk up with all that unwanted attention.

Ennyway, I skinned the bear an divided the meat four ways. But when Lorinda cooked a hunk, it looked an smelt so much like dog that I *could not* eat that bear. Turned out the same thing happened ta Clarence an ta Earl.

But Ed Meyer said "We like it!" An it ain't long before Ed an Olga had all that bear meat for themselves.

But I was proud a that bearskin. It was perty stiff becuz I tanned it myself. Eventually it ended up on the seat a the old Dodge pickup, an it stayed there until jest about all the hair wore off.

That's the only bear I ever shot.[2]

As long as we're talkin about huntin, I'll tell you at least one more story. If I kin think of one more. You know I don't like tellin'em. This one is about a plan. Now most plans, when it comes ta huntin, don't amount ta much. But this one did.

It's a big story. I ain't sure we kin even finish in one day.

It is the most precise thing I ever figgered out in deer hunting. I never figgered one out like that before or after. Never.

Maybe Birdy was twelve years old. I don't know. Maybe he was younger.[3]

Well, Art Axen used ta stop at the farm quite a bit. He was a older man, married, but he didn't have enny kids. An he was a horse nut. He farmed with horses till he retired. I think he might a been the last man ta come ta town with horses an wagon. I don't think he ever did buy a tractor.

Art Axen liked Birdy. An he knew Birdy wanted ta hunt deer. So Art brought'em out some old club of a gun. I didn't figger Birdy was ready for it, but there it was, an Birdy wanted ta go.

I spoze this musta been the opening morning a deer season. Toward the end a November. Somethin like that. I was milkin cows an Birdy's in the barn, buggin me already about huntin deer. The sun ain't even up yet. So I let'em take that old club of a gun an go back into the pasture. But I told'em, "That's a big woods back there. You stay on *this* side a the fence."

Okay. That was fine with him. An off he goes. Well, I ain't done with chores yet, an here he's back already, all hepped up. He'd seen a buck walkin. He was so excited he hadn't even thought about shootin. That buck had

---

2. As children, Birdy and I slept in an unheated bedroom upstairs. For a while that bearskin was kept in the attic. But I would get it and lay it on the floor on my side of the bed I shared with Birdy. The last thing at night and the first thing in the morning my bare feet were in that black silky hair. But my mother, it seemed, hated that bearskin and would put it back into the attic. I have no idea how many times we went through that bearskin dance from attic to bedroom and back again. Eventually the Dodge pickup won. S. B.

3. I called Birdy. He says he was nine or ten, at the oldest. S. B.

The Most Worthless Piece a Land

walked into the long alder swamp on what we still called Greutzmacher's forty. Birdy'd seen the buck, an he wheeled'er back to the barn ta tell me.

"You got ta help me get that buck!" he sez ta me.

Well, I told'em I wasn't done with chores yet, told'em ta sit down on a milk stool an rest a minute, told'em "When I'm done with chores, we'll go get that buck."

That was a perty big thing ta say to a kid. Or, easy ta say, maybe, but not so easy ta do.

So while I'm finishin up the barn chores, I'm thinkin of how I'm gonna try ta make that promise come true. An somehow I got it inta my head that that deer was gonna head north, an I even had a idea a which ridge he was gonna try'n cross.

So I sez ta Birdy, "You got ta sit right here for one hour." Now that's a long time for a kid ta sit when he's all hepped up. I gave'em my pocketwatch ta look at. An I told'em, "When the hour's up, you walk down the road until yer past the alder swamp, an then you come north through the woods. I believe that buck is in there bedded down. He's gonna come out ahead a you. He's gonna go north. He's gonna go a long way. You follow his tracks. I'm gonna be waitin for'em."

Well, that's a big patch a woods for a little kid, so I gave'em a empty rifle shell, an I showed'em how ta blow it an make it whistle. "Once you jump that buck," I told'em, "you keep right on his track"—there was snow already—"an every now an then you stop an blow on this shell. That way I'll know where you are. You won't hear me, but I'll hear you. So don't worry about gettin lost. I'll know where you are. You ain't gonna be lost. Now you stay put for one hour before you come." An he agreed ta do that.

So I got ready an grabbed my .303 an hightailed it down the road ta Frostbite Avenue an up about a mile. I figgered that buck was gonna cross a ridge jest to the west a Eiden's pond. The pond's surrounded by a alder swamp, then a ridge, an then another swamp. I was gonna be waitin on that ridge. An I walked fast ta get there.

Well, it ain't long after I'm there I kin hear Birdy's whistle way off to the south. There wasn't much brush on that ridge fer me ta hide in, so I stood real still, watchin the deer trail that came in from the south. I was watchin quite a while.

All of a sudden I saw that buck comin, an jest like that he swung back south an disappeared. I think he musta got a wiff a me. Well, he swung back south, but not far, cuz Birdy was on his trail. An so he started ta go around

A Windfall Homestead

that swamp to the west a me—on the far side, a hunnerd an fifty yards away, maybe—always in the edge a the brush. I could see flickers of 'em, but I couldn't get a good shot.

But I noticed there was a little opening jest ahead of 'em. So I dropped my rifle sights inta that little hole an I waited for 'em ta come in, an when he did I pulled the trigger. An he disappeared again.

I thought I had 'em, but I wasn't sure. So I walked real careful kiddy-corner acrost that swamp, ready for 'em ta jump up, but there he was, deader 'n a fart.

I could hear Birdy blowin his whistle, so I took the empty shell I'd jest used ta shoot the deer with, an I answered 'em. An then I started walkin toward his whistle. Perty soon we met up in the brush, an he was one happy boy. He was jest plain tickled. He didn't know where he was, but he was tickled.

I took 'em over ta see the buck. I spoze you could say that it was, in a way, Birdy's first deer. It was one a those times when everything worked out exactly right. That's what you kin get fer thinkin like a deer.

I'll tell you another one that didn't work out so good. This time you were hunting with me, Seedy. Jest you'n me. An I was gonna make a drive for you.

I was standin there waitin while you got around ta where you were spozed ta go. A course, I had my eyeballs open, lookin at everything. An perty soon here comes a buck walkin kiddy-corner towards me. Long as he was comin, I jest stood there waitin.

Well, he walked behind a little knob an all I could see of 'em was his back—three, four inches of his back. That's all. But I figgered that's enuff. I'll hit 'em in the spine, an he ain't goin nowhere.

So I up an shot an he disappeared—only instead a goin down, he turned an ran. I got one more glimpse of 'em in the brush, an I threw a shot at 'em, but I missed.

I felt so bad about it, I jest stood there an bawled. That's the truth. I jest stood there an bawled.

Jack, ya know, was the scholar. He was the smart one. I spent lots a money on his education. I don't think he ever finished college, but he got perty close.

The Most Worthless Piece a Land

He kinda liked ta plan things out. I kin remember he made a big map upstairs in his bedroom, a whole lot a paper taped together, an it had a big hunk of our hunting territory all marked out—Foster's Clearing, Little Fritz's, Kelly Crick, Sad Sam's Stand, Florence's Stand, Popple Ridge, the Boulder River. I think there were a few years in there, after yer mother died, when hunting season is what Jack lived for.

So, ennyway, I took'em back a Doc Sievert's one hunting season. It was a beautiful sunny day, an I posted'em on one a those tall hills an made a loop around ta make a drive for'em, from east ta west. I think he might a been sixteen, seventeen years old. Somethin like that.

I was maybe halfway through makin that drive when I heard'em shoot—once, twice, three times. Well, three times usually means you've got'em, but I jest stood there, ennyway, watchin. An perty soon I heard'em holler, "It's a buck! He's comin!"

An, by golly, it was a buck an he wasn't wastin enny time, either. I up an gave'em a poke an down he went.

Well, Jack comes over an he's all excited. That buck'd come right by'em, fifty feet away, he said, an it stood there lookin at'em. He shot at that deer three times, an he missed every shot. Oh! He was perturbed!

I think he was glad I got'em, but he was so mad at himself I think he cudda wrapped that gun barrel around the nearest tree. I think he had buck fever. I didn't laugh at'em becuz when I was his age I used ta get it so bad my whole body'd shake.

Some things ya jest can't plan out.

16

Way Too Fast

I WANT TA TELL ya how in 1950 I came ta buy my first tractor, that Farmall C. But sittin here thinkin about tractors an horses (an what else is there fer me ta do, Seedy, but sit here on my ass an think?), I kin remember, when I was a kid in Dawson, North Dakota, a tractor my Uncle Hugo bought.

Hugo had a bachelor farmer for a neighbor, an that neighbor bought himself a three-wheeled "bull tractor." Everything was "bull," ya know. An people want what their neighbor's got. So Uncle Hugo wanted a tractor.

(Maybe you think all this is a lot a bull—is that it, Seedy?)

Now Dawson was too far west ta be good wheat country. It was too dry. Well, some years it was good. Most years it wasn't. I know one year Pa did good. Other years he planted, but there was nothin ta harvest. You can't make a livin that way. You jest go broke.

Uncle Hugo's tractor came in on the train. The station was maybe a half-mile from where we lived. Uncle Hugo used a team of his horses ta pull that tractor down to our place. An there it sat for a week or so. Jest sittin in our yard. Gettin used to the prairie air, maybe.

Then Hugo came ta start it, ta drive it home, ya know, with its three big metal wheels all fitted out with lugs. He cranked an cranked. I think he was jest about ta lose his temper when that tractor finally popped. An then he drove it home—two, three miles from where we lived.

Now most people used horses, but every now'n then you'd see a tractor. Once I counted thirteen plows—*thirteen* of 'em!—hangin behind one

Way Too Fast

big tractor. An there were steam engines, steam tractors fer threshin wheat, big coal-burnin outfits with long belts runnin from the engine over to the threshin machine.

So this kinda thing was jest comin in. An I remember my Aunt Annie tellin my Ma that her daughter Pauline could plow jest as much land in a day with the horses as Uncle Hugo could plow with his new tractor.

So it seems like whenever the farmer had a little extra money, there was always somebody there ta take it from'em. A course, Uncle Hugo *wanted* that tractor. Yer neighbor's got somethin an perty soon you want what he's got, or somethin like it. You got a fresh dose a envy an perty soon somebody else is gonna get yer money. Advertising jest kinda greases up the whole process. That's jest the way it goes.

See, first the white man chased the Indians off the prairie, an then they killed all the buffalo. All a that happened only twenty, thirty, forty years before I was born. An then they brought in cattle. An that worked good in the summertime, but what are ya gonna feed'em in the winter? Buffalo wandered ta where there was somethin ta eat. But that didn't work with cattle an private property.

At first, when the railroad came through, all a those little towns had stockyards. Dawson had one. But they didn't last, either. In fact, I kin remember that Pa had the job a tearin one of'em down. In Dawson.

So the cattle—most of'em, ennyway—went out an the wheat came in. Everything was movin way too fast. In fact, if there's one way ta describe what was happening in the whole country, it's that everything was movin way too fast. Once there was railroads an tractors an electricity an telegraphs an all that kinda thing, life jest speeded up. Changes that used ta take—I don't know—a hunnerd years, say, now happened in a month. You ain't got enny time ta think about things, ta get used ta ennything, before somethin new comes along an makes yer old thing obsolete. That ain't enny way ta live. Think a those Dakota Indians. Thousands a years, maybe, livin on the prairie, most a that time in tipis, without enny horses, an all of a sudden here comes the white man an their whole way a life is wrecked before ya got time ta spit.

Way too fast. That's all I know what ta say about all a that. Way too fast.

You showed me that book once, Seedy—what was it called?—*The Day of the Bonanza,* by Hiram Drache, with all that stuff in it about "bonanza farming" in the Red River Valley. That kind a farming came to a end when the First World War was over. Until then, Europeans needed wheat and lots of it. After that, I guess, they got back ta raisin their own. Kinda had enuff trench warfare for a while. An that was the end a "bonanza farming." Over there fellas lined up ta kill each other, and over here the bonanza farmers made a killin. Funny use a words, ain't it?

Ennyway, it seems ta me I remember from the book that one a those Red River land companies had over forty thousand acres under plow, an a picture of a horse barn with eight-hunnerd head a horses in it, an a bunkhouse with a hunnerd beds an a cook shanty ta match. It was like lookin at a giant lumber camp, only instead a threshing timber, they were logging wheat.

So if the price a wheat fell with the end a the First World War, Seedy, what do ya spoze happened to farming after 1929? When the Depression came? The Town a Boulder was jest pocked full a little farms.

If you can't find a job, you still got ta eat. You still got ta have a roof over yer head an a stick a wood ta burn. An that means yer gonna hoe some potatoes, milk a cow, pick enny berries you kin find ta pick. My folks had thirteen kids, an every one of 'em got hungry every day, two, three times a day, an what are ya gonna do about it? Teach'em ta hoe in the garden, milk a cow, cut a stick a wood, that's what.

There wasn't enny money fer ennybody ta be fartin around with tractors. Oh! I did it with that Model T tractor I bought from Dan Young's widow, the one Daisy drove in the new field I planted potatoes in. The same one my brother John was drivin when it buckled under him with me behind with the handplow. But that didn't amount ta much.

There were lots a horses around, but most of 'em were tired old plugs that weren't enny use in the loggin camps ennymore. If ya got a cheap horse, that usually meant you got one a those tired-out horses some lumberjacks had used for skiddin an played 'em out—the way Gunnar Anderson played out a horse when he was skiddin fer Oscar Krause an me. Maybe you could get a horse like that ta work for half a day, but then he'd jest stand there with his head hangin down, an you might as well take the harness off of 'em an let 'em be, cuz you ain't gonna get a nickle's worth a work out of 'em ennymore that day.

An I think I told you about that kickin horse I had, the one that stood an kicked an kicked until all her harness was off an wrecked, except for her collar an the hames. It took me three days ta fix 'er harness. An then

Way Too Fast

I led'er ta town an sold'er at a auction for twenty-five dollars. An I had ta pay the auctioneer a commission out a that. So you kin see I was really inta "bonanza farming" too. It's how I made my first million stones.

By the end a the Second World War, I had a perty good team. One a those horses had been half of a team owned by Ned Fox's older brother Allie. Now Allie an his brother Bert were bachelors who lived with their mother, over in the Doering area. The brothers shared a barn, but each of'em took care of his own cows.

One day Allie was haulin a load a firewood poles, an his horses ran away with him an the wagon. When horses get spooked or get ta goin like that, it's one hell of a job ta get'em ta stop. An Allie apparently didn't notice that one of those poles was, with all the bouncing, working its way back in the load. An when that pole slipped off the front bunk an jabbed inta the ground, with those horses goin like a bat out a hell, that pole swung up like a catapult an hit Allie on the head an killed'em.

Well, it wasn't long an those horses were for sale. But they were a runaway team that involved somebody gettin killed, so they had a bad name. Nobody wanted'em. But Ned bought one of'em, an I bought the other. I liked'em all right, but that horse a Allie's had short ears an I jest couldn't trust 'em.

I think I paid Allie's mother five dollars a month. I led that horse all the way from Doering—twenty miles, probably, or more—until somebody relieved me.

Now in that same nick a time I bought a young mare from Mike Stevens. I think I paid a hunnerd an twenty-five dollars for that horse. An then I had a real team.

But that mare from Mike Stevens was young an only half-broke. I had a hell of a time with'er. Plus she an Allie's horse didn't seem ta like each other. They'd stand in the pasture with their hind ends pointed at each other an kick an kick an kick. I can't remember that they ever hurt each other, but they sure could put on a show.

Well, Ned came over an helped me. He liked workin with horses. We hooked both of'em to my handplow. They wanted ta run, but it doesn't take long ta bring'em to a walk with a plow jabbed inta the ground behind'em. Gallopin an plowin jest don't go too good together.

Wasn't long an they were a perty good team. An we *worked*. I always said, if *I* got ta work, *they* got ta work. An, by golly, they did. A horse that wouldn't work wasn't of enny use ta me.

Well, you can't get old an expect ta get away with it. Not if yer a horse. Though I spoze the same thing could be said about a ninety-six year-old man.

I don't know what yer smilin about, Seedy. Wait until yer ninety-six and see if *you* can get away with it.

Ennyway, I had that team quite a while. An then, on the mare I'd bought from Mike Stevens, her right hind hoof started ta come off. I never saw such a thing before or since. I even got Ed Meyer's Pa Louie ta come over an take a look at'er, cuz Old Louie fancied himself somethin of a horse doctor. An he said he hadn't seen ennything like that before, either.

There was nothin ta be done. But on top a that problem, the white horse with short ears I'd got from Allie Fox's mother was gettin old an tired. He wasn't enny good for a day's work ennymore. Half a day an he was all played out.

Well, I was lookin at two, three hunnerd for a perty good horse, an now I needed not one but two. Mike Stevens' horse, the strawberry roan, had ta go to the fox farm, an now what was I gonna do?

I looked at a little tractor down at Leek's Hardware, but that little tractor didn't have enny sleeves between the pistons an the engine block, an I wouldn't buy it. But there was a man who worked for Kamke Implement who had a little farm in Pine River. This fella was a good mechanic, an Kamke wanted'em full time. An he had a Farmall C, with cultivator an reversible plow, an he put it up at auction.

Now I liked ta go to auctions. Sometimes I'd go jest for the fun of it, jest ta hear the auctioneer stand up there an blab, especially if it was Art Shiniky wearin his gloves an duster. Oh! that man could talk!

But this was serious. I still didn't know what ta do. So I went to the Lincoln County Bank an told the man there what my problem was. He jest sat an listened while I told'em about my horses an about not knowin whether ta get a new team or buy a tractor. An, besides that, I told'em I didn't have enny money.

Well, he jest sat an listened until I was done talkin, an then he kinda leaned toward me an said, "Buy the tractor." An, with that, I got up an left.

When that auction came up, I was there. I think it might a been Lorinda who came with me, an we had a trailer hooked behind the car. I meant business. An when that little tractor came up ta auction, I waited till everybody else had bid it as far as they were gonna go, an then I took over. Same for the cultivator an plow. I think I had ta bid about seventeen hunnerd dollars for all a that. An when I walked in where the clerk was sittin, an he asked, "How are ya payin for this?" I jest sez to'em, "Lincoln County Bank an me are in this together." An he sez, "Drive it home!"

Which is exactly what I did. But first I got a couple fellas ta help me load the cultivator an plow on the trailer.

That's a long drive from Pine River through Jensen an out to the Town a Boulder, especially in the spring a the year. I think I damn near froze ta death. An when I got home an went inta the farmhouse ta warm up, I looked out the window an there's Birdy up on the tractor seat an he's got the tractor runnin in low gear an he's goin round an round an round out in the yard. An I jest stood there an laughed. That was a happy day.

When Birdy was seven, eight—somethin like that—he wanted a horse. I mean, he *wanted* a horse. (I don't think you ever wanted ennything, Seedy. You were different. You jest stood back an watched.)

Ya see, about that time there was a horse-ridin fad. The time a workhorses was comin to a end. Almost all of us little farmers were gettin tractors. But there was, I don't know, a kind a prosperity after the war, an it seems like when somethin is comin to a end, what used ta be fer work an fer real all of a sudden it's fer fun an fer play. Horses became a hobby.

Maybe people jest couldn't let go a horses, jest like that. I mean, we all got little tractors, so we didn't *need* horses. Horses ate grass that a cow could jest as well eat. They took up space in the barn.

But there's a funny kind a emptiness in yer life when all of a sudden you ain't workin with horses ennymore. Somethin's missin. Somethin's different. I think people felt that. Horses were part of a farm, part of your life, an maybe ya didn't know how much they were part of your life until they were gone. Maybe that's why horse ridin got ta be such a fad. An, a course, when somethin like that gets started, seems like everybody's got ta get in on it. That's jest the way it is.

Well, Birdy wanted a horse. (Maybe *I* wanted'em ta want a horse, too. But that's gettin too complicated fer my old head.) I felt kinda pushed into it, in a way. Didn't have enny money, as usual. But I went to a horse auction.

Ya know, Art Axen might a had somethin ta do with it. He used ta stop by a lot. I think I told you that him an his wife didn't have enny kids.

A Windfall Homestead

An I think Art wanted a son, wanted a boy, an I think he liked the kind a boy Birdy was—strong-willed, ya know, always wantin ta *do* stuff. Art liked boys like that, but he liked horses better. Put a good horse an a strong-willed boy together an Art was a happy man.

For all that Art Axen was a horse nut, he was not a rider. I got'em up on a horse once, an he rode'er out the driveway an back, but I could tell right away he wasn't comfortable up there. He liked ta *drive* horses. He wasn't interested in *ridin*'em.

But now that I think about it, I believe Art Axen had *somethin* ta do with Birdy wantin a horse, though it's hard ta say jest what that somethin was.

Ennyway, I went to this horse auction. Cudda been a couple hunnerd people millin around, everybody lookin at maybe a hunnerd horses. An all of a sudden I see somebody leadin this bay horse—all brown, ya know, except for a black tail, black mane, black lower legs, and a patch a white on her forehead—an there were three little kids on'er, bareback, one sittin right behind the other. An I thought, "*That's* the horse fer Birdy!"

So I kept my eye on'er, an when she came up fer auction, I bid'er right up. A course, as usual, I didn't have enny money, so the auction people had ta finance me. But that horse cost me less'n a hunnerd dollars.

She was Daisy. That's what we called'er. I ain't sure ennymore how she got that name—whether she brought it with'er, or if we gave it to'er. But she was a Daisy.

Well, somebody hauled'er home in a horse trailer. An Birdy, a course, right away had ta get on'er an ride. But she'd only walk. Walk an eat, walk an eat. An perty soon he's kinda disgusted. "That horse kin only walk," he sez, an he's not too happy about it.

So I sez to'em, "Let me try." He got off an I got on'er and I gave'er the razz an we went around the garage in high gear. But on the west side a the garage she slipped an we both went down. She fell an I fell right with'er. But, both of us jest got up. I petted'er neck an told Birdy, "She's all right. See, she can go fast."

Now Lorinda's brother Martin had married Laota Culver, an their oldest daughter Bonnie was a year or so older'n Birdy. An that girl loved ta ride. She could really make that horse go. An I think Birdy got courage from seein Bonnie make Daisy run.

I can't remember fer sure, but I think they said at the auction that Daisy was with foal. It seems ta me we got'er in the summer, maybe fer Birdy's birthday, in July. But I seem ta remember that filly being born the following winter. We called'er Rowdy an she was one gangly horse. The stallion must've been a perty big workhorse cuz Rowdy was big-boned and clumsy—tall like a workhorse, but not as heavy. She had big feet an could trip over her own shadow. Oh! She was one clumsy wretch.

Eventually I modified the old harnesses ta fit those two horses, an I even skidded firewood with'em one winter. But it was like drivin a team a squirrels.

I think I jest liked horses.

There was a lot a magic in those ten years. From 1940 ta 1950, I mean. Got married, bought a woods forty an built the barn, built a silo, had two boys, built a new house an bought a worthless forty fer pasture (at least it was a place the cows could go ta get lost an ta drag their tits in the mud), bought a new car, bought a tractor. In those ten years, the farm jest *blossomed*.

17

Comin Home With Both

SOMETIME IN THE EARLY 1950s—I think it might a been '53—we decided ta take a trip out ta Washington. I can't remember what caused us ta go, exactly. I hadn't seen most a my family for goin on twenty years. I guess that was reason enuff.

It was late in the winter or early in the spring. No field work ta do yet. Always that space a time when yer walkin around suckin yer fingers an lookin out the window.

So I bought train tickets an we went—you an Birdy an Lorinda an me. (I think I got one a Mary's boys—Huntz—ta come an do the chores while we were gone.) Ennyway, we got on the train in Jensen an I think we went ta New Lisbon an then ta Minneapolis. Once yer on the train out a Minneapolis, you stay right on it all the way ta Washington.

That's a long trip. Yer ass gets tired sittin on a seat, an ya can't go ennyplace. The train's always rumblin an rumblin. Ya take cat naps an that's about it, day'n night, day'n night. All of it on a shoestring, ya know, always afraid yer gonna be broke an have nothin left.

But we went.

I think the biggest thrill was goin through the mountains—first the Rockies an then the Cascades. I spent almost all my time up in the dome car, lookin. *That* was somethin for the eyeballs. It musta been in the Cascades, in the mountains, where there's one railroad runnin *above* the other. That musta been quite a deal, puttin trains like that right through the mountains.

But everything is strange. The train is strange. The people are strange. It's too long, too far.

An when ya get there, it wasn't the thrill ya expected. Yer folks are old an bent over. All a those little kids are grown up already, an they ain't the same to ya ennymore. When we got there, the weather wasn't too nice, either—no snow, but it was damp an windy.

Ya had ta keep yer shirtcollar over yer ears ta keep from freezin ta death.

I think we stayed with my folks. Pa wasn't workin ennymore. They had some poor old rented house right next to the railroad track. Hardly enny money.

In some ways, these kinds a trips are a pain in the ass. I mean, yer lookin forward ta seein people again, an that's good. Gets ya goin inside. But after a half-hour a talkin, ya know, ketchin up on the news, you ain't hardly got ennything ta say to each other ennymore. An then what are ya gonna do? Ya still got another week or ten days ta kill before ya kin go home.

Yer wore out when ya get there, nobody's got a damn thing, an once ya see'em fer a few minutes you ain't got nothin more ta say. Oh! There was a coal mine between Chehalis an Centralia, diggin on both sides a the road. But we jest kept on goin. An I saw'em haulin logs right through town, three logs on a truck. Big log in the middle an two little ones on either side ta keep the big one in place. I'd never seen nothin like that before. But it ain't long an all yer doin is killin time.

I don't know how ta say it, but I felt like—Well, yer the ones that wanted ta go ta Washington. An what good did that do ya? Like I told my mother in the fall a '36, the log shack's the best home I ever had. The Little Hobo ain't goin ta Washington. An it didn't take long a bein out there in the spring a 1953 an I knew I wanted ta come right back home again.

It wasn't the log shack ennymore, but it was still the best home I ever had, an family kin get ta feel almost like strangers when ya don't share a life with'em ennymore. There's sadness in that, but there's a funny sort a agitation in it, too. All I know is, I came back home with both feelings.

Well, here's one I can't ferget. It jest worked out too good.

Now I can't remember if we got a television before Jack was born or after. But it was somewhere in the middle '50s. A little black'n white deal. An you two older boys always wanted ta watch yer outlaw movies on TV. But you had chores ta do. An those chores had ta be done first.

A Windfall Homestead

One a those chores, in the evening, was diggin loose hay out a the hay mow, an pitchin it down to the plank floor—enuff for the next morning. That was not a easy job. The hay has got to be taken out kinda like it was put in. So even though ya might think it's a job that's got no skill to it, that ain't so. You got ta pay attention to the patterns of how the hay is layin, an you do that as much by how the lifting *feels* with yer pitchfork as much as it *looks* to yer eyeballs.

A course, I'm talkin *loose* hay here, not baled. I was still making hay in the summertime with the hayloader. I hadn't got modern yet. I still didn't have a baler ta curse at an buy parts for.

Ennyway, you boys had chores ta do before I'd let ya go watch yer cowboys. An sometimes you were in a hurry, an even though you said you'd dug out enuff hay, sometimes you hadn't. I always had ta check.

An this perticular time—late in the fall—I went up ta take a look. An there wasn't enuff hay dug out. So I climbed up in the hay mow ta dig out more. An while I was up there, I heard a shot. A course, I couldn't stand ta hear a shot an not investigate. So I climbed up the inside of the south barn wall an looked out the little window hole way up at the peak. I was jest perched up there, lookin south, in the dark.

Well, south a the farm was the county road (which was gravel then), an south a the road was a big spruce swamp, an south an a little west of that swamp was one a Dick Hahn's fields. From up in the peak a the barn, I could see all that, even in the dark.

An what do ya spoze I saw? I saw a light come on for a little while back in that field, an then it went off. Well, I thought, if Old Dick kin ketch a little meat that way, why can't I? So I climbed down, finished diggin out the hay, kissed all the cows goodnight, an came up to the house.

You boys were jest done watchin yer shoot'em-ups, gettin ready ta go ta bed, but I sez ta Birdy, "Put yer jacket on. I got a job fer you."

Well, that was unusual. He wasn't used ta that. But he did what I told'em, an he didn't ask enny questions. I got my .22 an we went out an got the tractor. We headed west into the hay field I'd been usin for a late fall pasture.

I had a single-wire electric fence around that field, an the deer were comin in from a certain place from the north. They'd already started ta make a trail. I'd noticed that. Once they make a trail they jest keep usin it. They'd been comin in so offen they'd sometimes knock the wire down. So I was always havin ta fix fence.

Comin Home With Both

Well, I drove us back to this certain spot an I told Birdy ta get on the seat. I kept the motor runnin jest about idle, an the tractor's lights were shinin on that spot where the deer trail came in. I told Birdy, "Jest sit there watchin. All you got ta do when a deer comes in is put the tractor in low gear, turn the wheels, an keep that deer in the lights."

I think we stayed there maybe ten minutes, lights on, tractor jest purrin, when here comes a nice spike buck. I was standin by one a the rear tires, waitin. An when Birdy got his eyes on that little buck, he kept'em in the lights, jest like he was spoze to.

Plink! One shot an down he went.

Well, now it's time ta work in the dark. I put a chain around the deer's neck an we dragged'em back to the barn, behind the tractor. Jest like nobody's business. An then I told Birdy, "All right. Now you kin go ta bed."

But, ya know, I still had a little more work ta do.

Here's one I fergot ta tell ya. It's kind of a stinkin story. This one happened, I think, back in the early '40s. My memories ain't all in exact order. But you might a already noticed that, if you've been payin attention.

Ennyway, I think I told you that Lorinda was close to her Uncle Paul an Aunt Rica. But she was also perty close to her cousin Esther, who was one a Rica an Paul's oldest daughters. An Esther got married to Emil Oestreich. That was one a the connections that put me in contact with many of the Oestreich brothers. Martin. Paul. John. Emil, a course.

Shortly after yer mother an me were married, Emil an Esther came over, an Emil an me went huntin. We were up by Little Fritz's Clearing, by that old tote road that ran from Little Fritz's over toward the mouth a Kelly Crick. It was late in the fall, an we spotted a little animal trail that ended by this hole in the ground.

Well, a course, I had a long nose, an I wanted ta know what was in that hole. So I laid on the ground an reached in, clear up to my shoulder, an I could feel fur. So I groped around in there, got my hand around a animal, an pulled it out.

It was a sleeping skunk!

Well, I tossed it aside an Emil smacked it on the head an killed it. But I kept reachin down inta that hole an pullin out skunks, one of'em by the ear—five, six of'em. All of'em were sound asleep, except the very last one.

That one was startin ta wake up, an when I pulled'er out, she lifted'er tail an pissed all over me.

Now you kin imagine what I smelled like!

But we gathered up all those skunks an carried'em home an skinned'em. The hides were worth a buck apiece. After they aired out a week or so, we took'em ta town an sold'em to Abey Block.

Everyone a those skunks in that den was a female. After that I heard that male skunks don't den with female skunks. Usually in February you start ta see skunk tracks in the snow. That's gonna be a male, out lookin for a den a females ta crawl in with. How he knows where ta look, I do not know. But he seems ta be able ta figger it out.

I know Lorinda wasn't too keen on havin me in *her* den, after I'd come home with Emil an all those dead skunks. I jest can't imagine what the problem might a been. I thought I smelled jest right, like a man is spozed ta smell.

Yer askin me about Jack bein born, Seedy, but in order ta tell ya about that, I got ta tell ya that the old dug well wasn't deep enuff ta keep the cows in water. Fifteen, twenty minutes a pumpin an the well'd be dry, an then you'd have ta wait a while till more water trickled in.

So I decided ta get a new well drilled.

Now the old well was jest off the northwest corner of the farmhouse, an I had the new well drilled jest south a that. All a that got done jest a day or so before Jack was born—early July a 1954—an that well-drillin rig was still sittin there the day Jack arrived.

Lorinda was in the hospital, in Jensen, you older boys were sittin in the living room—jest waiting, I spoze, an I was at the sink in the kitchen, shavin. It was rainin, an all of a sudden lightning struck that well-drillin rig. At least I think that's what it hit. It was powerful, like a rifle shot, only worse.

I put the razor down an walked in ta see you boys, an you were jest sittin there, quiet as mice, scared ta death. Then I noticed a white dust comin up from behind the mopboard. I bent down an took a look. Smoke!

I ran down the cellar an there was a band a fire along a stretch a floor joists, on the west end a the house. See, not only was that well-drillin rig out there, so were two metal bottles a propane gas. The copper tubing from those gas bottles came into the house through the wall an ran along one a the floor joists an up through the floor to the kitchen stove. The lightning had blown a hole *in* the gas line *and* it had lit the gas on fire. So I was standin there lookin at a lightning-made blowtorch ready ta burn the house down. If we'd been gone, the house wudda burned to the ground.

But there was a pail a water sittin by the waterpump an tank. I grabbed that pail a water an threw the water on the fire. The fire went out, jest like that.

I ran back upstairs, out the door, an shut off the valves on the gas bottles—gas was jest a hissin out of that punctured line in the cellar. An then I ran back downstairs an emptied water out a the watertank an really doused those floor joists. Even though the fire was out, there were bright, glowing orange coals still stuck on the joists.

Well, when all a that was taken care of, an I was sure I had'er licked, we went ta town ta see Lorinda an Jack. But before we went to the hospital, I had ta stop by Les Kanitz's gas station ta get gas in the car. He looked at me an started ta laugh.

A course, I wanted ta know what he was laughin at. An he sez, "Do you always go ta town, Hank, with only half a yer face shaved?" An then he laughed some more.

Clean-shaven on one side, whiskers on the other—that's how I looked when I went in ta see Lorinda an Jack.

I think Jack's been scared a me ever since.

Yer askin me about discipline, Seedy, an I spoze yer thinkin that stupid remark about Jack bein scared a me becuz a my whiskers is really true. Is that it? Or are ya jest tryin ta splice together some ends too short ta use? Maybe like a box a whiskers.

Well, I know that Pa didn't discipline us kids fer ketchin fish. Discipline, ya know, is fer one thing but not another. An when it came ta spearin fish, Clara was the ringleader. She was the gutsy one. Nobody disciplined us fer that, except the game warden might've—if he wudda caught us.

Ya know, I think Old Ed Bosworth cudda caught us if he had really wanted to. But I believe he was a sympathetic man. I think we were more afraid of him than we should a been. I believe he knew exactly what we were doin. He knew, but he turned his back.

We were poor. Didn't have enny money. Didn't have nothin. But we had ta eat. What good would it a done ta have us pinched? There was no money ta pay a fine. Put somebody in jail? Put Pa in jail? What good wudda that done?

A Windfall Homestead

But I think my Pa was always fightin with himself, fightin a battle in his own mind. First of all, I believe he was Gramma Buckberry's boy, jest like Uncle Hugo was Grampa's boy. An when we lived in Dawson, in North Dakota, Hugo had a perty good-sized ranch an three kids that worked, while Pa had a small house on the edge a town an ninety-nine kids all wantin somethin ta eat. Well, maybe not ninety-nine, though sometimes it felt like it. Pa was always behind, always in the tail end. Instead a things gettin better, they always seemed ta get worse. Hugo had a ranch. Pa had kids. An Pa'd go chasin after somethin he never managed ta get.

Our parents, ya know, never sat down an talked with us kids about this kind a stuff. Nobody said ennything straight out. So I'm tellin you what I *think* might a been the case. An it might be better if you didn't write enny a this down. What good does that do? This ain't exactly history. Maybe this is what they call "psychology," which is scratchin yer head over what yer tryin ta figger out but don't know for sure.

Every now an then Pa'd turn on me an say, "I'm gonna cuff you up." An then he'd give me a couple swats on the head. Sometimes when he'd do that I didn't even know what the swats were for. That hurts a fella's feelings. (Was he cuffin me jest ta get some frustration out of his system? Though he'd also give me a lickin if he smelled smoke on me, like when I'd been off with Jake Karban, and Jake had rolled us a cigarette ta share.)

I know we were walkin together one time—I was a big kid already, practically growed up—when Pa stopped an gave me a cuff on the head. I don't know why. It made me so mad I said to'em, "That's the last time. I ain't takin ennymore cuffs from you." An it *was* the last time. He never hit me again.

Now I kin remember givin each a you boys one spanking, an I kin remember why I did it.

With Jack, it was on the school bus I was drivin. He wanted some a yer lunch, Seedy, an you wouldn't give it to'em, so he swore at you. I jest pulled over an stopped, got up an gave'em a couple swats on the ass. It was his swearin that made me do it.

With you, it happened when one a the neighbor boys was over an the two of you kept runnin in the barn when I was milkin cows. I told you several times ta stop that runnin, but you didn't listen. So the next time you came runnin through, I grabbed yer arm an gave you a couple swats on yer ass. After that, you didn't come runnin in the barn ennymore.

Comin Home With Both

With Birdy, I was out hoeing potatoes an he wanted ta help. I told'em no. But he kept buggin me. He kept sayin he wanted ta hoe. So finally I told'em ta go get a hoe. But I also told'em, "When yer done, you got ta go hang yer hoe up." Well, he agreed ta that. Off he went an perty soon he was back with a hoe. He chopped at the weeds a couple a times, but he soon learned it wasn't as easy or as much fun as he'd thought. So he dropped his hoe on the ground an walked away.

"Wait a minute," I told'em. "If yer done hoein, you got ta put yer hoe away." But he jest said "No," an he kept walkin. I told'em three times, an he said no three times, an then I caught'em an swatted'em. Then he *did* put that hoe away.

But those are the only times I kin remember givin you boys a licking. I ain't sayin that those are the only times you had one coming, but they are the times you each got one.

18

Changes on the Farm

Now you want me ta tell you about the 1950s? About changes on the farm?

Well, the first thing is the tractor. I finally got ta sit on my ass while plowin. Unless you've plowed by hand behind horses, you maybe can't understand what a change that was. But that little Farmall had only a one-bottom reversible plow, so it wasn't like now when ya see guys turnin over four, six, eight furrows at a time. This was one furrow up, one furrow back. But it was a good plow an a good little tractor, an it made me feel good ta sit up there an watch those furrows a dark earth rollin up, one after the other. I was on top a the world.

Ya know, the whole forty acres had been nothin but a bunch a brush—brush an stumps an rocks. An I was the one responsible for everything that got done. Oh, I had help buildin the barn, an that sort a thing; but I cleared all the land, most of it with a team a horses, a stoneboat, and a handplow, an it all started with that little clearing in the spring a '33.

When I had that little clearing ready, I didn't even know what I was gonna plant in it. An Harry Eberhardt said he'd sell me ten bushels a potatoes for thirty-five cents a bushel. So I bought'em, an then I was broke again. I hauled all those potatoes—six hunnerd pounds of'em—over to the log shack in the back a my Model T, an its ass was jest a draggin. I cut those potatoes an planted'em all by myself.

Pa was not interested in my log shack. Except for helpin me put the rafters up (inta that peaked, beehive shape, which I didn't like, but I kept my

Changes on the Farm

mouth shut)—except fer that, he didn't have nothin ta do with my log shack or my forty acres a land. I think he was sick a Wisconsin an wanted ta go back ta North Dakota. I don't think he wanted ta do ennything that seemed ta tighten up his stayin here. He wanted ta get out.

But that summer a '33 I was gone, workin for Universal Engineering, an when I came home, all covered with soot from ridin the coal tender, the land was black from the forest fire that had come through. Pa was still fightin fire, or maybe jest chasin smoke. Ma an the kids were diggin my potatoes. Her garden had dried up over summer. She took a hunnerd bushels a potatoes home that fall, an I had maybe fifteen or twenty left fer Gramma, Grampa, an me—cuz that's the fall they lost their brick house in Jensen an moved in with me, into the log shack.

I think those potatoes were the most important thing that ever happened on the farm.

Okay. All right. Well, I realize you'd like me ta say somethin about changes in the '50s. Is that what you got in mind, Seedy? Is that why yer squirmin in yer chair? Askin me about silo filling an threshing an making hay? Is that it?

Well, I'm gonna tell you what got me disgusted about silo-filling rings an threshing crews an all that sort a thing. See, I could work twenty-five hours a day. I worked all the time. An when ya get called ta come on such an such a day ta help somebody fill silo, say, an ya get there an he ain't ready or some piece of equipment is missin, an ya got ta stand around for two, three hours waitin, I couldn't stand that.

Once Floyd Peterson asked fer help ta put up a little barn, an some guys didn't come. So we jest sat an waited. Eventually I jest got up an walked home. I didn't see how I could help somebody if he wasn't ready ta be helped. When I went somewhere, I went ta *work*, not sit on my ass an gossip. I jest couldn't stand ta fart around like that.

As far as silo-filling goes, I went an bought a used silo filler an a corn binder from Mike Stevens. (Mike was always lookin for a fast buck. After he quit farmin, he bought an sold horses. An after that he went into the used equipment business. Always chasin the fast buck, but I don't think he ever caught up with very many. Maybe there are jest different kinds a buck fever.) An then I filled my own silo. I didn't have ta wait fer nobody. I farted around a little while with a little, used combine—I think it only cut a five-foot swath—but that was more trouble than it was worth. So I started ta hire guys with good combines ta cut my oats. An, later, when my silo filler

A Windfall Homestead

went ta pot, I hired the Wendt brothers, Kurt an Bob, ta come over with their equipment ta cut corn fer me, an in a couple a days time they had the silo filled. No fartin around.

An one year I hired Fidelis Hahn ta bale hay fer me. Well, actually it was his wife Marion who did the balin becuz Fidelis was workin for the county highway department. But Fidelis had a little farm an he'd bought a new baler an it worked good. No trouble. Next thing I knew, I bought a used baler, an that was a pain in the butt. It was *always* breakin down.[1]

---

1. I sometimes feel like I'm maybe sticking my nose too much into Henry's stories. But I have something to add to this baler story. I also seem to have a "point of view." Maybe it runs in the family.

We boys worked on the farm year round, mostly evenings and of course weekend chores during the school year, but a lot more in the summer. Rock picking usually took a couple weeks in early June. But haying typically didn't start until close to the first of July. That always left a couple of weeks for . . . something.

When we were big enough and able, we frequently helped Henry peel popple pulp during those two weeks between picking rocks and making hay. As I recall, Henry hired Fidelis—Marion, really—to do the baling for him because the pulping job he'd taken was bigger than anticipated.

Henry got the cutting and raking of hay done while Birdy and I did evening chores; and the next day, while we were gone to the woods, Marion would come and bale. That evening, besides the regular chores, we'd go to the field with tractor and wagon, pick up the bales, haul them to the barn, and stack them in the hay loft.

That year, the haying and the pulping got finished almost exactly at the same time. Of course, Henry had to pay Marion—Fidelis, really—for the work. And I remember Henry saying, rather disgusted, that the baling had cost him almost exactly what he'd made peeling pulp. It made him *so* mad that he went to town and bought a junky used baler, which only added to his woe.

Later, I took this pulping-haying-baler incident to be a kind of watershed, a marking point, rather like Lorinda's working in a pea canning factory, in Jensen, in order to make enough money to get rid of the round oak table in the kitchen and to replace it with a formica-topped table with aluminum legs. Out with the oak chairs. In with plastic cushions. Both of these situations, these choices, in my opinion, are examples of the pernicious side of "progress."

Now there were steps in this "becoming modern" that were practical and useful. But there also were steps that just lured people into a financial and consumerist hole. Some things beckoned with imitation elegance from the pages of glossy magazines. Other things promised mechanical efficiency and speed. It was all part of the huge commercial package called "progress," sophisticated bait for people who were steadily becoming "consumers" more fully and more deeply than they were remaining "citizens."

Was making loose hay with a hayloader really that much harder than making hay with a baler? A hayloader just rumbled along behind the wagon, its knobbed wheels providing the traction—the energy—by which the windrowed hay was pulled up the metal incline of the hayloader and slid into the wagon. Horses were powerful enough to pull the wagon *and* the hayloader. But a baler needed tractor power. And the little Farmall C wasn't big

Changes on the Farm

Ya know, it's gettin harder fer me ta pull things apart. When yer young, ya think nothin of pullin the wings off a fly or shootin sparrows. But when yer older, you start ta think that even the tiniest, most worthless creature has got a life of its own, an who are you ta pull it apart or snuff it out, jest becuz you happen ta feel like it? What gives you the right ta play God or Devil?

Maybe it's different with memories. You ain't askin me ta shoot a neighbor's cat, Seedy. Yer jest askin me ta reach down inta that musty old root cellar I got holed up inside my head, an see if there are enny potatoes in there that ain't got sprouts on'em a foot long, if enny of'em are fit ta eat.

Ever eat yer memories, Seedy? Some days I think that's all I do, though some of'em don't taste too good, while others maybe get sweeter all the time.

Well, okay. Yer wantin ta know about ennymore trips ta Washington.

---

enough for the job. So Henry had to buy a larger tractor—a Farmall H.

Where was the place to stop? How was a person to know when enough was enough? Subsistence things like kerosene lamps, a woodburning cookstove, a large garden and home-canned food, a flock of chickens, home butchering, a smokehouse, and consistent neighborhood cooperativeness—all began to be dropped or abandoned. Some "cooperation" certainly involved aggravation. That's true. But there was a notion that this intensive focus on production, on *real* farming, on "progress," was leading somewhere, that it was or promised to be a real improvement, and that each of these little farmers who stuck it out and did everything possible to make these little farms *work* was building something important and valuable to pass along to their kids. Almost without exception, this proved not to be true. Just the opposite. We kids left.

In my estimation, the signs of rural failure were showing up already at the end of the Second World War. A house with no eaves is a house based on a suburban magazine concept, as is a kitchen table with aluminum legs. Pure ungrounded consumerist fantasy. And did increased mechanization really accelerate the farm's productivity or significantly reduce its labor? By 1957 or so, the Boulder School was closed, and those of us still attending were bussed to the Copper—which, in turn, was closed for good in 1960 or '61. The increasing commercialization of home life and the increasing industrialization of farming were backdropped by the atrophy of neighborliness and the closing of the country schools. Small-scale farming and one-room schools committed suicide hand-in-hand. (Or were they murdered?) (And, if so, by what or by whom?)

The noose was tightening. Subsistence skills were going out the window. Mechanization seemed irreversible. Local community was getting thinner and thinner. The Modern World became more and more alluring. People with no cow manure on their shoes knew what was what. We youngsters were on a certain trajectory into some sort of Technological Future. Henry's farm, for all its vitality, was slowly getting strangled. Having money, being modern, and not knowing when enough is enough were three strands in that strangulating rope. And most small farmers could hardly wait to try on that fancy new necktie. By the time the knot was tight enough, both the little farmers and the little schools were completely out of breath. S. B.

A Windfall Homestead

I must a drove ta Washington at least four times. But the only time I did that when Lorinda was still alive wudda been in June a 1957.

I am, ya know, ninety-six years old. Ain't I entitled ta begin ta ferget a few things? My head ain't gettin enny bigger. Some stuff has got ta go ta make room fer ennythin new—like knowin what day a the week it is or whether it was the sun that came up this morning or jest a great big yellow light bulb. A fella's got ta make a little room fer somethin new. Maybe I need ta clean out that root cellar.

What I can remember is that there wasn't ennything in perticular ta cause that trip. No special reason. Except, maybe, that my folks weren't gettin enny younger. Go see'em one last time.

It must a been the '47 Chevy that we took. An I think Mary went with us, an I believe her youngest son. That wudda been Glen. An yer mother an Jack an you, Seedy. Birdy stayed home an did the chores.

I thought about takin the cows along, but I couldn't figger out how ta get'em all in the car. An yer mother wudda worried about all their dresses an such. Nightgowns.

All I kin tell you about that trip is that it was a lot better than takin the train. When yer jest along fer the ride, it's like somebody's leadin you around by the nose. You ain't got nothin ta say. But when it's nineteen hunnerd miles starin you in the face, you got ta pay attention.

I know we made it to Chehalis in three days. The first morning we left the farm before the sun was up, an we stayed at a motel on the Dakota side a the Montana border. That's one long day a drivin. An, a course, it's a big thrill drivin through the moutains, once ya get to'em. Montana, ya know, is one big state.

I believe we stayed with Daisy an Jim in Chehalis.

I guess that's about all I got ta say.

I think it musta been 1980 before I went out there again, an that wudda been with Mary, jest the two of us, in that red pickup Jack bought when he was thinkin about takin over the farm, an that I ended up with. (Well, you ended up with it, Seedy, all wired up an snortin.) I went elk huntin an didn't see a damn thing. Except, way back in the timber with my brother Bill, I found a really nice perty stone, an when I asked my brother Bill what it was, he said it's a "leaverite."

"A 'leaverite'?" I asked'em. "I never heard a that."

Changes on the Farm

"Leave'er right where you found'er," Bill sez. But, a course, I had to put that stone in my pocket an carry it out. It never was much good ta eat, but it sure has kept well.

When Mary an me came back, we got caught in a snowstorm in the mountains. The road was packed an glazed, an I never in my life saw so many cars in the ditch. An we ended up bein one of 'em in the ditch.

So I'm standin there, in the ditch, thinkin what are ya gonna do now, Hank, an here comes the wrecker man, an he jest stands there lookin down at me, waitin ta see if I'll ask'em ta pull me out. But I don't like those guys. Oh, they kin help ya out, all right, but they sure are awful expensive. They hook right onto yer wallet an haul away everything that's in it. So I jest looked at'em an said, "I'm gonna try it first."

A course, I had a shovel along, an I did quite a bit a diggin around the wheels. An then I got out the tire chains an put'em on. But instead a tryin ta get right back up to the road, I backed'er up first, ta get a run at'er. An, by golly, up we went.

I jest waved to that wrecker man an then we had ta wiggle around a couple a semis jackknifed kiddy-corner acrost the road. An then we kept right on a goin.

Thirty-five miles an hour for a long time after that. I think I wore out the tire chains on that road. Took us an extra day ta get home.

19

Too Big ta Ketch an Swallow

I KNOW YER WANTIN ta kind a wrap things up, Seedy, an yer sayin you want ta do that by askin me about Lorinda's illness an her death. Her cancer. But, ya know, I'm glad when I kin ferget some things. Now some things I *like* ta remember, an those are the stories I *like* ta tell. Even some a those I like ta tell aren't all full a fun, but neither are they full a pain. There's some good in 'em. Somethin a *life*, somethin a *hope*.

When I think a the difference between Lorinda's dyin an my—well, I ain't exactly convinced I'm dyin, even if I *am* ninety-six years old. A little wore out, maybe. Not exactly a spring chicken ennymore. (You ever been ninety-six, Seedy? I hope ya get ta try it sometime.)

But here I am, having gone through that fuss a last December when I thought I *was* gonna kick the bucket, an now I got a nurse that comes ta see me every week an wants ta know "Do you have enny pain, Henry?"

What do ya think, Seedy? Do ya think you kin get ta be ninety-six years old an not have enny pain in yer life? What a joke!

So a nurse comes ta see me, an a nurse's aide comes an soaks my feet an shaves my whiskers, an a lady chaplain comes ta listen to my stupid stories, an all a that's nice. I like it. I like them. They're nice people. An they're all gettin paid by Uncle Sam. Otherwise they wouldn't be here.

What's a old man's life worth, Seedy? I must be a valuable old bastard. I like the attention. I really do. But what's a old man's life worth? Kin you answer that?

Too Big ta Ketch an Swallow

When yer mother was dyin, there was nobody ta help. There was a time when I didn't know if I was walkin or on horseback. Doctors all the time. No insurance a enny sort. Hospitals. Madison. Marshfield. Wausau. The bills jest kept comin. Pay'n pay'n pay. An when I was out a money, those bills still kept comin, until finally I had ta go to the Lincoln County Bank, an they said the only way they could help was if I mortgaged the farm. Which is what I had ta do.

Other than the times she was in the hospital, an one week in the county home after her last time in the hospital, she stayed at home. We had two beds in our bedroom. One fer her. One fer me. I used ta get up in the middle a the night an give'er her shots.

I was drivin school bus on the side. I asked Fred Doepke a lot a questions—besides ownin the busses, he also was a lawyer. He gave me lots a advice, an he never charged me ennything. He even got me a set a rear tractor tires at cost, cuz mine were wore out. Cost me seventy-five dollars apiece.

Like I said, the county home wouldn't keep'er, didn't want'er, an from then on she was at home. She realized then that she couldn't be helped, that she was dyin, an I think she was dwelling on it all the time. Afraid of it an couldn't do a thing about it. An I think she let it get the best of 'er, so everybody else had ta suffer a little, too.

A course, I spoze that's easy fer me ta say now. I'm a ninety-six year-old man, jest slowly fallin apart from old age, but she was a young woman then, less'n fifty years old, with two kids still at home, with what should a been a lot a years still ahead of her, too young ta die. An I think that cancer jest filled'er full a pain. So it's a hard job, sometimes, ta try'n put yerself in somebody else's shoes. Especially when those aren't the kind a shoes yer eager ta be standin in.

All I kin tell you is that I did the best that I knew how ta do. Nobody came ta help. I was strictly on my own.

On the day she died—it was early in February a 1963—I called the doctor at four o'clock in the afternoon. She was in terrible pain, but it wasn't time ta give'er a shot yet. An the doctor said ta go ahead an do it. By six o'clock she was dead. Did that extra shot kill'er? Does it matter if it did?

All that suffering, an all of a sudden it's over. It makes ya wonder what's the point a all that pain? What's it good for?

Lots a times now I can't sleep at night. Jest sit here in my chair an think. Rememberin things. But I ain't afraid a dyin. Cemeteries are full a dead people. One more don't make much difference.

A Windfall Homestead

So I jest sit in my chair an rock an hang on. An when the paper comes, I look an see all those people dead at sixty, seventy, eighty years old. An here I am still alive! Maybe I've outlived my usefulness, that's all.

Damn it, Seedy, at least you kin smile about it! What else is there ta do? That's jest the way I feel about it. I don't even want ennybody ta preach a funeral over me. What's the use a all that nice talk about Old Mister So-an-So an what a holy man he was? Most a that is nothin but a pile a crap.

Maybe these stories are my obituary, Seedy—you ever think about that? Here you thought you were writin down my *stories*, an all the time all you were doin was scribblin out my *obituary*!

Don't look so—I don't know what—*shocked*, maybe. At least ya kin smile about it.

I ain't no saint. I'm jest a sinner.

That's jest the way it is.

I think that last story is jest a little too sad an dreary ta end with, Seedy. So I'm gonna tell ya one more. But you heard about this "jest one more" business before.

You might say this one is about the tote road that was still perty easy ta see when we first moved out here in the brush, in 1922. Not that I saw it right away or followed it as far as I could, but it did help me get ta know the country.

See, the county road that went north past our bunkhouse, which was down by the Boulder River, jest kept goin north, up Karban Hill an then straight up (in a brushed-out trail sort a way) to the Anderson Homestead, where we used ta cut hay when I was a kid. It was jest a trail, good enuff fer horses an a wagon an not much else.

But up past Old Man Karban's place, about where Wangen Road now butts inta the county road, is where the old tote road came acrost. That tote road, I believe, was put in before Kinzel put the railroad in, back in the days when they were takin out the pine. So we could be talking the 1880s maybe. I ain't sure. I wasn't there. I asked'em once if I could come along ta watch'em cut the big pine, but they said, "No. You ain't old enuff till after yer born." So I guess that settled that.

The tote road went close ta where Oscar Wangen's house used ta be, but a course Oscar wasn't in there yet. An it kept on goin east, more or less, until it hit the Wisconsin River, jest upstream from Bill Cross Rapids.

Too Big ta Ketch an Swallow

You could wade acrost the rapids there, or jest above'em, if you were careful. Water up to yer knees an fast. But if ya took yer time, you could make it over an back. I know, becuz I did it. (Though it was gettin hard ta see wagon tracks an hoof prints in the river ennymore. I think the fish brushed'em out on purpose.) But I never followed up the tote road on the east side a the Wisconsin River. So I don't know where it went from there. Probably swung south ta Jensen.

But from the end a Oscar's road, that tote road jest kind a meandered off to the northwest, not too far from Happy Jack's an on acrost that little crick that flows between Happy Jack's an Dan Young's. There had been a log bridge acrost the crick, but it was washed out, jest a big log here an there on the downstream side—one a those places I later learned ta come smellin around fer trout, cuz they liked, ya know, ta hide under those logs an watch the world go by. An sometimes I'd help'em take a little trip inta my fryin pan.

Ennyway, the tote road went up through what's now Jankowskys' land an right in front a my log shack (or, maybe I ought ta say, where the log shack eventually got built) an up acrost the farm to Kelly Crick. I can't remember enny sign of a bridge acrost Kelly Crick. Maybe there never had been one or maybe it got washed clean away. An, from there, that tote road kept on to the northwest as far as Camp 30. So I spoze that tells you they were haulin stuff to the logging camps by horse an wagon, all the way from Jensen. Ya know, underarm deodorant an that sort a thing. Aftershave lotion. Stuff ta curl yer hair. Things that lumberjacks needed. Frozen pizzas. Lottery tickets.

So followin the tote road was part a how I learned the country when I was jest a kid. Later, a course, after the forest fire in '33, when everything was burnt black as the ace a spades an the whole country looked like a coal-dust prairie, I stuck my nose inta every little pothole, mostly lookin fer deer, but also keepin my eyeballs open fer windfall logs. I found quite a few of'em that way—two of'em so big, up back a Doc Sievert's, that I had ta use the horses ta roll'em on a sled—an one was even layin in that grass swamp between this place an yer log house, Seedy. If I found a sound log or a windfall or a rampike, I didn't ask ennybody enny questions. I jest went an got it. The whole set a farm buildings was mostly built out a windfall "residuals." You might even call it a windfall homestead.

If there was a trail, I went down it. I had a long nose. An since that nose had got stuck on the front a my head, I didn't seem ta have enny choice but ta go followin it. It took me lots a places.

A Windfall Homestead

I walked that tote road lots an lots a times. An one time I was headed up towards what was gonna be my Windfall Homestead (I think I'm gonna start callin it that, Seedy, jest fer the hell of it, though I never called it that before), an I was near that washed-out bridge on the crick back a Happy Jack's, an here's a bird about the size of a robin, not enny bigger, sittin on a branch about as high as my head, an she ain't movin. So I walk right up to'er an look'er in the eyeballs an she jest sits there glarin back at me, eyeballin each other.

Well, I thought, ain't you a little puffed-up ball a feathers, brave as a lion or stupid as a cow, an I raised my arm an put my hand right up to'er head an she reached out with'er beak an gave me a sharp peck on the finger, an then she flew away. Not far, but she flew.

Well, I thought, somethin's fishy here—but it ain't trout. So I jest stood real still an started lookin around. After a little while I spotted a nest a naked little birds right on the ground, right alongside the tote road. Okay. *Now* I knew what was goin on, what made'er so brave and bold.

All a those hungry kids at home an here comes a really big piece a meat, jest wanderin down the trail like nobody's business. Mama Bird must a sat on that branch tryin ta figger out how she could handle me. I think she wudda liked ta have fed me to'er babies, but I was jest too big ta ketch an swallow. An it must a made'er mad ta think a all that good bird food goin ta waste.

It's kinda like the stories I still could tell ya, Seedy, if only I could remember'em. Ta think a all that history goin ta waste.

But I guess that's jest the way it is. That's jest the way it goes.

It does make ya wonder, though, whether there ain't—what would you call it?—some kind a cosmic record of all the amazing things that've ever happened in the world and that nobody seems ta know about.

Maybe that's yer next project, Seedy. Sometime when yer nappin, you gotta think about how ta go about tappin into that "cosmic record."

I ain't about ta tell ya how yer gonna get that one done, cuz I don't know. But if ennybody kin do it, you can. I never saw a fella take ta naps the way you do. There ought ta be a passageway ta pure wisdom in that napland somewheres.

All I got ta say—when ya think yer at the end a yer rope and it's as black as the ace a spades, keep yer eyes open—even if you are asleep.

Seedy Buckberry's Afterword

THESE ARE HENRY'S STORIES, not mine. But, as his stenographer, the guy with the pencil, I'd like to say something about why I provoked and instigated this project, starting with *Get Poor Now, Avoid the Rush*, and concluding (I think) with this present volume.

I moved to inner-city St. Louis in the summer of 1967 and continued to live there until June of 1976. Don't ask me why because I still don't know. Call it aimless alienation. I do know that by the end of that period, I was totally burned out on urban life. But, before I got to the "total" phase of burnout, I had begun to ask smart people to explain to me why small farms were dying. I was missing rural life, spending way too much time in the elephant house at the zoo (elephants smell something like cows), and I was increasingly aware that small farms were taking a beating. I wanted to know why. My background and nostalgia ("homesickness") made my interest deeply personal and not simply academic. I *really* wanted to know. Please, will somebody tell me? Why are small farms dying?

The answers I got did not satisfy, to say the least. Looking back, I think I can honestly say I was asking an eighty-pound question and getting only three-ounce answers. The truth seemed to be that hardly anybody was interested in the plight of rural culture or had given it any serious thought. I thought people were even mildly aggravated when asked such a stupid, useless, trivial, and irrelevant question. Who cares? Rural culture?! What's *that*?

By the time I had lured Henry into telling me his stories (about as difficult as coaxing a horse into a stall with a bucket of oats), I had already arrived at a set of answers to my St. Louis question. So I wasn't exactly looking to Henry, or to his stories, for an answer. By then, I already knew the answers—or at least I thought I did.

A Windfall Homestead

Answers to the why-are-small-farms-dying question had come primarily from thinkers and scholars whose works never seemed to have made it into the mainstream. (I'll list some names and book titles, pretty much in the order I discovered them, in case anybody is interested in a little bedtime reading: Paul Goodman, *Growing Up Absurd* and *Compulsory Miseducation*; Martin Buber, *Paths in Utopia*; Norman O. Brown, *Life Against Death*; E. F. Schumacher, *Small Is Beautiful*; Lewis Mumford, *The City in History*, *The Myth of the Machine*, and *The Pentagon of Power*; Wendell Berry, *The Unsettling of America*.) The deepest of all are Lewis Mumford and Norman O. Brown. Mumford especially takes his readers on an awesome historical tour, with or without seat belts buckled.

Now, in order for me to be willing to grasp the dynamics of agriculture historically, I had to face up to something nestled snugly inside of me—an induced religious blockage. Although I hadn't been raised an explicit fundamentalist, I had been taught Bible stories as literal history (the Garden of Eden, Noah and the Flood, Moses parting the waters of the Red Sea—all that sort of thing), and no one had ever said those stories weren't literally true. So religious stories and real history were all jumbled up in my mind. (Public schools avoided separating the two for fear of provoking the righteous wrath of religious taxpayers who might raise holy hell on behalf of their delicate china shop understanding of God and heaven.)

So I essentially entered adulthood with an underlying emotional and mental notion warning me that to even think about history *before* Adam and Eve was to diddle and dabble with *evil*. Why "evil"? Because to think about history outside of or prior to God's Holy Word was to disbelieve the divine accuracy of God's Holy Word. And that was strictly forbidden. Talk about an Iron Curtain! I had one inside of my head!

Now I wasn't the only person with such a metallic affliction. That affliction was so common as to be a cultural convention. Almost everybody I knew shared it. It was one of the reasons why people weren't interested in the history of agriculture. Agriculture's actual story contradicted Genesis, and most people couldn't tolerate the internal conflict. To think about real history felt wicked. It was simpler and easier to just pretend such history didn't exist, had never happened, or was irrelevant. The human mind is a curious critter. The power of religious mythology is pretty amazing.

But I *really* wanted to know why small farms were dying, so I *really* had to learn about the origins of agriculture and civilization, even if it scared me half to death. That meant I had to begin reading serious history, and that's what I found especially in Lewis Mumford's books.

As I got deeper and deeper into this investigation, I began to realize I'd grown up in the final stage of peasant culture, at least in the United States, an inheritance of self-provisioning that went back in time to our truly ancient hunting and gathering ancestors. By "final stage," I mean that the ancient culture of agrarian self-provisioning (thousands of years old) was dying at the hands of civilization. That is, the death of small farms, of small-scale farming, was also the death of rural self-sufficiency—the death of rural life, the death of agrarian culture—whatever we might call it. This was the termination of a kind of folk culture that went back thousands and thousands of years. And its final death rattle occurred in my generation.

Henry's stories were, for me, the purest, most concentrated expression of a transition from buckboards to space stations, from home canning to Wal-Mart, from skinny-dipping in the river to Super Bowl Sunday. As local folk culture died, civilized nationalism (with all its commercial appendages) sucked up human allegiance. Where we used to love our home place and village life, we now "loved" capitalism and the empire military adventures of the flag.

But Henry never got pulled into civilized nationalism despite his attachment to biblical literalism and the philosophical fundamentalism of the Seventh-Day Adventist Church, which he joined somewhere around 1970. Oh, he was nudged along by "progress," like virtually every human being I've ever known, certainly including myself; but he was a stubborn old farmer, a woodsman, a lumberjack, a horse handler, a fish netter, beaver trapper, and deer hunter. He knew how to do too many things—some legal, some not so legal—to be a modern "consumer." And he was much too grounded in real life and real people to be terrified by the calculated propaganda of people like Richard Nixon, Ronald Reagan, or George Bush I and II.

If Henry Buckberry had a major flaw in his thinking, it was (in my completely modest opinion) the same one I needed to break through in order to answer the question about the death of small farms: biblical literalism. But, at age 96, a breakthrough was hardly to be expected, and maybe shouldn't be encouraged. I don't know. I do know that the grooves our thoughts run in are pretty well established by the time we're in our twenties and thirties, and perhaps even sooner.

These mental grooves, channelled and pressurized by biblical literalism, commercial ideology and civilized nationalism, virtually guarantee that the country as a whole is headed rather speedily toward a whole series of terribly disruptive crises—in the economy, in international relations, in global ecology, in our energy habits, and in our everyday "lifestyle" and patterns of thought. I used to think we'd wake up in time to avert the worst of the crises, but I'm finding it harder and harder to believe that. We love our grooves too much to change voluntarily. Or, if we don't exactly "love" those grooves, we're afraid to openly examine or crawl out of them.

We all grew up thinking we were free and independent. Nobody was going to tell *me* what to do. But where do we suppose the thoughts we think come from? Corporations do not spend billions of dollars every year on advertising just for the hell of it. Nor are they inclined to throw money at advertising if advertising didn't increase corporate profits. Politicians wouldn't flap the flag in our faces if we wouldn't reward them with our votes. Preachers wouldn't preach hell and damnation if *fear* wasn't a core emotion in all of us, just waiting to be exploited. And as folk culture has shriveled and died, the Big Three (corporations, politicians, and clergy—with programmed baby-sitting from the school system maybe nudging in as Number Four) have polished to a high sheen the mental grooves our "independent" thoughts get to slide in.

Anyway, I think we're quitting with Henry's stories. Maybe it's mostly me who's quitting, although I think it's mutual. I think from here on out it would not be stories, but an ambiguous blend of spiritual discovery, intellectual broadening, and painful (but liberating) psychotherapy. But that's beyond our pay grades.

Chronologically, these stories end with Lorinda's death in February of 1963. Henry was fifty-one years old.

In June of 1964, Henry married Viola. (I was one of two people late for the wedding.) Although Viola brought enough money to the marriage to first ease and then eliminate the mortgage on the farm, theirs was not a relationship rooted in tenderness, reciprocal understanding, or love. They had a blue-collar class affinity that masqueraded (at least for a while) as reciprocal affection. But troubles were rife and came in many ways. Almost forty years of tough-it-out unhappiness followed, before Viola's death in April of 2004. Not unhappiness every day or in every way, but overall there was anger, sorrow, grief, and resentment.

Quite a few people were adversely affected by this constellation of woe. The person whose sorrow most touches my heart is my brother Jack. I won't say that nothing would be gained by picking the scabs off the wounds of those years; but, if nothing else, I'm not sure I have the medical expertise for the job, a tough enough stomach, or the necessary spiritual discernment. (Once again a pay grade problem.) Plus, I left home in September of 1964, and I didn't return to Boulder to live until the summer of 1976. (My second wife Athena and I built a shack in the pine woods, in the Greutzmacher forty, in the fall of '76.) So not only was there a twelve-year block of time when I was largely absent from the scene, the home situation had significantly altered over that period.

Henry was still Henry, but the farm was not as psychologically accessible, not as peasant welcoming, as it might have been. Love, perhaps, might've had big enough arms to wrap around everybody and everything; but we were all individual creatures protecting ego and turf. Besides, Viola had brought into the marriage a daughter and an adopted son, both of whom had troubled lives. Jack was squeezed between a rock and a hard place. Our mother had sickened, shriveled, and died while Jack was a mere boy, and Viola never had the maternal warmth to even begin to heal or overcome that great psychic wound.

So I think we're quitting with Henry's stories. The psychotherapy will have to wait. The farm stayed in the Buckberry family—Jack tried to make a go of it for a couple of years of near drought, in the late 1970s, before turning it back to Henry—until the farm was sold, in 1980, to an Adventist couple from California whose fantasy was to make it bigger and "more successful." Henry, meanwhile, mostly out of used lumber, built a new house, on the Greutzmacher forty, over a two-year period, from 1974 to 1976.

After the farm was sold, Henry and Viola lived continuously in the "new house." The people who bought the farm—all of it except the east half of the Greutzmacher forty—threw in the towel before 1990, and Henry's farm got chopped into four separate parcels. It's one of—I don't know—twenty or thirty little farms that have bit the dust in the Town of Boulder. It's another integer in a larger statistic of small-farm collapse and failure. It's a tiny chapter in a hugely long history of small-farm squeezings that go back through every "mature" civilization to the rise of civilization itself. (The Roman Empire was the product, at least in part, of the death of small-scale farming during the late Republic. So it's not the first time small-scale farming got bonked on the head.)

Civilization got its start by stealing the "surplus" production of small farmers. With industrialization civilization discovered it could simply do away with farmers altogether and produce food with machines, chemicals,

A Windfall Homestead

and fossil fuels. Peasants were obsolete. Peasants were liquidated. Stalin was just the most brutal of the liquidators.

Another argument in favor of calling it quits is simply this: Henry's most vivid stories are overwhelmingly those that occurred in the era and aura of workhorses, kerosene lamps, snowshoes, and woodburning cookstoves. The stories that coincide with electricity, tractors, school busses, and supermarkets just don't quite cut the mustard, even if told with the same narrative energy. They're no longer true peasant stories.

If this is true—it's true for me—we have to ask why that's so. We have to look for reasons why the "modern" is so sterile and boring. We have to try to explain why shacks contain more vitality than carefully constructed houses built from blueprints, why a big garden and jars of home-canned food generate more psychic energy than supermarket coolers full of plastic meat and aisles loaded with colorful cans and toilet paper.

At the risk of appearing academic or pedantic or (as that cunning racist politician George Wallace used to say) pointy-headed, I want to invoke the historian Henry Steele Commager who said, in his 1950 book *The American Mind*, that the 1890s were the great watershed years in America. What happened before the 1890s is fundamentally different than what happened after. (I recommend, too, *The Populist Moment* by Lawrence Goodwyn, a book that covers the same period in greater detail.)

So what are the particulars? Before the 1890s, America was overwhelmingly rural and agrarian. After the 1890s, America became urban and industrial. The key political event occured in 1896 when the People's Party, the party of ordinary farmers, the so-called "Populists," was defeated in the presidential election. McKinley won. Bryan lost. With that defeat, agrarian America began to disintegrate.

However, to say that agrarian America began to fall apart does not mean that preindustrial culture died an instant death or that elements of folk life did not survive into the twentieth century—and even into the twenty-first, as Henry Buckberry proved out at the sawbuck with his bowsaw, cutting county forest gleanings into hunks of firewood, at the age of ninety-five.

But agrarian America, certainly from the Civil War on, was being vigorously squeezed. It survived on millions of small farms and even enlarged its population and cultural space as a consequence of industrial depression in the 1930s. And it survived longest where agriculture was the most marginal, where soil was glacial and rocky, where growing seasons were

Seedy Buckberry's Afterword

short and frost unpredictable, where tiny farms were carved out of cutover logging land and reclaimed in the aftermath of forest fires. The Great Depression gave a temporary boost to subsistence, to big gardens, to a couple cows in a shed, to shacks and neighborliness, to sneak hunting in the brush for wild meat.

I grew up in the very tail end of this small-scale agrarian subsistence culture, and I got a big enough dose of it to realize, later, that I had caught the sunset of European peasant life in America, the last gasp of authentic agrarian folk culture, before it was totally sucked up into the new industrialism, complete with satellite dishes and electric garage doors.

Of course, being my father's son, I want to say a few things about the significance of this transformation. (Henry became, you know, a lay preacher in the Seventh-Day Adventist church.) The first thing to say is that the anthropologists and archaeologists have been saying for a good century and a half that agriculture was created primarily by women gatherers who were the first people to deliberately plant seeds and to concentrate in a small area the sorts of plants they would later harvest for food. I'm talking ten thousand years ago here, plus or minus a few birthdays. (If you want the big picture, very readably presented, go find two back-to-back books by the late historian Lewis Mumford. I mean The *Myth of the Machine* and *The Pentagon of Power*.)

When food abundance got solid enough, predictable and reliable enough, thanks to the women farmers, the domestication of a number of animals began—the cow, the sheep, the goat, the pig, the chicken and duck, the horse. And out of that came agriculture proper, with oxen pulling wooden plows. And when this combination of plant and animal domestication had generated its even-greater food abundance, along with settled villages and all kinds of new inventions (like the wheel), then this decentralized village life was unexpectedly overpowered, either from without or from within—probably from without—by armed male bandits who established themselves as a ruling class—an aristocracy—and turned the relatively well-off and nonviolent villagers into half-starved, oppressed peasants whose food was systematically stolen and whose boys were forcibly conscripted into being soldiers for the king and whose girls (as it says in 1 Samuel 8:13) were coerced into becoming "perfumers." Hence cities were created in what's now called the Middle East. Cities, kingdoms, empires—which is what we all were taught, when we learned about the

A Windfall Homestead

Glorious History of Civilization. (We were taught to celebrate Civilization, of course, not to look at it carefully or critically.)

This pattern of peasant and aristocrat went on in various ups and downs until the eighteenth century. Then two things happened almost simultaneously. One thing was the sudden outburst of revolutionary democracy, as in America in 1776 and in France a decade later. The other thing was the industrial revolution, which is often dated from 1760, in England. (See E. J. Hobsbaum's *The Age of Revolution: 1789–1848*.)

Now in America there was a big fight between Thomas Jefferson and Alexander Hamilton. Jefferson wanted small-scale farming to be *the* dominant form of cultural life, while Hamilton wanted no obstacle placed in the way of the maximum growth of finance and industry. By 1896, Jefferson had lost and Hamilton had won. Since 1896, except for the pause created by the Great Depression, Jefferson has kept losing and Hamilton has kept winning. Agriculture has been transformed into industrial agribusiness (which is "farming" without farmers), and Jefferson is confined to a mental hospital, babbling incoherently, undergoing electroshock "therapy." Alexander Hamilton decided to occasionally change his name, and has been known as Bill Clinton, George W. Bush, and Barack Obama.

Anyway, here's the point I want to make. The culture of hunters and gatherers is so old it goes back to time out of mind. Hundreds of thousands of years. Old. Really old. Older than any "antique" you've ever been tempted to buy at your favorite flea market. Compared with the culture of hunters and gatherers, agrarian culture only goes back about ten thousand years. (We haven't been encouraged to think or talk about this stuff very much because religious fundamentalists go ballistic with their biblical-literalism hissy fits. Anything older than five or six thousand years is "evil." This evasion and avoidance suits the political elite just fine. Why? Because the elite worship the civilized, aristocratic palace; and if "peasants" can be kept in the dark about how wealth gets concentrated in so few hands, about when and how this aristocratic theft and murder occurred, then this wonderful system of industrial capitalism can just keep chugging along—until oil depletion, rampant pollution, climate change, military mayhem, and economic collapse combine to wreck this historic house of cards.)

Civilization (which is city organization deriving from the rise of an armed and deadly bandit aristocracy) only goes back about five thousand years. With its kingdoms and empires, civilization has always tried to get bigger and bigger, get more control, take over more people and more land.

Seedy Buckberry's Afterword

But in the larger scheme of things, noncivilized people were more numerous, and lots of land was not controlled by civilized intrusion. Civilization was a self-important nuisance, but it wasn't to be taken too seriously. Even the Roman Empire collapsed.

But it didn't take very long and Europe redeveloped civilization. Europeans with their sailing ships, swords, and cannon proceeded to conquer *the entire world*, beginning in earnest with Columbus. Within four hundred years more or less—say 1492 until 1896—the Western Hemisphere went from "wilderness" to civilized, with Jefferson's small farms permitted to "domesticate" the wild landscape before being economically strangled to make way for agribusiness, which is the modern name for technological agrarian slavery, which is maximized food production under the economic control of financialized corporations. All indigenous cultures were overpowered, squashed, or smashed.

See, the "populist" farmers in the People's Party of the 1890s wanted small-scale farming to thrive. Jefferson believed small-scale farming was humanity's true calling, and the Populists agreed with that. A lot of late nineteenth-century farmers recognized that civilized industry was their enemy—the huge banks and corporations. In order to control the banks and corporations, the farmers spelled out (are you ready for this?) a platform of *socialism*: public control of banks, mines, utilities, railroads, corporations—everything that by virtue of its very size was simply too big to be owned and controlled by private wealth—"too big to fail." Such massive private wealth, the Populists believed, was ushering in a new form of aristocracy, an aristocracy temporarily hiding behind corporations; and they saw that this new aristocratic wealth could buy politicians the way a farmer might buy a batch of baby chicks. (Of course, banks and big businesses fought back against the populist farmers, and they engineered an awesome propaganda campaign that made socialism equivalent to devil worship. Guys like Rush Limbaugh are their current mouthpieces.)

There's another thing to say here. Democracy insists that power resides in the people. But in order for that statement to be politically meaningful, the people must be able to exercise power in more significant ways than by occasional passive voting for candidates bought and paid for by Big Money. In my estimation, that means democratic socialism, just as the farmers of the 1890s said. But it also requires a huge revitalization of small-scale farming—for two reasons.

A Windfall Homestead

First, the charge invariably leveled against socialism is that it always becomes dictatorial, with a tiny clique of brutal bosses at the top who tell everybody else what to do, who line grumblers up against the wall and shoot them down. Socialism, however, will be *democratic* if *farmers* control it, if the bulk of the economy is vigorously small-scale and in private hands.

The second reason for revitalizing small-scale farming is that such farming is the basis of our actual living with nature, for we are biological and evolutionary creatures who simply must live with animals and weather and woods and dirt. It's our biological and cultural heritage, our medium—ashes to ashes, dust to dust, dirt to dirt. To live on the fiftieth floor of the economic skyscraper is to live in our technologically abstracted, utopian heads, which is the aristocratic arrogance we inherit from our infatuation with civilization. To become civilized you must consent to have the peasant squeezed out of your soul and shift your allegiance from cooperative community in nature to the arrogant technology of the city-state, from Jefferson to Hamilton, from the peasant to the aristocrat.

Put the reasons together and we can come to this conclusion: socialism in the hands of small farmers is a huge impediment to fiftieth-floor dictators. Democratic socialism is the logical and necessary expression of the agrarian community taking political control of the industrial large-scale. Either civilization controls folk culture or folk culture controls civilization. It's one or the other. I am one-hundred percent for the latter.

I want to point out a couple more things, then I'll quit. First, the brilliant pointy-headed economists never did figure out how to control the Great Depression. The forces that triggered its suspension (not its end) were Germany and Japan. That is, the Second World War created a permanent war economy, with absolutely huge government deficit spending on the military (or on what Eisenhower later called the "military-industrial complex") continuing right up to the present day. (See James Carroll's *House of War* for a guided tour.)

What do you think would happen if the plug suddenly got pulled on Pentagon spending? I predict we'd be right back in the Great Depression, only this time with a huge hunk of the world royally pissed off at us for all our bloody meddling since (at least) 1945. I don't say that because I want Pentagon spending to continue. I believe such spending is leading us to disaster, both in terms of impossible debt and in terms of international military mayhem—including, with WMDs, to possible mammalian extermination. The industrial economy collapsed in on itself in 1929 and has been on military life-support since 1941. The only kind of (modest) industrial economy that's sustainable, without militarism, is a socialism that's ecologically prudent and in the collective democratic control of small farmers.

Second, the term "globalization" represents something absolutely new in human history. Until now, civilization strutted its stuff in fits and starts, here and there. It was mostly local, sometimes (like Rome) regional. It was *never* global. But now it is global. And our very own red-white-and-blue America is the current key player in this globalization. Civilization, with its power-hungry aristocracies, always dreamed of controlling the entire world; but never, until now, was it able to pull it off.

The crisis of the twenty-first century is whether agrarian folk culture can take over and reformulate the meaning of civilization, or whether civilization will totally devour all forms of organic folk culture the world over. That's the battle that's going on. When push comes to shove, I think I know where Henry Buckberry stands, and I sure as hell know where his bushy-bearded son Seedy has planted his big flat feet.

I can't begin to tell you how *grateful* I am to have been raised in the fading sunset of peasant culture. If anything has kept me from getting sucked up in the cheerleading for American Empire, it's the residual cow manure on my shoes. And it is my fervent hope that when civilization crashes and burns, agrarian culture will be there to clean up the mess.

Forgive me my self-interest in the matter, but I nominate Henry Buckberry as a patron saint of simple living, an American peasant who slipped below the electronic radar and made it into the twenty-first century. Or, as Henry might have said, imitating an illiterate lumberjack Swede he once knew—"Yust barely."

Henry Buckberry's Obituary

Lest there be any well-intentioned persons who do not perceive the difference... between religion and the cant of religion, piety and the pretence of piety, a humble reverence for the great truths of Scripture and an audacious and offensive obtrusion of its letter and not its spirit in the commonest dissensions and meanest affairs of life, to the extraordinary confusion of ignorant minds, let them understand that it is always the latter, and never the former, which is satirized here. Further, that the latter is here satirized as being, according to all experience, inconsistent with the former, impossible of union with it, and one of the most evil and mischievous falsehoods existent in society...

CHARLES DICKENS, *PICKWICK PAPERS*,
PREFACE TO THE FIRST CHEAP EDITION, 1847, PAGES XI-XII.

HENRY BUCKBERRY PASSED AWAY on Wednesday afternoon, August 26, 2009. It was a beautiful day, sunny and warm. But not all issues or matters of interest passed away with him. As with a scruffy dresser stuffed with holey socks and threadbare underwear, there's a fair amount of sorting and sifting still to be done, most of it with some degree of resistance and reluctance.

So this is, among other things, a peek into Henry's religious closet, partly to see what's in there, partly to record Seedy Buckberry's state of being as he gazes at all the boxes of dusty audio tapes, old "Amazing Facts" newsletters, and used sermons wrapped in brittle rubber bands. Oh my gracious goodness! This will require some serious meditation. Maybe two or three stiff shots of Geritol. Here goes.

Henry Buckberry's Obituary

Henry was the third of thirteen kids. It's therefore fitting that this alleged obituary should be divided into thirteen sections, bits, pieces, or fragments of folly—one, we might say, for each Buckberry sibling. But it seems to me that this entire project—Henry's stories in and of themselves, how I guided or conducted the interviews, even my busybody notes and presumptuous Afterword—would be incomplete and perhaps even misleading without a religious appendix. (Of course, there will be a few smart-mouthed cynics, perhaps like my dear exaggerating cousin Efrazima Fiddlehead, who would, at this point, mockingly feign a severe bellyache and claim it to be a near terminal case of religious appendicitis. But let's just ignore the theatrical scoffers.)

It's obvious, however, that I avoided the subject of religion as much as possible when I worked with Henry on his stories. (For those who knew him well, the omission is brazenly obvious.) It was the *stories* I was after, not rants on "what the Bible sez." But now it may be time to poke around a little in Henry's closet of rants to see if we can pull some dust bunnies out of the religious hat.

Henry's main beliefs circled back on themselves like rabbit runs in a swamp. Stand still long enough (like Henry with his Pa's single-shot .22) and Gyp the dog was sure to bark a rabbit by sooner or later. My wife Susanna tried oh! so hard to engage Henry in a discussion of how Jesus had given his friends a much fuller idea about love, how love was at the heart of the Gospels, how radical servanthood and radical stewardship were spiritual instruments for achieving cultural transformation. In fact, seeing how badly I had failed in my attempts to converse with Henry about religion, Susanna went into her conversations with him feeling more than a little cocky, for she thought she'd seen how I'd done it wrong and how she, therefore, with confident insight, was going to do it right.

Well, big surprise. Those rabbits were so well trained that even being shot through the heart with a bolt of female love wasn't about to slow them down. Susanna was close to tears.

Now when we boys were kids on the farm, we played various chasing games. In some of them, if you made it to a certain place—a tree, a portion of a wall, a fence post—you were in a safe zone. We called that safe zone "gool." (Which word may have been an evolution of "gaol," for that's the British way of spelling "jail." And, in a kid's mind, maybe jail—or gool—is a safe zone, a goal free of all parental expectations and overbearing demands.)

A Windfall Homestead

Anyway, Henry's *gool* was Exodus 20. There Moses went down onto the people and spake unto them: remember the sabbath day; six days shalt thou labor; but the seventh day is the sabbath of the Lord thy God; thou shalt not do any work.... So, according to Henry, if you *love* God, you will *obey* God; and if you *obey* God you will *keep the sabbath*. Case closed. All the rest was just "doctrines a men." The rabbit wasn't even out of breath.

Well, being Seedy, you know, always interested in public wrangles (maybe like the Irishman who wanted to know "Is this a private brawl or can anyone get in?"), I wondered, given all the tinkering with the calendar over the centuries, if there might be some uncertainty about which day of the week thou shalt do no work. Suppose the Seventh Day is actually Thursday? Or Monday? What if somebody got it wrong? What if it's been wrong for centuries?

If so, why take a chance of getting on God's bad side by doing work on *any* day of the week? Why risk the possible draft board, you know what I mean? So, like the Englishman who said that whenever he felt an impulse to work he'd lie down until the feeling passed, I too cultivated an epicure's sensitivity to the variety of naps possible on any given day.

But let's get serious, even if it only lasts for a fleeting moment.

Religion is kind of an odd duck. Well, maybe religion *and* politics are odd ducks. (For one thing, when they fly upside down they quack up.) Religion, like bad jokes, gets on our nerves. It boxes us in. It pisses us off. Those who yammer at us about religion often piss us off, especially if we don't know how to answer back. So we don't want to hear about it. Religion even makes our trigger finger itchy.

But that isn't fully true, either. We *do* want to hear about things religious—or, if not "religious," exactly, then *spiritual*. But we'd like good bread to eat, not a rock to suck on; a good hunk of baked fish, not a coiled rattlesnake staring us in the eye and flipping us his orthodox forked tongue. We'd like our religion a little more open-ended, please, not a crudely disguised deadfall designed to bonk us on the noggin before being taken captive and dragged to the Cave of Conviction for further indoctrination and forced "conversion."

Religion, however, has become a box of rocks, a pit of snakes; so you're either really into it or you detest the whole stinking mess. What's needed, says our modest Seedy, always waiting patiently to be asked, is a new folk discipline of religious anthropsychology. We've got to get *inside* this rocky box of slithery snakes and make an effort to find out just what the slithering hell it means. Are religious images arbitrary and worthless, or are they anthropsychological emblems of our cultural and political psychodrama? (On occasion, I take perverse pleasure in big words. Maybe you've noticed.)

Having largely steered clear of the subject of religion in Henry's stories, and touching into it only lightly in the preposterous Afterword, I, Seedy B. hisself, am going to blithely diddly-doodle in the swamp of religion in this here goofy, haphazard obituary. I invite you, dear reader, into the muck as well. Mosquito net, if you want, hip boots, chest waders, scuba suit and snorkel—whatever tickles your fancy. Just no four wheelers, jet skis, or cell phones, please.

Consider it an Irish wake, a happy brawl open to the public, a mud wrestle until the last dog dies. Just don't quack up.

II

Norman Cousins in his book on Albert Schweitzer called, simply, *Dr. Schweitzer of Lambarene*, says every age has need of saints. Cousins goes on to say that a saint becomes a saint when he is claimed by other people as their own, when the "saint" awakens in others a desire to know the best that's in them, the desire to morally soar.

Well, I'm not about to tell you that Henry Buckberry was a saint, at least not in the usual sense. Or, if he *is* to be considered a saint, it's precisely that our age has an acute need for his seemingly bottomless, versatile peasant skills. (Now I know that peasants never get to be saints—it's against the rules, for peasants and pagans have the same Latin mom called *pagus*—look her up in the dictionary, if you don't believe me—and pagans are automatically excluded from consideration from sainthood. But let's see if we can bend a few rules and regulations.) So it's more or less up to us to democratically claim Henry for a saint, insofar as he can awaken in us an awareness of how badly we are in need of his "obsolescent" skills and talents. Whether anybody will get to go for a saintly moral soar in some supernatural ether is altogether a different notion and a more difficult matter totally beyond my pay grade.

With people who work so hard to be *moral* (as Henry, in some ways, did), it doesn't take a backhoe to dig up some underlying impulses that run in the opposite direction, impulses identified or simply rationalized as *im*moral. Henry was a hoarder and a penny pincher. He wanted to talk about sex with his hospice nurses. (He had *hospice* nurses because he was supposed to be dying, for Christ's sake!) Henry sometimes hid behind patently false "doctrines a men"—like the insupportable idea that the Bible is the inerrant Word of God—in order to *avoid* difficult moral dilemmas. Or, to put it differently, Henry was an erotically hungry man, but his religion kept his appetite chained.

Henry had a working-class, man-sized libido. He was a big, strong fellow whose "capital," we might say, was his physicality. Given who he was, and that he was raised with such a fierce sense of *obedience,* his libido, that healthy, powerful body of desire, was kept on a leash with the tensile strength of a logging chain. Raised with truly fierce parental strictness (in a larger world where such fierceness was the social norm), compelled at an early age to be economically responsible not merely for himself but for his entire family (remember how Grampa Coster "borrowed" seventy-five dollars he never paid back?), Henry naturally gravitated toward a religious conviction that laid great stress on *obeying* God's Law. We might say Henry was preprogramed for such gravitation. Obeying was the armor of responsibility. This tendency eventually shoehorned Henry into becoming a fundamentalist. And, from my invariably modest and humble perspective, Henry's fundamentalism was the shadow side of his opposite, very strong capacity to give and share and provide.

Henry's quest to be moral manifested itself in his need to be obedient. But this business about obedience is like a trapdoor on a gallows, for *dis*obedience will snap that trapdoor open, and there you'll hang by your necktie until the crows come home. What I mean is, the compulsive drive to be *obedient* seems to be rooted, not in love, but in an unresolved *fear.* And, since God is supposed to be love, not fear, we got ourselves a real theological problem here, Houston; for if God is love, how come so much religion runs its engine on the fuel of liquid fear?

Fear made Henry avoid conflict with people or with circumstances he was afraid of, even as it made him, in tandem with his awesome work ethic, something of an authoritarian presence to his children. This affected us three brothers differently. From my totally neutral, detached, objective, humble, and modest position as middle child (plus, let me remind you, I'm the guy with the pen), I would say Birdy developed a concentrated dose of filial resentment as a result of Henry's failure to stand up for him when Birdy was repeatedly bullied at school. This concentrated resentment seems to have been put to use by Birdy as a kind of nuclear fuel rod in his internal power plant, still feeding off its radioactive anger after more than fifty years of slow but steady burning. Birdy did business by concentrated application, concentrated wits, and endless drive.

Jack got a different package. Some of what I'm going to say about Jack is circumstantial and conjectural; but, what the hell, here goes. I think the youngest child often gets a more relaxed affection, especially from the father. By the time the youngest kid rolls around, Daddy has to some extent learned (one hopes) from his prior mistakes, is less uptight about being Daddy, has already realized that sharp-edged expectations about shaping his children to his strict satisfaction is as achievable as packing quicksilver into snowballs; and besides, he is weary of the daily tension of being the aloof and authoritarian Dad and is (somewhat secretly) eager for a little easy companionship.

If all that is more or less true, Jack's situation was hugely compounded by the cancer our mother developed when he was still a little boy, with the terrific strain her suffering put not only on the entire family, but more specifically on her relationship with him. Their relationship was stretched painfully thin by her suffering and emotional withdrawal.

Jack was born in '54. By the late '50s, our mother's cancer was well-advanced. Birdy graduated from high school and left home in '61. Our mother died in '63. In '64 I graduated from high school, Henry married Viola, and I left for a brief stint at college. Jack was hurried through repeated variations of abandonment, isolation, and stress. Troubles never seemed to end.

There are, I think, some parallels between Birdy being bullied at school and Jack feeling bullied (or at least pushed around) at home. With Birdy, this resulted in a clear and decisive anger toward Henry. Birdy felt let down in a big way, and nobody was gonna bully Birdy ever again. But, with Jack, the dynamics were far more deeply conflicted. On the one hand, Henry did not firmly stand up for Jack with the sudden importation of an entirely new and not altogether compatible step-family. On the other hand, Henry's relationship with Jack, with ample opportunity for companionship on the farm, was Jack's dependable reservoir of reliable affection. So they developed a peculiar friendship, an oddly intimate companionship, but a relationship operating within the psychological limitations of Henry's obedience, his sense of perpetual responsibility, and his fear of conflict with his new wife (no shrinking violet) and her children.

It wasn't until Henry died—on August 26, 2009, that beautiful day— that Jack realized, as he put it to me over the phone, "how much Henry was inside my head." So if Henry is a kind of folk-culture saint (that's the picture I seem to want to paint of him), a person whose life can serve to awaken others to the practicalities of homemade subsistence and the pleasures of sufficiency, he was not a *spiritual* saint. He was here one hundred percent conventional.

Ethically and spiritually, Henry moved into an even tighter box of obedience when he became a Seventh-Day Adventist, somewhere around 1970. (I think it has to be said that Adventism provided Henry with an opportunity for gender self-defense and even a kind of odd aggression in his deepened obedience—male prerogative with divine sanction. That opportunity came via a new level of salvation authority his Adventist affiliation offered. Now he *knew* he was in God's inner circle of obedient sons, and that certainty gave him both a freedom from self-doubt and a sense of religious entitlement with which to bully others with his new depth of conviction.)

I often pondered what it might've been like to have been the proverbial church mouse under the pew when Henry was first confronted with Adventist certainty. I suspect he got himself quickly backed into a biblical corner, was bullied by the Bible (or those who brandished it), intimidated by a threatening God with hellfire in his eyes, and was successfully processed through a form of religious boot camp and came out a gung-ho grunt for the Sabbath. I suspect the psychological underpinnings of the boot camp ordeal meshed almost perfectly with Henry's interior vulnerabilities, with his fear of authority and the feeling of security that comes with obedience—being in on the inside skinny of the Big Boss's Plan. Once in, Henry was locked for life. God had him in a box from which he could never escape.

But, all in all, the local Adventists were not a bad lot. Quite the contrary. They were honest, hard-working, working-class people, many of whom were farmers or blue-collar craftsmen with their own small and independent businesses. Henry's work ethic and working-class life fit in perfectly. He found male companionship and a new level of purpose as elder and lay preacher. He read and reread the Bible with rare diligence. He *worked* at the Bible like a detective sorting out clues. He was tracking down God's Plan.

Jack was pulled along on this journey to God's Truth, and he even went to an Adventist college for a while, after graduating from high school. Birdy, meanwhile, was loosely affiliated with a nondemanding Methodist congregation in Minnesota—vaguely "liberal" in its vague theology—while I was in a state of total uncertainty and dedicated flounder, close to being uncontrollably hostile toward and perversely contemptuous around sanctimonious piety, both fascinated and repelled.

It took years for Jack to peel off the restraining Lazarus bandages with which he'd been laid in the Adventist tomb. Birdy slowly but steadily shed the foggy, rather cloying moralisms of the Methodist cloud bank and eased himself, it seems, into a fuller acceptance of agnostic uncertainty. No more church for Birdy. No more ponderous, guilt-laden abstractions from financially self-interested clergymen calculating their retirement funds or promoting a building project as a monument by which to immortalize their contribution to the architecture of the aesthetically pleasing but practically irrelevant Beatitudes.

By the time Henry died, all three sons had bitten deeply into the bitter apple of divorce, although yours truly Seedy B. had bit, not just once or twice, but *three* times, and that just might shed some light on his peculiar fight with God our Father, amen. Well, let's see. If I say "Seedy" or "his" rather than "I" or "me," perhaps my natural disposition toward the neutral, detached, objective, modest, and humble will be honed to an even more gleaming sheen. (Of course the opposite view, that I might be tempted to lie through my teeth—what's left of them—would simply be mean-spirited and unnecessarily humiliating. I am offended even by the thought.)

I think. . . . Excuse me, *Seedy* thinks he came to realize, through the profound theological exposition called *The Wizard of Oz*, that "the wizard," AKA God, was a fraud, all Hollywood special effects, and by no means a real down-to-earth prairie tornado. Now this was no sudden, all-at-once dust-storm revelation, no instantaneous, top-to-bottom flash of wind-blown enlightenment. Enlightenment rarely, if ever, happens that way. Or, if you do get struck by a giant bolt of transformative lightning, chances are you will be absorbing and assimilating that giant strike by thousands of little afterflashes for the rest of your life. And,if you get zapped by a series of Really Big Ones, you might end up feeling like a perpetual hippie-dippie psychedelic light show for the rest of your born days, even to the point of dragging a copper ground wire down and out of your pants leg for fear that the next Really Big One might fry all the remaining circuits.

Now I vaguely recollect that this is supposed to be Henry Buckberry's obituary. But if the sins of the fathers are passed on down to the third and fourth generation—this is biblical, folks, don't look so skeptical—then seeing how shrivelled, frazzled, and frayed the first-generation sons are just might be an incentive for tracing the stray voltage back to its source,

A Windfall Homestead

although it's probably not possible to snoop all the way back to its family roots because those trees, with their raw lightning scars running full-length down the trunks, have long since toppled over in the woods and gone back to sleep as good, clean forest dirt. Both Nature and Spirit seem heavily invested in recycling. Ashes to ashes.

Both Seedy and I, in our schizophrenic, Siamese, love/hate cleavage, suppose this toppling over into dirt brings us right smack up against the matter of heaven. (If heaven has matter, in the more scientific sense of the word, which is yet another pay grade problem.) And maybe this is where the nub of the difficulty lies. Maybe it's not heaven versus hell, God versus Devil, but a craving for ego immortality in our current bag of worms (to borrow a sublime simile from Martin Luther), versus an acceptance of recycling our very own bodies into good, clean compost. Now this raises the question of *obedience,* and obedience raises the question of *fear.* Or, in other words, just what the hell is it we're afraid of? Are we afraid of Hell? Are we afraid of dissolving into dirt? Are we afraid of daring to stand straight and act real?

I take it as true—Seedy takes it as true enough—that all living things not only live until they die (which may be a self-enclosed solipsism or even a needlessly redundant tautology), but all living things also work at staying alive, while some higher life forms of the animal sort will actually flee or fight in order to stay alive. As if you didn't already know that. But the underlying question therefore seems to be: Do all living things *fear* death?

If you, dear reader, say Yes, our very own Seedy B. says No.

And since S. B. has stolen every single pen, pencil, magic marker, crayon, and piece of chalk in the entire neighborhood, broken every laptop and jammed 911, we're stuck with having to listen to what that motormouth bonehead has to say. So listen up, people.

Seedy says the effort to stay alive, even if, when, or where it involves flight or fight, even if your heart rate cranks up several involuntary percentages in an incident of danger or an instant of crisis, is not the same as fear of death. Such alarm is not inherently connected to a craving for heavenly immortality or a fear of The Hot Place where a nasty mean guy with a pitchfork will keep prodding you back into the coaxing and hungry flames. If we can pull a representative word out of our collective semantic hat here, a word to scare the holy bejesus out of us, that slimy little semantic critter with the pitchfork might have the Latin word *pagan* printed front and back on his grimy sweatshirt.

Henry Buckberry's Obituary

When Birdy, Seedy, and Jack were kids, anybody who was a *pagan* was headed to The Hot Place with a one-way ticket and no possible refund. Frequent flier, one way only. No deposit, no return. Everybody who wasn't a Saved Christian had better buy an asbestos casket, procure several oil drums of sunscreen, and hope for the very, very best.

We're talking Hell here. Fear. Real fear. And no kidding around, either. This will sere, fry, cook, bake, both macro- and microwave you in torment for ever and ever, amen. *This* was a load of existential anxiety you could take on as a kid and be trapped under for the rest of your life. Heaven might be sunbathing on cloud tops for all we knew—boring, maybe, and pretty devoid of entertainment or excitement—but perpetual torture by frantic fire forever was no frigging joke.

So let's just say that any anxiety about dying had a massive additional overlay of pure fear of fire. And that meant fear of God-the-Father's wrath, a hot, endless, never forgiven volcanic wrath. And that meant (though this was subconscious and unspoken) the Devil actually *was* God in His Abu Ghraib/Guantanamo night job. God not only would throw you into the eternal torments of Hell if you failed to pass the obedience test, He also took perverse pleasure in your eternal torment, for once you were in the roaster you were in *forever*.

We're grownups here, more or less. Let's face this seamy picture. I think it's about time, don't you? Or do we want to go on playing Cosmic Bogieman just for the secret pleasure of peeing in our pants?

III

Maybe it's time for a little digression, perhaps even a small diversion. I want to say a word (I hope it's the last word) about Efrazima Fiddlehead's rather sour (I won't say supercilious or scurrilous) Introduction to this volume of Henry's stories.

Efie is the daughter of one of Henry's younger sisters. (I won't say who. There's no need for that.) She became an irrepressible flamboyant hippie over forty years ago, changed her last name to accomodate her new status and identity, and moved to an organic-foods, Buddha-chanting, love-peace-beads-and-candles commune in the Cascade Mountains of Oregon, somewhere southeast of Eugene and northeast of Medford, between Crater Lake and Klamath Marsh. I hear she has hair to her butt, rolls her own cigarettes, and hasn't strapped on a bra for all of those forty years.

A Windfall Homestead

Maybe I caught her in a bad mood when I sent her both volumes of Henry's stories, explaining how long it had taken me to get them done, and asked (I thought politely) if she'd be interested in providing a short Introduction to the second volume. I was trying, you know, to be inclusive and nice. Family values, and all that. Sharing the pleasure.

Whoa! Did I get an Introduction! But, having asked, I felt obliged to accept what she wrote. Stupid me. Done with Family Values, I can tell you that.

However, when Henry read Efie's Introduction, he had this (to me) bewildering and inexplicable look on his face, dreamy and far-off, the most discernible aspect of which seemed a kind of heartfelt longing. I was puzzled. What was *this* about?

In the subsequent months before he kicked the bucket, Henry would occasionally talk about his visits to Washington, especially those visits in the early 1980s. And once he let slip that he'd been to "this funny little shack" up in the Oregon Cascades, with Efie. I started to ask him to tell me more about it, thinking there might be a story here worth putting down, but he clammed up so tight, so fast, I thought he was going to bite my head off and chew on my neck. He had so few teeth left, and those mere ragged stubs, I felt we couldn't risk the dental damage.

I don't think there's much point in asking Efie what went on at her psychedelic shack. She's not going to tell—not to me, anyway. So there are some things we'll just plain never know. Did Otto Buckberry, for instance, offer his buckboard to the Dawson vigilantes when they hung that drifter from the stockyard gate in Steele? Did Efie roll Henry one of her home-grown, wacky-weed, herby cigarettes and show him a sunset he'd never noticed before? Your guess is as good as mine. *Something* happened up on the mountain among all those beads and candles, that I know. But *what*?

But thank God for life's little mysteries! They give us something to think about, especially when we're on the verge of getting bored. A fuller explanation of Henry's dreamy expression is totally up to Efie. Just don't hold your breath waiting for her reply.

Bill Clinton said he didn't inhale, either.

IV

Well, let's get back to work.

"Work?!" you ask, sputtering. "What's *work* about this bullshit, except for the *work* of having to read this crap?"

Henry Buckberry's Obituary

Hold your horses, folks. Don't let a little stick in your bee bonnet get you all discombobulated. Just relax and allow Old Seedy to walk you through his little carny side show. You can argue later about whether it was worth your measly inflated nickle. But, for now, just come along for the bumpy ride. And don't look so frigging sour.

We could probably get into one hell of a food fight if we seriously entered into a discussion about how we got into this pickle, but let's acknowledge that there are more than enough atomic weapons ready to go, on land, sea, and air, to do us all in—the entire human race and a lot of other critters right along with us. That is, our kind—folks with two legs and an overrated, much-admired big brain—now have the capacity to undo millions of years of groping life-evolution because of our amazing weapons. Fair and balanced. That is to say, because of our brainy *fear* combined with an incredible conviction that we have the *right* to unleash this apocalypse! We who are mere creatures of Life's evolution on Earth are now in a position to poison, perhaps beyond recovery, that very evolution.

So let's stop making believe that our *fear* doesn't have real consequences. End-Of-The-World is no longer a fanciful, hysterical hallucination of those people whose minds got glued in the Book of Revelation or ate too much loco weed by mistake. Such "hallucination" as we now have is firmly packed in bombs and missiles, ready for instantaneous launch. *Fear* is the common denominator of our globalized specialty in homicide. Planet murder.

So, dear friends, this can't help but bring us back around to Henry and this wierd allegation of an obituary. Henry's determination to be *obedient* was sitting on top of a smoking volcano of *fear*. Henry's religious convictions were built largely on the simmering and shimmering lava bed of volcanic fear. It's the same emotion—if "emotion" is the name to give it—that fuels the ICBMs with their payloads of mammalian extinction. End-Of-The-World stuff. For real. Forever.

In Henry's apocalyptic anticipations, God was very soon going to kick the crap out of unbelievers (including phony Christians), blow the world to hell, and send all the pagan goats to The Hot Place. The Navy, Army, and Air Force have a similar game plan, although with their plan we get to fry and die right at home. No passports or exit visas required. No standing in line. No waiting your turn. No otherworldly rapture. Pure democratic extermination.

What I'm trying to say, people, is that unless we get a grip on this *fear* that seems to be in control of our civilized destiny, we're cooked. See,

A Windfall Homestead

I believe Henry's religious expectations of Heaven or Hell are pure fiction, pure, undiluted fantasy. But they are also very, very common fantasy projections into very real political attitudes and actual technologies, and they are far more common among Christians who identify with the Christian Right. The Christian Right also represents the single biggest bloc of voters who not only support but actually insist on the most massive military capacity possible to man. And the most massive military, having lavishly detonated its destructive payloads in Vietnam, Central America, Iraq, and Afghanistan (to provide only a thin set of examples), has as its crown jewels tightly packed canisters of radioactive extermination. (And how "fail-safe" are these atomic jewels? How fully are they governed by prudence and wisdom? Well, take a good, hard look at the military track record from Vietnam on, and then tell me how safe and secure that makes you feel.)

The Christian Right tells us it's Hell for everybody, except for a very select, discrete few who'll get to go to Heaven—or maybe into a palatial bunker built into the Rocky Mountains near Colorado Springs. Those who have a one-way ticket to The Hot Place, as Henry frequently pointed out to the hospice nurses (when he wasn't telling hunting stories or broadly hinting at the importance of sex), were "as the sands of the sea." Given the numerical magnitude of the human race, past and present, you can do your own mathematical calculation regarding our chances of holding a winning PowerBall ticket. Get yourself a calculator with a really big screen because the odds against getting a harp on a cloud are absolutely daunting.

If the whole shebang is going to go up in a giant ball of radioactive fire, and if this ball of fire is God's Great Design, then you tell me what's to distinguish God from the Devil—? I'm listening. I really am. Does it make a difference whose roasted weenie you are?

Here, people, is at least one way to talk about the eye of the needle, the throat in the hourglass: *Where in the world does this volcanic fear come from?*

There are, it seems to me, two main avenues of exploration here. One is to say that fear has been embedded in the human species from the get-go. It's our animal heritage. If that's so, human behavior governed by fear is, literally, millions of years old. The other avenue of explanation is to say it's something relatively new. If it's the first, if it's millions of years old, we're probably cooked, for the simple reason that if fear is so deeply embedded in us, there is probably no way to unembed it or get over it. But if it's the latter, if it's realively new, we might just have a spitting chance of getting out of this pickle alive.

So hang on a minute while I go lasso my hobbyhorse and saddle up. Take a breather.

V

Well, wouldn't you know? My hobbyhorse is tied up for a bit. He's out mowing the lawn with his wooden dentures. In the meantime, I'd like to clear up any possible misunderstanding about whether you're getting a raw, antireligious rant here, some down-and-dirty snarl of back-alley atheism or, maybe, not.

The answer may be yes or it may be no, depending on your point of view. Allow me (I'm the guy with all the pens) to sum up Old Seedy's perspective in a few bold or sloppy strokes.

Our primary subject here is Christianity—or, rather, it's one of our primary subjects. Until the astronomers, geologists, biologists, anthropologists, and archaeologists came along with their explosive discoveries and dynamited our collective mythic imagery of the past, virtually everybody under the sway of Christian conviction believed that the Genesis account of creation was, more or less, true and actual history. That is, God supposedly made everything in six twenty-four hour days. And then He took a long nap. All the rest of the stories were true, too— the Garden of Eden, the sneaky serpent in the garden, Eve eating the forbidden fruit, and so on. The whole nine yards. God hung out a Do Not Disturb sign and slept through the entire seventh day. And then the trouble began.

And how did we know God or have an image or understanding of God? We "knew" God through the stories. The *stories* told us exactly who God was and what kind of truly awesome power He had. We knew they were stories. That part was obvious. But we thought they were *true* stories— true, basic, factual, blow-by-blow accounts of real and actual history. The real, rock-bottom stuff.

And then, a little later, a mere few thousand years, after everybody believed all those Bible stories to be true and actual history, here came some unintimidated natural scientists who said, "Well, people, we've got some good news and some bad news. The bad news is that our inherited Big Story is not exactly true, at least not as factual history. The good news is that the story of how everything got here—including our very own selves—is much more complicated, interesting, and exciting." The real point of all this religious stuff (since it isn't in the ballpark of historical accuracy) must therefore be in the realm of ethics. Maybe we're supposed to actually take this love-your-neighbor stuff to heart. You know, actually believe it and live it (as best we can) and turn it into the underlying, core principles of our economics and politics. Imagine that!

The Christian world immediately split into two major parts. One part said, "You stupid scientific atheists don't know what you're talking about. Your 'wisdom' comes straight from the Devil. We don't believe a word you say." The descendants of these refuseniks are our present-day fundamentalists and their "conservative" cousins whose self-appointed job seems to be to "conserve" these illusions.

The other part of the Christian world entered bravely into uncertainty and honestly into confusion: If God wasn't really as we were taught, who or what *is* God? Does God "exist" at all?

In other words, the fundamentalists hunkered down in rather rigid righteousness, protecting their biblical image of God from the sinful thoughts of scientific atheists. The nonfundamentalists, meanwhile, have been wandering for several centuries in the foggy wilderness, no longer knowing, exactly, which end was up.

If Henry was pretty much in the first camp, we sons have all ended up in the second camp. If you, dear reader, share Henry's fundamentalism (though not necessarily his particular Seventh-Day brand, for Seedy B. recognizes that there are lots of fun flavors on the market), then you probably can't help thinking that Birdy, Seedy, and Jack have all gone to the dogs—and "dog" is God spelled backwards. Whatever that's worth. Barking up the wrong Tree of Life, perhaps.

Now just to say Birdy, Jack, and Seedy B. are in the same camp doesn't necessarily mean we're sleeping in the same sagging tent. There are lots and lots of sagging tents in the Camp of Theological Confusion. That camp is something of a sprawling refugee outfit, and it's full of interesting homeless characters. As God collapses, the number of refugees just keeps getting bigger and bigger.

Birdy and Jack will have to speak for themselves about which tent they're holed up in. But before I make an attempt to describe my tent, I would like to point out that in the Camp of Theological Confusion there are lots of people who don't have a clue which tent to sleep in. You might call them the True Theological Homeless People, the T.T.H.P.s. In my perfectly accurate but strictly unofficial national survey (conducted by calling people totally at random, at all hours of the day or night, with or without cell phone access), there are a whole lot more T.T.H.P.s than there are "conservative" fundamentalists. But because the True Theological Homeless People are so chronically disorganized, so fractious, diverse, bewildered and aimless, the fundamentalists keep holding the dead center of political power, just as a handful of organized cops can overwhelm a peaceful demonstration and crowd the demonstrators into a tiny "free speech zone" bordered with razor wire. In the ongoing game of capture-the-flag, fundamentalists remain rugby champs, as fierce as berserker Vikings surrounded on a spit of land, their ship adrift and on fire, with no hope of rescue except from Thor and his magic hammer. End-of-the-World stuff, once again. Puff the magic dragon.

At the point where the T.T.H.P.s finally get their shit together and get a grip on their commonality, there will be a massive transformation of political consciousness, a real sea change in how we understand the divine—for how we understand the sacred or the divine directly determines our politics. Maybe we'll get to yak about that, too, later, before this alleged obituary runs out of ink.

VI

Seedy's tent is real simple, folks. If you bother to read Norman Cousins' book on Albert Schweitzer, mentioned somewhere near the beginning of this seemingly endless and pointless "obituary," you'll get some of the basics. If the biblical stories don't hold water, much less contain an entire Flood with an odoriferous Ark filled with seasick animals smelling of soiled poopies and barf bags, then perhaps the *ethical teachings* of the prophets and the Gospels contain all the "living water" you'll ever need—though we're all totally free to sip from other spiritual wells, springs, rivulets, or geysers just to see if we like the taste. In other words, it's not Adam and Eve, Cain and Abel, Noah and the kangaroo, but love, compassion, sharing, and forgiveness that constitute the heart of the matter. Ethics is the heart of the matter, not myth. That's point one.

Point two is that if fundamentalism teaches us that we'll get an accurate image of God by believing the stories, the Camp of True Theological Confusion teaches that we'll begin, slowly but surely, to get a new, deeper, and richer impression of the divine as we live out the spiritual ethics and make them not only our "lifestyle" but the rock-bottom basis of our politics. In other words, it's myth versus ethics. And ethics has to win. Or we're cooked.

A Windfall Homestead

That's it. That's Seedy's tent. It's small enough and light enough that you can roll it up and stick it in your hatband, like a colorful feather shed from the bird of paradise. Rainbow and Green—the survival politics of Planet Earth. Maybe, like Cousin Efie, you can even roll it up and smoke it.

VII

Well, okay. The hobbyhorse has finally got his belly full of lawn grass, and he's done picking dandelions out of his wooden teeth with a screwdriver. Let's get on and rock, baby!

Whoa, Seedy! Before you get to galloping off into the dust of history, let's just remind folks that a lot of what you were about to say (I almost said "going to shoot your mouth off about"—sorry) can be found in the Afterword that Efie apparently found so aggravating and disgusting. (What *is* Efie's problem? Did she neglect to run a copper wire down her leg? Too many afterflashes?) Remember how important that question was to you, Seedy, way back in the Stone Age of St. Louis, when you just had to know the answer to "Why are small farms dying?"

It's *civilization*, stupid. Civilization invented kingship, militarism and slavery, and it invested the king with the divinity of God. If you crossed the king, you were chopped liver. If you crossed God, you were toast. Combine and internalize these dynamics over centuries of brutal behavioral enforcement on peasant, serf, slave, and peon, then compound it with a religion (I mean Christianity) that started out as a peasant liberation movement (under the slogan "kingdom of God") and ended up (under the slogan "City of God") as the oppressive official state religion of the same empire that murdered its founder, and you get—what? Well, after crusades, inquisitions, witch burning, and assorted religious wars, you get modern-day fundamentalism built on a cauldron of fear. But not just any old fear of snakes or spiders, mice or bats, but a fear so cleverly packaged that even the impulse to examine what's inside the package is prohibited by fear. It's an *untouchable* fear, a *total* fear, an *utter* and *complete* fear, a fear so big and so persuasive that its hapless victims will voluntarily blow the world to hell when their fear finally reaches the tipping point of being unendurable. Instead of compassionate ethics with which to spiritually reformulate wholesome life on Earth, we've got a huge wad of bone-crunching myth to terrify us into everlasting death.

Henry Buckberry's Obituary

I would say we're well down the path of being terrified to death. Farther than we care to imagine. Much farther. Maybe near a real fiscal or flagitious cliff. Therefore there really is a Global Crisis. We might say it's weapons of mass destruction, or climate change, or species extinctions, or rampant overpopulation. But its real magma is *fear*. Unless we resolve the issue of *fear*, we're only diddling with symptoms. ICBMs are only the nose cones of our *fear*. Try slipping a condom on that.

VIII

Especially for those who weren't present, I suppose I ought to describe how Birdy, my wife Susanna, and I organized the events in the immediate aftermath of Henry's death, even though we've still got a little unfinished business to attend to on the so-called "theoretical" side of things. If getting ready to blow the world to hell is to be called a "theory."

Now nearly all the funeral planning got put off until the last minute, so to speak, for two main reasons. First, Henry really didn't want to deal with it. Oh, he had a spot already picked out and paid for in St. Paul's Cemetery, butted up against a corn field in the Town of Corning, right next to our mother, Lorinda, and two doors down, so to speak, from Viola. (Kitty-corner across the highway from the cemetery is The Drinking Gourd Bar. This tavern, once owned by my maternal grandparents, had recently changed hands, and its cloth banner proclaiming UNDER NEW MANAGEMENT had been blown off the building, swept across the road by the wind, and had gotten itself stuck on the framework of the supporting posts of the sign that said ST. PAUL'S CEMETERY. So the new configuration was a little puzzling and somewhat disturbing. It read:

ST. PAUL'S CEMETERY
UNDER NEW MANAGEMENT

Theologically speaking, this was something of a conundrum and a bit unsettling.)

Henry had an almost relentless contempt for funerals—all the drippy, pious hush, the piped-in music, the dim lighting and cheap plush, and, of course, the human carcass in the wildly overpriced, fancy casket, the stiff all doozied up with rouge, an expensive set of useless clothes, and hands folded as if in pious prayer. Plus, the real rocket fuel in his aggravation was the goody two-shoes sermon with Uncle So-And-So reputedly looking

A Windfall Homestead

down from his airy cloud, all happy and sweetly missing his dear family and his bowling buddies who hadn't yet climbed aboard the padded heavenly express. Soon. Three strikes and you're out.

Henry believed in heaven, of course, but he also believed that only the cream of the crop—a very tiny dab of the most *obedient* cream of the creamiest crop—would be permitted entry into The Good Place, and then only after physical resurrection at the End of Time. For Henry there was no immortal soul getting sucked up instantly by God's heavenly vacuum pump. No bullshit about Uncle So-And-So peeping benignly in on his very own funeral proceedings, with a wistful tear slowly leaking down Uncle's foggy cheek. Not for Henry. No way.

The stockyard gate was narrow, by God, and only a few of the bawling critters were going to be able to get through. You had to really *want* to get through, but pushing and shoving and jabbing your neighbor out of the way with your Texas longhorn headgear wasn't going to increase your likelihood of slipping through the narrow gate one iota. God was gatekeeper, and nobody was going to slip in on a fluke or a con job. God didn't make mistakes. God has flawless antennae for *obedience*.

The other end of the corral has a wide gate, and I don't need to tell you which broad path that leads down or what its terminus is: nothing but red-hot branding irons in Hell's Stockyard and Slaughterhouse (HSS or "hiss," for short) forever and ever, amen. (When Mark Twain was asked where he wanted to go after death, he thought a while. Then he said, well, one place for friendship, the other for climate.)

The other dragging foot that helped to put things off was the emotional awkwardness of planning Henry's exit while he, deaf as a post, was patiently waiting, in his red recliner, for somebody even slightly willing to listen to another of his hunting stories. It felt, you know, a little unseemly to be planning his slide into dirt while he was eager to tell about the time he shot six deer. Or pulled half a dozen skunks out of a den.

But when Henry had a warning stroke somewhere in the wee morning hours of August 15, and then another one three days later as Susanna was helping him eat a late breakfast, all awkward hesitations evaporated. It was time for the rubber to hit the road. It was now or never. No more procrastination.

I'm not going to bore you, dear reader, with the details (or bore myself trying to remember them all or line them up in proper order) but, rather, I'll make an effort to give you the gist of things. First, it was Birdy, Susanna,

Henry Buckberry's Obituary

and I who cobbled the funeral process together, piece by stray piece. It started with asking our tough-talking friend Wayne, a log house repairman by trade and a really fine carpenter, to make Henry a coffin out of popple lumber that (until we tore the stack apart in search of the right boards) was meditating in a quiet, unplaned pile behind Henry's house. These boards had been sawn from logs windblown in Henry's woods, about as homemade as it's possible to get. A windfall casket.

Wayne took those boards, had a somewhat crusty guy named John Allen plane and mill them tongue-and-groove, and delivered the finished coffin, complete with looped lifting ropes on both sides and both ends, on the very morning of the day Henry died, August 26. Cutting it right down to the wire. Wayne delivered the popple box in his pickup with bumper stickers that read Love Your Mother and Tree Huggers Make Better Lovers. Perfect fit, as far as I was concerned. Only in this case, the trees were going to be hugging Henry, not the other way around. (The man never did get enough hugging.)

The next question was whether to go for home burial.

Wayne had loaned us two books and a video. The books were *Dealing Creatively with Death: A Manual of Death Education and Simple Burial* by Ernest Morgan and *Caring for Your Own Dead* by Lisa Carlson. The video was called *A Family Undertaking: Home Funerals in America*. (Of course we didn't have a television or DVD player, so guess what? All we could do was stare at the plastic cover of the DVD, which wasn't very helpful.)

Birdy especially got cranked up about home burial. But when he called a local undertaker (shirttail relation through marriage), Birdy was told, "Good idea. You just started two years too late."

In other words, some things have got to be thought through and arranged ahead of time. Suppose you bury Uncle Harry or Aunt Elsie in the back forty. Fine. But in ten years, fifteen years, you find you've got to sell that back forty, even though you may not want to. So the new potential owner says to you, "I got the money in hand, but I ain't givin it to you until Harry's moved." And you just got yourself a problem.

For us that meant we'd have to start thinking about a neighborhood cemetery. But you don't get that done in two or three days while an old man is dying in the next room. So scratch home burial for Henry. Plus he did have a cemetery plot already bought and paid for, even if it was UNDER NEW MANAGEMENT.

A Windfall Homestead

We discovered three things in pretty quick succession, and those three things opened doors. First, it was legally possible to bury Henry without embalming. Second, the hospice people would help wash and dress Henry's body at home. Third (this was Susanna's idea, bless her soul), we could get Rick Dorn, a big, burly man with a walrus mustache, to show up with his Percherons and a wagon, and we could haul Henry, on back roads, in his homemade popple coffin, the seven or eight miles to St. Paul's Cemetery. (I added a fourth thing—asking Carl Uttech to sit on the wagon with eight or ten of us and play hymns on his squeezebox as the Spirit moved him as we rolled along—though that was frosting on the cake.)

On the morning of the day Henry died, Debra, the hospice nurse, arrived about the same time as Wayne, with Henry's box in the back of his Hug-Your-Mother pickup. Henry, by then, was in the hospital bed hospice had provided. Deb took Henry's vital signs—he could no longer talk—and she said he had, at most, twenty-four to forty-eight hours left to live. His heart rate was up to one-hundred twenty beats per minute.

At noon, as Susanna and I ate lunch (the living remorselessly continue to get hungry and to shamelessly eat), Henry's breathing became increasingly irregular. After lunch, Susanna went to our log house, back in the woods, to do something or other, and I continued typing a narrative of Henry's life for the memorial service soon to come. Shortly after two o'clock, I checked in on Henry. His breathing told me the end was near. I thought to go get Susanna, but I couldn't leave Henry. I hurried out to ring the huge Swiss cowbell, hoping she'd hear.

And then I went in and sat by Henry. The Old Man. My father. Or, as Birdy and Jack sometimes called him, Father Time. I thanked him for all he had done for me. I asked his forgiveness for all the stupid things I'd done that had caused him pain and grief, even for the things I'd written—*some* of them, anyway—that might or might not be exactly or precisely true. Close, maybe. I'm not sure about the cigar. I was crying. Tears were running down my face and washing my tangled whiskers in warm, salty streaks.

One last gasp, and Henry's incredible life was over. Dawson to Boulder in a mere ninety-seven years. A little after two o'clock, on a beautifully sunny and warm Wednesday afternoon, August 26, 2009. Not quite ninety-eight orbits around the sun. (Another week and he could've had one last Social Security check worth $619. Isn't that the shits?)

I sat with him a while, feeling a wonderfully full emptiness, then walked the crooked, woodsy footpath to find Susanna. I found her on her

Henry Buckberry's Obituary

way, headed back to Henry's house. I hugged her, crying, and we walked back together, then sat with Henry, with the body that was no longer breathing or telling stories, for—I don't know—another half-hour or so. Then it felt like time to spread the news.

I called Jack and Birdy. Jack was too choked up to talk, so I gave him the best telephone hug of which I was capable. Birdy immediately began discussing procedural details, a subject that, at the moment, I found myself incapable of handling, thus begging off for an hour or so. And then I biked down the road to tell Ned Fox's son Royal and his wife Gerry that Ned's old hunting partner had jumped off the cliff and wasn't coming back. When I returned—five minutes later, ten at the most—an overloaded motorbike was parked by the garage. Inside the house, crying by Henry's bedside, was our dear Vietnam-vet, Buddha-chanting friend Uncle Monk, down from the Tomahawk ghetto. The tears started all over again. (How did Uncle Monk know to show up when he did? Some weird, mystical Buddhist radar?)

Well, enough of this drippy stuff.

Susanna called Deb, who showed up in about an hour. Susanna and Deb took Henry's death clothes off, washed his body, and dressed him in the fresh things I'd chosen—a black-and-white checkered flannel shirt and a pair of my blue bib overalls, all well broken-in by use. He'd lived as a farmer and, by God, he was going to his grave as a farmer. No business suit and stupid tie for Henry. No false representations. (If heaven has a business-suit dress code—the ultimate, you know, in Gated Community—then Henry wasn't gonna get in. Plus he was barefoot. No shoes, no service.)

The next afternoon—yet another gorgeous day—over one hundred people came to the house to pay their respects. Sheer word of mouth. (The local radio station refused to broadcast a death announcement because it wasn't an official funeral parlor directive.) People who hadn't seen each other for years pulled up chairs in the garage and chatted about things they'd nearly forgotten. There were clustered conversations all over the lawn. There was more food than the table could hold, more than we could eat, and more food kept arriving. Henry lay on his hospice bed, in bibs and flannel shirt, the quiet center and unmoving hub of a busy wheel. All this company and he couldn't tell even one hunting story! What a bummer! What a dirty deal! No wonder he hated to think of his own death and funeral!

We'd more or less said the wake would last from three in the afternoon until seven in the evening. Deb the hospice nurse was back. The plan was to move Henry's body to the popple coffin, quietly waiting in the attached garage. By seven-thirty, twilight setting in and a fair number of people still hanging around—self-selected, you might say—we just rounded up whomever wanted in on the transport, surrounded Henry's bed, rolled the patchwork quilt he was lying on into long coils on either side of his body and, using the quilt as a litter, carried him out the front door, across the deck and down two rickety steps to the lawn. On impulse, I began singing the Shaker hymn *Simple Gifts* as we went down the steps. Susanna immediately joined in, and then others who could or would or weren't too choked up to try.

We were carrying Henry feet first toward the open garage door, but the idea was to turn him, when we lowered him into the popple coffin, so his head would be to the north. Spontaneously we began to do that turning even as, without a shred of planning or premeditation, we were singing "till by turning, turning, we come round right."

We came round right, by God, with balsam boughs under Henry and partially over him. Deb had brought a fistful of acorns from her home near Sayner. She gave them to me, and I handed them out, one by one, to all the kids who wanted one, including little Henry, Birdy's grandson, who could hardly see over the edge of the coffin. Little Henry stood on his tiptoes and dropped his acorn in by his great-grampa's bare feet.

I went to do something—I forget what—and when I returned Phil Herbig was smudging Henry's body and the popple coffin with smoking sage and sweet grass. Phil is a Vietnam vet, a former Marine from western Montana, who saw and did things in Vietnam I probably will never ask about or wish I hadn't if I did. He apparently lived inside his PTSD (Post-Traumatic Stress Disorder) for maybe thirty years before he discovered Native American religious practices and Edward Tick's classic PTSD book, *War and the Soul*. I walked straight up to Phil, stood in his way, and he smudged me end to end, side to side, top to bottom. Best smoke I ever had—better even, I'd guess, than the seventy-five-dollar cigar Grampa Coster gave Henry in exchange for his bankbook, back in the 1920s, or the sneaked home-rolled cigarette Henry sometimes shared with Jake Karban on a raft (or maybe it was Henry's deadhead speedboat) in the Boulder River.

Next morning when Rick Dorn drove his magnificent grey Percherons into the yard, with a rumbly wagon hooked behind, and swung them in a full circle, facing out, I once more started to bawl. It was a weird joy all shot through with grief—and, as I became aware as the day progressed, my

Henry Buckberry's Obituary

state of being was increasingly well-larded with crooked slices of emotional exhaustion.

Birdy, with a neighbor's battery-pack drill, drove down the screws Wayne had preset in the coffin lid, but not before everybody who wanted—thirty, forty people, probably—got to see Henry in his popple box, one last time. Susanna, at my request, got out her violin and played some melancholy tunes as we lifted the closed coffin, carried it to the waiting wagon, and slid it in the long way between facing benches. And then we self-selected once again as eight or ten of us climbed up into the wagon seats, including Carl Uttech with his black suspenders and silver concertina.

Rick Dorn, wearing a big, black hat and black duster, sat high on the driver's seat, talked to his mares Nell and Fran, tightened the reins, and off we went—seven or eight miles, trot, walk, and rest, trot, walk, rest, five or six cars slowly following, trot, walk, rest, people in oncoming vehicles with a look of pure astonishment on their faces as they drove past.

I gave a running commentary on Henry's life as we drove by the field whose pine stumps he once blasted for Dan Young, the site where he cooked booze for ten dollars a month, Frostbite Avenue where he learned to shoot dynamite with Tony Zillman, the house where Happy Jack operated his speakeasy, the hill where Old Man Karban had his shack, the gravel pit he helped Oscar Weaver open with shovels and a worn-out truck, the forty acres (with the Boulder River flowing through) that his parents owned, the bridge off which he and two of his sisters jumped when they first learned to swim, the driveway down which the bunkhouse used to sit (and, beyond that, the huge garden on the flat by the Boulder), the remains of the old railroad bed where steam logging trains used to chuff and rumble and alongside which Henry drove crosshaul teams loading logs, the alder swamp where Gyp the dog barked up rabbits, the place where Henry saw his first bear, the field where, picking wild strawberries, he looked up into the hypnotic eyes of a timber wolf, and the place where, a little over eighty-seven years ago, he walked in snow behind a bobsled to an empty frame house in the dead of winter—February of 1922.

In-between my gabby recitations of Henry's narrative, Carl played hymns on his concertina, to the steady, rhythmic clip-clop of horses' hooves on asphalt. Trot, walk, rest. Here and there, presumably with advance warning, people sat and waited for our cavalcade to roll on by. A few people in oncoming pickup trucks pulled over on the road's shoulder in respectful courtesy. (I believe I saw Fred Schulz's grandson, Steve, in one of those trucks.) Rick asked my son Woody to ride up top with him for a mile or so; and, when Woody got down to walk the last stretch to the cemetery, Rick asked me to climb up.

It took us two hours to get to the cemetery. In a field we saw, believe it or not, in the company of grey sandhills, a white whooping crane, one of the rarest birds in North America. Like Henry, one of the last of a magnificent breed.

And then there we were. The end of the line. Henry's last horse-and-wagon ride. Stop and snort. There was the grave with the casket-lowering gizmo perched on top, reminiscent of a gallows, perhaps. (I was involuntarily reminded of Henry's last morning in his favorite red recliner, the chair he practically lived in. He could no longer stand, nor support enough of his own weight, even with the walker to lean on, to pee standing up. So Dawn, the curly-haired hospice aide, engineered our moving him from chair to hospital bed. Henry was sufficiently alert to understand its significance, for he had previously said something that indicated his recognition that, once he was put into *that* bed, he would never get out of it alive. So he looked at the bed. He looked at us. He looked straight at me. He was deaf, remember, so I put my finger on his chest and then pointed to the bed. He looked again at me and—not one word—nodded. There was a look on his face I will never be able to describe or forget. He knew exactly what the bed meant. And I felt in that moment like a prison warden as he straps a death-row inmate on his final transport, on his way to the gas chamber. Or, oddly enough, the face of my children at the moment of their birth.)

The popple box was itself heavy, and Henry was not a little man. But strong arms pulled and lifted, and (once again) a self-selected gang of pall bearers carried Henry in his wooden coffin to the apparatus that would shortly lower him down to the gritty level where his wives were waiting.

Welcome home, Henry. How've you been? What's the weather like? Is it cold out?

We began to gather round.

IX

I suppose I should say that Birdy, Susanna, and I had decided two things early on regarding the local Adventist congregation. First, the Adventists could have the graveside service. In fact, we asked Alan Iattoni, a handsome, working-class man, a mason, if he would give the eulogy. Second,

Henry Buckberry's Obituary

we decided—and, truth to tell, I was the one who pushed the issue—that the memorial service to follow was *not* to be held in the Adventist church. The Adventists would get to give Henry a graveside send-off or let-down, depending on your point of view (it seemed appropriate after Henry's forty years of tithing for the Adventists to twitch him up or down), but the memorial service was for the rest of us, not subject to any opportunistic preaching from an Adventist angle. Not that that was truly likely to happen, but I saw no need to set up the juicy fruit of temptation. Such juiciness, once taken advantage of, even without premeditation, can leave a sour aftertaste. There was no need to tempt the Sabbath-keepers to slip some select slices of fruity admonition in at the last moment. No. The premeditated answer is no. We'll do the memorial service elsewhere.

X

So we gathered round, fifty, sixty people—Birdy, his former wife, their three kids and families; Susanna, with her second daughter and her family; yours truly Seedy B., with two of his three children (both unmarried); and a whole host of others, including several people from Viola's side of the family, plus friends, neighbors, and some collection of folks who were anybody's guess. Alan, with some throat clearing, called us to order, told everybody he'd been asked by the family to say a few words, that he wasn't no perfessional preacher, but he'd written down, in longhand, some notes to keep himself on track. (I glanced over and saw a couple sheets of yellow paper inside Alan's Bible—the Bible had bright red covers—and when he pulled those yellow pages out and opened them, I could see they were indeed handwritten, crossed out and pencilled in, exactly the sort of draft I'd produced a hundred times or more when working on Henry's stories.)

See, I'd thought at first to tape record Henry—and I did, for what became the Introduction to volume one. But as anybody who's read that Introduction knows, I'm not smart enough to operate a tape recorder reliably. So everything after that initial interview in the dusty pickup—if I might be so bold as to call that failed experiment an interview—was done by asking questions of Henry and jotting down his responses in a weird kind of almost-legible, homemade shorthand, followed by reconstructing those incredibly dismaying fragments into a handwritten narrative, followed by brutal editing and seemingly endless sessions at the manual typewriter: not only not smart enough to operate a tape recorder, but also not smart enough

A Windfall Homestead

to work an electric typewriter, much less a computer keyboard. Not quite Stone Age, maybe, but definitely a throwback, an atavism, a reversion to a primitive type. (Maybe that's what pissed Efie off. Maybe she's a computer geek who only reads from a glowing electronic screen. I only met her once, when we were kids, out in Washington, and she made relentless mockery of my crewcut. She goaded me beyond endurance. Maybe she found my photocopied typescript a trifle medieval, you know, stubbornly pre-Gutenberg. Maybe she had an awesome crush on Henry and just plain resented the fact that *she* was not his daughter and I, a mere crewcut bimbo, was an oblivious and undeserving son. Who knows? But—and I realize this is not exactly the right moment to ask this again—did she or did she not get Henry stoned at her shack somewhere east of Crater Lake? I would *really* like to know.)

Anyway, Alan gave a warm and friendly talk on Henry, mostly about his engaged involvement in the church—Alan and Henry were both baptised by immersion in the same tank on the same day—I'm not sure who got the used water—but he also talked about Henry the farmer, Henry the hunter, Henry the willing helper available whenever there was something to be done. Of course, Alan also had to slowly slide into a little Bible explication of the you-know-God's-waiting-to-see-if-you-make-the-right-decision sort of thing, but all in all his comments were extremely light on the fire and brimstone stuff. Which was fine with me. It was already a warm day, no need to heat things up even more.

Now Alan had brought along the new Filipino preacher, a small, slightly chunky fellow (the only person present with a necktie), who not only had an acoustic guitar strapped on (and led us in a hymn or two) but managed to stroke a "closing prayer" into a mini-sermon in which God was invited—three times, if I remember correctly—to come and take us all *Home Now* rather than put it off until later. But God, or a swift fleet of pickup-and-delivery angels, failed to materialize, the requested rapture was a fizzle (just try and imagine the cemetery sexton's puzzlement as he discovered the popple coffin, its lid ajar, still perched on its catafalque, surrounded by rumpled heaps of clothing and an acoustic guitar!), and so we s-l-o-w-l-y dispersed, but not before standing by while the coffin-lowering gizmo guy steadily eased the coffin down the hole, with Susanna's homemade wreath still tacked onto the lid.

When the coffin had finally settled into the cement vault (which we didn't want to buy, but the cemetery sexton made us get, though Birdy had a hell of a time persuading the vault people this wasn't a pre-Halloween prank), those who wanted got handsful of dirt and sprinkled Henry's box with a final farewell. In the end, there has to be One Last Thing, and sprinkling the homemade popple coffin with dirt was it.

Goodbye, Henry. Goodbye, goodbye, goodbye. Dirt and tears. That's all we've got left to give you. Tears and dirt. Dirt and tears.

XI

The memorial service, at the Methodist church in Jensen, was almost too much. But it was, I think, necessary, and it went off astonishingly well. Carl Uttech, with his black suspenders, grey ponytail, salt'n pepper beard, and gold tooth, sat up front with his concertina and led us in (I think it was) four old hymns. Birdy's tall son Tim played a more or less religious medley on his trombone, with his wife Jennifer accompanying on piano. (I had no idea Tim was such a good musician!) And Susanna's four grandchildren, home-schooled and therefore unburdened by the typical slouchy sullenness of contemporary school-ruined childhood, sang *The Irish Blessing* in lovely harmony, a cappella, beaming with self-confidence. I read aloud the narrative of Henry's life I was working on the day he died. Don Entenman, the Methodist pastor (who's really a Quaker), read a long section from the final chapters of Job. (Job 17:1–10. Well, actually it wasn't that passage, but right now it fits my mood.)

There was a block of silence out of which people could speak, if they wished. A few people did speak, including Birdy's Tim, who gave a brief account of how Henry not only built his new house, in the mid-1970s, out of used lumber, but spent hours straightening used nails and salvaged spikes. And then Carl Uttech played the final hymn, *How Great Thou Art*, and while we sang "the rolling thunder" a very real rumble of actual thunder shook the stained glass windows. Maybe the fleet of angels had been detained elsewhere when they were being summoned to the cemetery, were frustrated to be late, and were letting off a little aggravated angelic steam. Hard to say. Shit happens.

Henry loved chicken, so of course we had to have the obligatory fried chicken parts and mashed potato funeral meal downstairs. Cole slaw. Buns. The usual. Totally normal. There were pictures of Henry up on easels. People sat at long folding tables, chowin down. There was a certain festive atmosphere.

A Windfall Homestead

By the time I got home, I was cooked, maybe an inch and a quarter from some sort of emotional collapse. I retreated to my bed, after stuffing in a greasy pair of orange rubber ear plugs I sometimes remember to wear while gnawing at firewood with the old, red chainsaw Henry and I bought together in 1984 for a popple-peeling job. Within an hour I managed to stretch my margin of collapse to three and a half inches. The evening with family wasn't over yet, not with the ragged ends of funeral business still in need of attention. We managed, somehow. Birdy ran the show.

The house felt empty, hollow, vacant, grey, and weightless without Henry's presence. Or maybe the twilight zone was simply closing in on me.

XII

Well, it feels like it's time to wrap this up. I don't know if I can truly explain why Henry Buckberry might be considered a folk-culture saint, except by saying (as he said early on in the first volume of his stories) that it was *the times* he lived through, the life circumstances he embodied in such a representative way, that made him a somewhat larger-than-life figure. And that he was so strong and healthy is certainly no incidental matter. He had the body with which to do the things he did.

While it's true that Henry got suckered by Progress, as all of us have, one way or the other, he never left off being or thinking like a dirt-poor homesteading peasant farmer. He knew how to hoe potatoes, file a saw, milk a cow, harness a horse, fix a tool, change a tire (or a diaper), saw a board, cut a tree, hunt a deer, spear (or net) a fish, trap a beaver. It was, simply, his life. He had big hands, a strong body, and a thousand useful skills. He was a man of subsistence culture.

The world, however, changed so much, so fast, especially in the aftermath of the Second World War, that it left him stranded on a smaller and smaller sandbar of agricultural irrelevance, working harder than ever just to stay even, an island of sand eventually reduced to a wealth of stories and a poverty of religious convictions. His was the last generation of unselfconscious homesteading endeavor, the last gasp of an agrarian way of life far, far older than the rise of civilization and, in the end, an agrarian way snuffed out by the utopian, rationalizing economics of the same civilized system that had coerced free farmers into becoming expropriated peasants five or six thousand years ago, the same system that killed Jesus before coaxing his followers to make aristocratic Christianity a state religion.

Henry Buckberry's Obituary

Part of my aggravation with Henry's fundamentalist convictions was how those convictions prevented him from fully grasping the historic process by which he had been dumped off in a Big Box parking lot. He knew things were screwy; he remained convinced that another Big Depression is just around the corner; he recognized, as only Earth-bound folks can, that the larger economy was floating on a cloud of hot air, with downright dangerous manipulations occuring from On High. He just wasn't able to actually explain it, and some of his attempts at explanation made a person groan; but his feeling-sense was right on the money. So to speak. Derivative swaps. Too big to fail. Utopia forever.

Well, let's think about this a moment. Henry wasn't able to get a grip conceptually on the nature of the larger economy because, at least in part, he was so completely locked into biblical inerrancy as the touchstone for his understanding of history. It made him—forgive me for being so brutal—intellectually stupid. Willfully blind. Blinkered and blindered. And, insofar as biblical literalism sits on the bedrock of unexamined fear, it was *fear* that blinkered Henry's grasp of history. Fear of hell is the psychological barbed wire fence protecting biblical inerrancy. Henry was afraid to cut the fence. Henry was afraid to let go of his fear. His obedience locked him in to a false understanding. That understanding said we're nearly into the End of the World, there's no future for or on this Earth, get your heavenly seatbelt fastened.

So Henry Buckberry, in a sense, has been my at-home case study for how and why religious fundamentalism is such a huge political and spiritual problem. Fundamentalism blocks or blunts an accurate grasp of history even as an accurate grasp is crucial for dealing adequately with global crises, and it stubbornly misidentifies what's important, urgent, and in need of sustained attention. (For example, the precivilized Stone Age is seen to be an evil fiction, therefore there's no need to study ancient history. And, since God is about to bring the world to an end, there's no need to get cranked up about global warming, climate change, or nuclear weapons. God's got it all planned. Chill out.) And because as a kid I got seriously dosed with fundamentalism myself, working through my own fears has enabled me to see (or at least think I see) how fear is lodged in others—how *deeply* it's lodged, sometimes below the threshold of consciousness—and how, in mass political behavior, it translates into public policy that's both dangerous and deadly. (Don't take these remarks as simply anti-"conservative," however, or as sly or covert endorsements of the so-called "liberal" side of

A Windfall Homestead

the political spectrum. If George W Bush was beholden to oil companies and the Christian Right, Barack Obama has obviously been beholden to the Wall Street golden-parachute artists who imploded the entire economy and whose "punishment" consisted of billions—or is it trillions?—of taxpayer bailout dollars, all wrapped in yellow ribbon marked "Too Big To Fail—Too Rich To Jail." As good old Ralph Nader tried so hard to tell us—Ralph, you know, is one of our living prophets—there's one political party with two heads. But, with our everyday A.A.D.D.—American Attention Deficit Disorder—we refuse to pay attention. The only solution is to start voting for Green socialism.)

Maybe here's where we get back to the T.T.H.P.s, the True Theologically Homeless People, who had better get their shit together soon or the two-headed "major" parties of Empire and Empire Lite are going to bury us all in a snarky pile of debt and debris. Unpayable debt. Radioactive debris.

Henry presents us with a bit of a contradiction. On the one hand, his actual life was in many ways in substantial accord with what a homemade, earthy life will be like in the not-too-distant future, when cheap oil takes a real header and we go back to hoeing potatoes. On the other hand, his religious convictions are—or were—a hard knot in need of patient, methodical untangling, a knot in need of spiritual loosening and liberation. To undo the knot means letting go the fear of death or, rather, the fear of eternal punishment and pain. For a lot of people that means letting go their fear of an angry, judgmental, and violent God. That means to cease being preoccupied with your fate after death. That means learning to live more fully and more simply on Earth. That means soaking up real history rather than fake religious "history" dressed in apocalyptic fear. That means recognizing civilization, with its underlying aristocratic principles of arrogance, violence and economic entitlement, as the political entity needing to be dissolved, as that historic entity which cranked up our built-in flee-or-fight impulse into a totally trapped reservoir of sustained fear, with the aristocratic impoundment of the exploited peasantry capped and sealed by a glowering God who promised eternal hellfire for resistance or rebellion.

This also means—probably—that the three mutually antagonistic Abrahamic religions (Judaism, Christianity, and Islam) are on their way out, perhaps by systematically beating each other to death in the not-so-distant future. If God goes, then the male cheerleading squads go right along with Him. And that means, finally, that unless we all get blown to Hell first, we are going to have to learn to actually *live* democratically on

Earth as we discover a deeper, quieter, more peaceful and gentle spirituality that enables us to live with far less political conflict and far more ecological respect.

I, for one, believe Henry Buckberry, once he got free of his fundamentalist blockage and fear baggage, would be happy as a lark in the world that's coming down the pike. In fact, I think we owe it to the entire Buckberry/Coster clan to see to it that that world arrives safe and sound, insofar as any fragment of that arrival is in our power to enable. Potatoes, firewood, a clean Boulder River with crayfish, otter, northern pike, and some shameless skinnydipping.

At least that's the modest, humble, working opinion of Henry's shaggy son Seedy—if anything he's got his fingers in can ever be called "modest," "humble," or "working."

Buzz off, Efie. Go smoke yer herb.

XIII

Maybe there is one last little thing. Henry's drivers license didn't expire until his one-hundredth birthday on January 9, 2012. That license had no restrictions. Before we got to thinking about Rick Dorn, his Percherons and wagon, we briefly considered cobbling four bicycle tires onto Henry's coffin, tacking a bright orange slow-moving vehicle symbol on the tailgate, so to speak, and pulling the coffin-on-wheels to the cemetery behind a couple of the neighbor's goats.

But Henry, as far as we knew, had never driven goats, and we doubted if those little buggers, with their perky insouciance, knew or cared to know "Gee" from "Hah." We doubted, too, if Carl Uttech would've felt comfortable sitting crosslegged on the wobbly popple coffin, squeezing baleful hymns out of his concertina, with goats attempting to harmonize.

So horses it was. And although they sweated—Nell more than Fran, for Fran, being considerate and humble, was always willing to let Nell lead by a half-step or so—they never stopped to kick off their harnesses, the way Henry's first horse did when he was slushing out the basement dirt of his log house.

A Windfall Homestead

Given how tight Henry could be, we brothers, in filial obedience, are still intending to see if we can get a refund on the unused portion of Henry's drivers license. We're trying to get an appointment with a Motor Vehicles supervisor to see what the procedure might be. We'll keep you posted. Henry might be proud of us, yet. Provided we get some of his money back.

In the meantime, here's hoping you make it safely home in the dark. Don't forget to look up at the stars, and smile. And, while you're smiling at the starry sky, don't forget to meditate on Henry's sage advice—get poor now, avoid the rush.

That includes *you*, Efie.

The Buckberry Family	**The Coster Family**
Grampa John Buckberry (1841–1930)	Grampa Henry Coster (1863–1934)
Gramma Marie Buckberry (1841–1922)	Gramma Caroline Coster (1863–1953)
Uncle Hugo Buckberry (1871–1943)	Ma Gertrude Coster (1890–1958)
Pa Otto Buckberry (1877–1962)	Aunt Minnie Coster (1893–1980)

The children of Otto Buckberry and Gertrude Coster (married in 1907):

>Mary (1908–2003)
>Clara (1910–2003)
>Henry (1912–2009)
>Daisy (1915–2009)
>Nellie (1917–1997)
>Ethel (1918–2000)
>John (1919–1993)
>Melva (1921–2012)
>Alice (1924–)
>William (1926–2012)
>Jannette (1930–)
>Patricia (1932–2010)
>Paul (1932–1966)

Thanks to Jeanne Vanderwood, Wanda Jean James, and Patricia Jo Blank.
S. B.

www.ingramcontent.com/pod-product-compliance
Lightning Source LLC
Chambersburg PA
CBHW071442150426
43191CB00008B/1205